"There is only one way to avoid criticism:
do nothing, say nothing, and be nothing."
— Aristotle

Let Me Tell You How I Really Feel...Again:
More of the Best of Laura Wagner's Book Reviews from *Classic Images*

by Laura Wagner

BearManor Media

Albany, Georgia

Let Me Tell You How I *Really* Feel … Again:
More of the Best of Laura Wagner's Book Reviews from *Classic Images*
Copyright © 2015 Laura Wagner. All Rights Reserved.

No part of this book may be reproduced in any form or by any means, electronic, mechanical, digital, photocopying or recording, except for the inclusion in a review, without permission in writing from the publisher.

Published in the USA by
BearManor Media
P.O. Box 71426
Albany, GA 31708
www.BearManorMedia.com

ISBN: 1-59393-564-1

Printed in the United States of America

Let Me Tell You How I Really Feel ... Again:
More of the Best of Laura Wagner's Book Reviews from *Classic Images*

To my late mother, Fran Wagner,
the strongest woman I will ever know.

Table of Contents

Introduction/Acknowledgments	xvii–xxii
Atomic Blonde: The Films of Mamie Van Doren by Barry Lowe	1-5
The Batman Filmography: Live-Action Features, 1943-1997 by Mark S. Reinhart	5-7
Beyond Peyton Place: My Fifty Years on Stage, Screen, and Television by Ed Nelson with Alvin M. Cotlar, M.D.	7-9
Bogie: The Final Chapter by Eli Rill	9-11
The Boxing Filmography: American Features, 1920-2003 by Frederick V. Romano	11-14
Character Actors in Horror and Science Fiction Films, 1930-1960 by Laurence Raw	14-22
Charles McGraw: Biography of a Film Noir Tough Guy by Alan K. Rode	22-23
Confessions of a Hollywood Director by Richard L. Bare	23-24

Cornell Woolrich From Pulp Fiction to Film Noir 24-28
by Thomas C. Renzi

Dana Andrews: The Face of Noir by James McKay 28-29

Death on the Cheap: The Lost B Movies of Film Noir! by Arthur Lyons 29-40

Diane Keaton: Artist and Icon 40-43
by Deborah C. Mitchell

Didn't You Used to Be What's His Name? 44-45
by Denny Miller

Doris Day: The Illustrated Biography 45-50
by Michael Freeland

Evelyn Brent: The Life and Films of Hollywood's Lady Crook by Lynn Kear with James King 51-52

The Films of the Seventies: A Filmography of American, British and Canadian Films, 1970-1979 by Marc Sigoloff 52-54

From Shock Theatre to Svengoolie: Chicago Horror Movie Shows by Ted Okuda and Mark Yurkiw 54-56

George O'Brien: A Man's Man in Hollywood 56-59
by David W. Menefee

A Girl and a Gun: The Complete Guide to Film Noir on Video by David N. Meyer 59-62

Glenn Ford: A Life by Peter Ford	62-64
Gossip or Fact?	64-65
Growing Up on the Set: Interviews with 39 Former Child Actors of Classic Film and Television by Tom Goldrup and Jim Goldrup	65-67
Guest Parking: Zita Johann by Rick Atkins / **Chaplin's Girl: The Life and Loves of Virginia Cherrill** by Miranda Seymour	67-73
Harold Lloyd: Magic in a Pair of Horn-Rimmed Glasses and Other Turning Points in the Life and Career of a Comedy Legend by Annette D'Agostino Lloyd	73-74
Heaven & Hell to Play With: The Filming of *The Night of the Hunter* by Preston Neal Jones	74-76
Hiding in Plain Sight: The Secret Life of Raymond Burr by Michael Seth Starr	77-79
The Hitler Filmography: Worldwide Feature Film and Television Miniseries Portrayals, 1940 through 2000 by Charles P. Mitchell	79-80
Hollywood's Child: Dancing Through Oz by Caren Marsh-Doll	80-81
The Horror Hits of Richard Gordon by Tom Weaver	81-84

Joan Blondell: A Life Between Takes   85-87
by Matthew Kennedy

John Gilbert: The Last of the Silent Film Stars   87-89
by Eve Golden

The John Wayne Filmography by Fred Landesman   89-90

Journey Without a Map: A Memoir   91-94
by Gardner McKay

J.P. McGowan: Biography of a Hollywood Pioneer   94-96
by John J. McGowan

Kiss Tomorrow Goodbye: The Barbara Payton Story   96-100
by John O'Dowd

Lew Ayres: Hollywood's Conscientious Objector   100-105
by Lesley L. Coffin

The Life and Death of Thelma Todd   105-108
by William Donati

Lloyd Hamilton: Poor Boy Comedian of Silent Cinema by Anthony Balducci   108-110

The Lucky Southern Star: Reflections from the Black Lagoon by Julie Adams with Mitchell Danton/ **The Epitome of Cool: The Films of Ray Danton** by Joseph Fusco   110-116

Maureen O'Hara: The Biography by Aubrey Malone/   116-125
'Tis Herself: A Memoir by Maureen O'Hara with
John Nicoletti

Mercedes McCambridge by Ron Lackmann   125-127

Mickey Spillane on Screen: A Complete Study of the   127-131
Television and Film Adaptations
by Max Allan Collins and James L. Traylor

Movies Made for Television: 1964-2004 by Alvin H.   131-134
Marill / **The ABC Movie of the Week Companion:**
A Loving Tribute to the Classic Series by Michael
Karol

The Munsters: A Trip Down Mockingbird Lane   134-136
by Stephen Cox

My Fifteen Minutes / Five Minutes More / What's   136-141
It All About, Sybil? by Sybil Jason

Mae McKinney: The Black Garbo   141-142
by Stephen Bourne

Noir City Sentinel: Annual #1: The Best of the Film   142-145
Noir Foundation Newsletter, 2006-2008,
edited by Eddie Muller

Now a Terrifying Motion Picture!: Twenty-Five Classic Works of Horror Adapted from Book to Film by James F. Broderick / **Hardboiled Hollywood: The True Crime Stories Behind the Classic Noir Films** by Max Décharné / **No, But I Saw the Movie: The Best Short Stories Ever Made Into Film**, edited by David Wheeler	145-149
Out of Hollywood: Two Generations of Actors by Robert Dix	149-150
Paul Bern: The Life and Famous Death of the MGM Director and Husband of Jean Harlow by E.J. Fleming	150-153
Pier Angeli: A Fragile Life by Jane Allen	153-154
Radio Live! Television Live!: Those Golden Days when Horses Were Coconuts by Robert L. Mott	155-156
Rin Tin Tin: The Life and Legend by Susan Orlean	156-162
Savage Detours: The Life and Work of Ann Savage by Lisa Morton and Kent Adamson, with a foreword by Guy Maddin	162-163
A Sci-Fi Swarm and Horror Horde: Interviews with 62 Filmmakers by Tom Weaver	164-170
Scripts from the Crypt: The Hideous Sun Demon by Tom Weaver	170-172

Shadows & Light: Journeys with Outlaws in Revolutionary Hollywood by Gary Warner Kent	173-174
Space Patrol: Missions of Daring in the Name of Early Television by Jean-Noel Bassior	175-177
Stand Up for B Movies	177-180
Tough Without a Gun: The Extraordinary Life of Humphrey Bogart by Stefan Kanfer	180-186
Up from the Vault: Rare Thrillers of the 1920s and 1930s by John T. Soister	186-187
Virginia Bruce - Under My Skin by Scott O'Brien	188-191
Warren William: Magnificent Scoundrel of Pre-Code Hollywood by John Strangeland	191-195
Western Highlights: The Best of the West, 1914-2001 by Henryk Hoffmann	195-196
Western Movie Wit & Wisdom by Jim Kane	196-198
Whatever Happened to Prince Charming?: A Memoir by Jeffrey Stone, The Original Prince Charming by Jeffrey Stone	198-201
White Horse, Black Hat: A Quarter Century on Hollywood's Poverty Row by C. Jack Lewis	201-202

William Beaudine: From Silents to Television 202-204
by Wendy L. Marshall

The Z Files: Treasures from Zacherley's Archives 204-206
by Rich Scrivani with Tom Weaver

Appendix: Addresses of Publishers 207-209

Introduction

"Laura Wagner professes to be the be-all and end-all when it comes to film history," wrote one of my fans. "Her little column in *Classic Images* is a platform to hate every book published and point out the mistakes the authors have made throughout their work. Her ego and arrogance is off the radar." You are probably wondering, too, why it's *my* fault there are mistakes in books.

"As usual, Wagner gives HER opinion about everything," continues this critic of mine, who is obviously smitten with me. "She sticks her nose in with opinions that are unwarranted in an attempt to rewrite Hollywood history the way she thinks it should be."

I have never professed to be an expert in film. Like a lot of die-hard movie fans, I can spot blatant errors when I am reading a book. How hard is it to spell Joseph Cotten's name? Katharine Hepburn? Fredric March? Yet, time after time, these names are butchered. Somehow, I am a monster for pointing out mistakes— errors that should never have been made in the first place.

As *Classic Images'* book reviewer I have a higher profile than others who make similar comments elsewhere. Also, as a woman, I feel that I am a target of various aggressive "writers" who think they can intimidate me. Believe me, chums, I don't intimidate easily.

When I took over for the previous critic, Anthony Slide, it was thought that *Classic Images* needed more than one person to replace him. So, in the beginning, other reviewers joined me in the pages of *CI*. One by one, they dropped out, leaving little old me — alone. One of the reasons for my endurance has been my thick skin and sense of humor. Aggrieved authors occasionally write to *Classic Images* blasting me for giving them a bad review, and often-times editor Bob King has printed these missives in the Letters to the Editor section. The other reviewers did not enjoy being publicly "shamed" and soon departed. Me? My first letter came after my very first review. The author complained about my "hatched [sic] job." Oh, how I laughed. Since then, the letters have piled up; most of them attacked me every which way, and all have a special place in my heart.

Contrary to popular belief, I don't hate every book published. I have liked and genuinely loved quite a few in the thirteen years I've been reviewing. Bad reviews, however, hold a special fascination with my fans and detractors. I admit they are much more fun to write...but I have never given a bad notice to any book that I didn't feel deserved it. I am always being accused of personal attacks against authors. I've said it before, but this needs repeating: These authors could be lovely people in "real life"— I wouldn't know, because I do not know them. What I *do* know is their writing and their viewpoints. That is what I sometimes have to blast, not them. Of course, they go on to personally attack me when they write me hate mail, but I guess that's perfectly fine. One writer disparaged me multiple times by email, really nasty stuff, after I gave bad reviews to two of his books. Yet, despite that, I raved about his third book, even calling it one of the best of the year. Always, I try to be fair.

This fairness extends to writer-friends. I once got a letter saying that I gave actress Sybil Jason a good review because I knew her. Well, this notion was blown out of the water several times. I was much better friends with actress Virginia Mayo and I gave her autobiography a terrible review. There have been a few books where I was thanked in the acknowledgments but I gave a book a bad review. If you know me, you know I am honest; if you are my friend, you know I do not mean it personally.

Even giving a good review has gotten me in trouble. One author got extremely upset and angry with me over a rave I gave him. In the review, I listed a few minor things I had problems with, but on the whole, it was a wonderful review. Prior to it being published, I told this writer that I loved his book and said it would be among the best of the year. When he saw the review, he flipped out, claiming that I lied and betrayed him. So upset was he that he never spoke to me again. Everyone who read the review, including his publisher, was puzzled by his reaction.

I admit to being zealous in my love of film, which has gotten me into a lot of hassles. I have opinions, of course I do, and I share them in my column — after all, it is *my* column. If you do not like my opinions, don't read me, it's as simple as that.

In 2009, BearManor Media published my first volume of collected book reviews, *Let Me Tell You How I Really Feel … The Uncensored Book Reviews of Classic Images' Laura Wagner, 2001-2010*, which also included my hate mail. This book you hold in your hands is a follow-up, mostly reviews covering 2010 to 2014, with a few earlier write-ups thrown in. Yes, there are bad reviews, but also some very good ones. Also included are a couple of essays I wrote in my Book Points column, "Gossip or Fact?" and "Stand Up for B Movies," which will best show readers what I believe in and expect from film books.

I do wonder sometimes why I continue to review. It's a thankless task and makes me and the books I write targets. But then I get letters from *Classic Images* readers (Robert Milroy, for one) who tell me that I saved them money on a book they might have bought if not for my review. Other readers say they fell out of their chairs laughing about something I wrote. I realize that I am providing a service for other movie fans. Also, to be able to champion the unsung in Hollywood is always worthwhile. Someone needs to go against the standard thinking that is prevalent in Hollywood biographies. Some days it gets me scorned by troubled individuals, but in the end, it pays off in that I am standing up to those clueless and scandal-mongering authors who fill up the book market. And encouraging those writers who make an extra effort with their books.

Here's to another thirteen years — wait, what am I saying?!

Acknowledgments

I WOULD LIKE TO THANK THE FOLLOWING PEOPLE FOR THEIR CONTINUAL help, encouragement, and friendship: Alisa Ann Armes, Peggy Biller, Lisa Burks, the late Cass Daley, Sandra Grabman, Ray Hagen, Matthew C. Hoffman, Frances Ingram, Leonard Maltin, Ben Ohmart, James Robert Parish, Ruth Prigozy, Christina Rice, the late Steven Tompkins, Barry Virshbo, Archie Waugh, and Tom Weaver. My late friend and mentor Doug McClelland's spirit watches over me, I am sure of that. I have always been thankful that he came into my life, as he enriched it considerably.

My editor at *Classic Images*, Bob King, has to contend with so much, including a lot of my hate mail. He cleans up my own messy writing, something for which I am eternally grateful. It helps a great deal that he and I share the same viewpoints on film. His colleague at *CI*, Carol

Peterson, is very dear to me. She is (almost always) a kind, sweet and helpful person, and brightens everything up with her humor.

My terrific nephews, Jake and Luke Vichnis, are my whole life. I love them more than I can say, and I am very proud of their accomplishments. Thank you, too, to my awesome brother, Tom, who I surely do not deserve. He's always there for me, and I love him very much. I am also blessed to have two sisters, Debbie and Patty, who make my life interesting. To say the least.

A very big thank you goes out to Jackie Jones, my best friend and comrade in film. Since I met her she has always encouraged me and is unfailing in her loyalty. Jackie is always seeking out interesting, long-forgotten movies, often sharing them with me. I cannot imagine my life without her friendship. She's a great broad, funny as hell, and the most fascinating person I know.

The past few months have been very difficult ones for me, as my Aunt Charlotte died on December 7, 2013, and my mother Fran Wagner passed away on March 21, 2014. Both were strong and faithful supporters of my writing. My mother read every review I ever wrote and got mad when I received hate mail. (Oh, how she laughed when she read the Bread Head story in Tom Weaver's *A Sci-Fi Swarm and Horror Horde: Interviews with 62 Filmmakers* [q.v.].) To her, I was the funniest person ever and she considered me a genius. While I am certainly not, it's a wonderful thing to have your mother believe that you are. My mom was a big movie fan as a child; it was she who started me watching old movies and prodded me to write about them. Her influence on me will never die, nor will my gratitude for all she did for me. I am a very lucky person to have had two strong women guiding me all these years.

Laura Wagner
May 20, 2014

The Reviews

Scoff if you must, but I always preferred Mamie Van Doren to either Marilyn Monroe or Jayne Mansfield. To me, Mamie was always fun, even when the movies (*Sex Kittens Go to College, High School Confidential!, The Navy Vs. the Night Monsters, The Private Lives of Adam and Eve*) were somewhat awful. There was a sense of fun about Mamie, which was confirmed by her 1987 autobiography, *Playing the Field*, which is still one of the best of the star memoirs.

Now, Mamie has gotten her due in **Atomic Blonde: The Films of Mamie Van Doren** by Barry Lowe, with a foreword by Mamie herself (McFarland). "That she has never been given her due as an actress is apparent from entries (or lack thereof) in film histories," writes the author. "This book is an attempt to counteract the prevailing attitudes about Mamie Van Doren's film career . . . It's an attempt to place Mamie in the context of her era, to examine her good, bad and indifferent film output, and to show she was as much an auteur as any other actor in Hollywood." All his attempts are successful. His introduction goes a long way in explaining "why Mamie Van Doren has been overlooked."

Barry Lowe, in his first book, has given us some fun and informative reading. He's an excellent writer, knowing just what to include. So many times I read these kinds of books and I am greatly disappointed by the author's lack of good judgment regarding what facts to include, etc. Lowe is obviously a movie fan and he jam-packs his book with useful info, a sense of humor and extensive quotes from Mamie, all of which are entertaining.

The book is presented as a "Films-Of" volume, with an extensive biography, and each film gets ample space, including credits, song listings, cast, plots, notes and reviews. Mercifully, he keeps the plot summaries short and interesting. The note sections are crammed with fascinating details, many times boasting first-hand quotes from Mamie, via the author's interviews with her, and some of her co-stars. A long letter that Lowe received from *Girls Town* (1959) featured player Elinor Donahue is absolutely priceless.

The author also interviewed Peter Bogdanovich who (as Derek Thomas) directed Mamie in *Voyage to the Planet of Prehistoric Women* (1968). This section was my favorite. There are some terrific quotes about this movie regarding Mamie's fear of "shark-infested" waters. So scared was she that her then-husband stood, rifle in hand, at the water's edge patrolling for sharks. Other good stories: Bogdanovich wanting her to bite a fish's head off (". . . these weren't, like, top quality fish," Mamie notes), and finding seashells big enough to cover the buxom Mamie. All in all, Lowe gets some terrific, very quotable quotes.

And his obvious admiration of her films, whether good or bad, is contagious. So many authors make the mistake of talking down the movies. Lowe could have easily done this, but he doesn't; instead, he makes each and every one sound as fun as they were meant to be. I love the quoted film dialogue, like this one from *The Private Lives of Adam and Eve*:

ADAM: You can't just walk out on a marriage like walking out of a phone booth.
EVE: I'm tired of putting coins in the slot. Besides I kept getting the busy signal.

Mamie, contrary to malicious reports elsewhere, was *not* a bad actress. Catch her in *Yankee Pasha* (1954), as the (too) talkative harem girl, and *The Second Greatest Sex* (1955) to see what she could do when given the chance at some comedy material. In *Teacher's Pet* (1958), with Clark Gable and Doris Day, she practically steals the show as the singing bombshell in whom Gable is (initially) interested. She was a talented singer, as evidenced in *Teacher's Pet* and other films as well as recordings.

Extras are listings of her TV appearances and a comprehensive discography. There are 99 terrific photos, some quite sexy and revealing (yes, there's a nude shot), all of them as glamorous as hell. (My favorite, though, is the silly shot of her and Mickey Rooney, as the Devil, in *The Private Lives of Adam and Eve*.)

According to Lowe, "This book is a historical and critical homage to one of the great blonde bombshells of the screen. If her career never reached the heights of a Davis, a Crawford or a Garbo, Mamie is nonetheless as distinctive and iconic in her way as these other screen goddesses. To some of us, more so." I applaud the author for his efforts—and totally agree. You go, Mamie.

LW Note: Scoff, they did: My Book Points column is all about opinion—mine. The opinions there are purely my own. That said, I occasionally hear from readers, and authors, who disagree with me. Yet, for some reason, I got some rather harsh letters for a few months about my review of *Atomic Blonde: The Films of Mamie Van Doren*. Why?

Because, in my initial review, I dared to declare my preference for Mamie over so-called icons Marilyn Monroe and Jayne Mansfield. I dared to say that, contrary to popular belief, I thought Mamie Van Doren was a good, underrated actress who was deserving of more attention for her acting abilities. To me, Mamie was always fun; I've always enjoyed her sparkling performances, and she had a rare gift to make trash bearable.

Come on, people, she was more than a sex symbol and it is unfair to judge her for her private life, although I think it adds to her overall funness and makes her extremely cool. It's Hollywood's loss that they never capitalized on her comedy talents, although there is definite proof of her abilities on camera. Watch her in the western *Star in the Dust*; she was a perfectly capable leading lady. Musically, she was a good singer.

This is why I love *Atomic Blonde*, a fabulous book filled to the brim with solid info, a sense of humor and extensive quotes from Mamie, all of which are entertaining.

I know I'm not the only one who loves Mamie Van Doren. I will always champion this lady all that I can. I have nothing against Marilyn and Jayne or any of the blonde sex symbols, but, for me, Mamie had the sense of humor and the acting chops to make me a life-long fan. If this isn't popular with some readers, I don't care. It's worthwhile to stand up and defend what others don't deem popular or highbrow. Does anyone think I care if Bosley Crowther liked Mamie Van Doren? I like her, and that's all that matters to this film fan.

When I published the above in my column, the always-classy Mamie emailed me: "Thank you so much for the kind words. You brought tears to my eyes with your stalwart defense of me and *Atomic Blonde*. Your review was well thought out and you really did your homework. To be appreciated, especially by another woman, is really heartwarming for me. All too often, reviewers of my movies have missed the point entirely. And they've missed all the fun of my movies with it. You GOT it and I am grateful for your insight, your writing skills, and your good humor. I wish you much luck in your career."

***

Despite McFarland's no-frills presentation (zero photos inside and out), **The Batman Filmography: Live-Action Features, 1943-1997** by Mark S. Reinhart manages to exhibit some original thinking and a highly opinionated style. Whether or not this will go over well with Batman fans is another matter.

Seven films are discussed: the serials *Batman* (1943) and *Batman and Robin* (1949); *Batman* (1966); *Batman* (1989); *Batman Returns* (1992); *Batman Forever* (1995); and *Batman and Robin* (1997). The newest, *Batman Begins* (2005), was being made during the writing of this book, so it couldn't be analyzed.

The book's 64-page introduction is a marvel. In that short amount of space, Reinhart deftly, and quite amazingly, goes through the history of the Batman character, as created in 1939 for DC Comics by Bob Kane and Bill Finger. This is a beautiful retelling of Batman's history, clearly and efficiently thought out. The Batman of the comics, radio, film and TV is covered, as is the personal development of the character. I can't imagine a better chronicle of this legendary crime fighter. (I'd like to point out one aspect of the Batman character that Reinhart misses here. In the 1960s and '70s, there was a fairly popular wrestler named Batman [aka Battman], who dressed and wrestled in full Batman costume. The man under the cowl was Tony Marino.)

The problem with all this, however, is that the author reuses all this material from his introduction in his film chapters, often, more than twice. This repetition is a serious mistake and comes across as padding; the book is short to begin with, 213 pages (not counting chapter notes & the index). A smarter move would have been to merge the intro and the film sections together, instead of breaking them up in two sections.

As it is, the duplicating of facts and ideas gets annoying, especially since he uses the same words to describe what he's already described. Case in point: the groundbreaking four-part graphic novel from 1985-86, *Batman: The Dark Knight Returns*. On Pg. 38 he writes: "*Batman: The Dark Knight Returns* was a tremendous critical and commercial success, and this success was not confined to the relatively small population of comic book fans. Warner Communications, the parent company of DC Comics, released the series as a one-volume paperback through their publishing company Warner Books. This version of *Batman: The Dark Knight Returns* sold very well at major bookstores throughout the country, and paved the way for the general public to start taking Batman more seriously than they did when he was viewed as a campy TV show character." And, then again, on pg. 140: "*Batman: The Dark Knight Returns* was a tremendous critical and commercial success, and this success was not confined to the relatively small population of comic book fans. Warner Communications, the parent company of DC Comics, released the series as a one-volume paperback through their publishing company Warner Books. This version of *Batman: The Dark Knight Returns* sold very well throughout the country, paving the way for the general public to start taking Batman more seriously than they did when he was viewed as a campy TV show character." This happens several times.

The films get the big treatment, with extensive crew and cast listings and the author's commentary and background notes. And while I think he goes on too long with his plot summaries, he does makes some daring points — I especially liked his tirade against director Tim Burton and the approach he took with *Batman Returns*. I couldn't agree more, although this may be a sore subject with some Batman fans. Actually, I think the author has Burton's whole film career pegged, and I appreciated the stand he takes in the book regarding the mean-spiritedness that prevails in *Batman Returns*. He really explains well why the film was such a disappointment, but he tempers his disregard for the film with a balanced picture of the film's pros and cons. One problem with his

Burton argument, however, comes with this statement: "Stung by the *Batman Returns* debacle, Warner Brothers realized that Burton could no longer be trusted to helm their Batman franchise. They began their search for a new Batman director, one who would have a deeper respect for the assignment." Now, although Joel Schumacher directed the next two Batman movies, Tim Burton is credited as a producer on Schumacher's first, *Batman Forever*. Obviously, Burton still had a hand in the making of the film, to what extent I have no idea, since Reinhart fails to even mention Burton being involved.

Another terrific insight Reinhart gives us is his discussion of what was in the original script of *Batman Forever*, and what ultimately made it to the screen. It gives viewers a better grasp of the film's story, filling in the plot holes. Considering that it has to do with the film's interpretation of the Batman character and his overall psyche, I found this very important.

A perceptive (and funny) moment in the text occurs when he compares, to the hour and minute, the similarities between *Batman Forever* and its "literal retread," *Batman and Robin*. This really elevates his dissection of the films. As does his evaluation of the actors who portrayed Batman: Lewis Wilson, Robert Lowery, Adam West, Michael Keaton, Val Kilmer and George Clooney. This also extends to other portrayals in the films (Robin, Alfred, Batgirl, Commissioner Gordon, the various villains, etc.); he does a good job.

Overall, I liked this book tremendously. If you can overlook the repetition and the total lack of photos (and his obvious dislike or understanding of the serial genre), you'll be rewarded by the individualist thinking on a series of films that usually gets ignored by critics.

***

Ed Nelson, best remembered for a television role, Dr. Michael Rossi on *Peyton Place* from 1964 to 1969, has written his autobiography. **Beyond Peyton Place: My Fifty Years on Stage, Screen, and Television** (Word

Association Publishers), written with Alvin M. Cotlar, M.D., is a treasure. First, I must admit, I knew little about Nelson's personal life. I knew of his work, naturally, in movies and, especially, on episodic television. He's an excellent actor. A couple of years ago I had a chance to catch him on an early '70s episode of *Search*, "Countdown to Panic." He played a man who starts to lose his mind after being infected by a highly contagious disease during a deep-sea dive. It was a powerful characterization that greatly impressed me. Even better was his long-running role on *Peyton Place*. He stayed with the show for its entire run and it was his stability that anchored that series. His story arc with Lee Grant on *Peyton Place* was remarkable, not only because of the chemistry the two shared and how well they played off each other, but the emotion Nelson put into the moments of silence, his glances, and his voice inflections. His simmering feelings for her were supposed to be suppressed by him, unspoken, and he was wonderful.

It annoys me that Hollywood didn't give him a break in films as a major leading man. With his positive outlook, however, he made a solid career as a strong, capable character actor on film, a real professional, broadening his range on TV and the stage. One reason Nelson didn't become a bigger star is evident just by reading this book: He's too nice. The Ed Nelson that is revealed is normal, faithful to his wife, and loves his children. He was never ambitious to the point of stepping on anyone. He was just an actor loving what he did and going about his business. There are some marvelous stories here about the people he worked with, including Roger Corman, Suzanne Pleshette, Joseph Cotten, George Peppard, Ronald Reagan (who he was good friends with), Ricardo Montalban, Clint Eastwood, and Ida Lupino, among many others. He discusses his TV episodes of *The Untouchables* and *The Twilight Zone*, and there is extensive coverage about *Peyton Place*.

Remarkable, for me anyway, was what he had to say about his stage work, especially playing Truman in *Give 'em Hell, Harry!* — a surprising credit for the actor. The photos from this production are terrific. His story about working on his last movie, *Runaway Jury* (2003), is sad and really strikes home the problem veteran actors have these days working with know-nothing filmmakers who have no respect for the older actors.

My favorite chapter dealt with his hosting duties on a local talk show, where he met many celebrities and notable people. It was fascinating reading about what goes into putting together that type of show. The photos that accompany this chapter are priceless. All the photos are gems and there are loads of them, including some color shots on glossy paper. The book is attractively laid-out. While the volume is well written, interesting, and flows nicely, there are quite a few factual errors, misspellings (*Bullet* instead of *Bullitt*, etc.), wrong movie titles (*The Professor and the Bobby-Soxer* instead of *The Bachelor and the Bobby-Soxer*), and just plain wrong information (the whole history of *Casablanca* is inaccurate; Michael Landon starred in *Highway to Heaven* not *Touched By An Angel*). I didn't know what to think when he incorrectly stated that "The Professor and the Bobby-Soxer" starred Shirley Temple, Ronald Reagan and Rory Calhoun and it was renamed *That Hagen Girl*. Holy movie mix-up, Batman!

If you can overlook these blunders, there's a great deal to enjoy here, a lot of humor and good stories. Early on, Nelson tells a story about meeting Joan Crawford, before he came to Hollywood. "What are you going to do with your life, Ed?" she asked him. He answered, "I want to be an actor," to which Crawford replied, "You will be, and you'll be a good one." And she was right.

***

Many people today think they are writers. With the Internet, the prevalence of blogs, reviews on such sites as IMDb and the Internet Archive, everyone has an opinion or think they have a story to tell—whether they have talent or not. More often than not, they don't even have basic writing skills. I am also finding a number of books that are *way* under a hundred pages, mere pamphlets that publishers trick us into believing are biographies. Instead of being sensible and writing an article, these would-be authors stretch their stories into books so thin you can almost see through them.

One such volume is **Bogie: The Final Chapter** by Eli Rill (BearManor Media)—an aptly titled book, because the whole thing is about the size of one chapter. The subtitle is almost as long as the book itself: "A Firsthand Account From the Set of Humphrey Bogart's Final Film, *The Harder They Fall*, By His Acting Coach." (Don't ask me how they crammed all those words on the cover, but they did.) I am embarrassed to even say this, but the whole book runs 45 pages. The author should be similarly mortified. I'm not saying the writing and stories contained within are bad—they're not. The writing is basic, very bland, really nothing special, but the stories are one of a kind.

Still, Rill had no business passing this off as a book. He even cheats with the photos. This firsthand look at the making of the 1956 film *The Harder They Fall*, contains *not one* photo from that production. The photos are from Bogart's other movies, along with some portraits and at-home shots, but nothing rare, and no photos of the other *Harder They Fall* cast members!

Interestingly, Rill quotes a lot of his conversations with Bogart. While some of this proves insightful and brings up some interesting topics, I am always wary of authors who recount, word for word, whole long conversations. The bestselling biographer Charlotte Chandler has made a career writing books based on her "friendships" with Groucho Marx, Federico Fellini, Katharine Hepburn, Billy Wilder, Bette Davis, Joan Crawford, Ingrid Bergman and Alfred Hitchcock—pages and pages, mile upon mile, of same-sounding, "revealing" quotes from people who never, ever trusted another person with such revelations before. I am *not* saying I don't believe Eli Rill. I am only saying that it's hard to trust long-ago memories of conversations, and it's expecting a lot from your readers, too. Our suspicions have been aroused too many times by writers such as Chandler and Darwin Porter in this regard.

Another shaky recommendation, only because *Bogie: The Final Chapter* will have some new stories for Bogart fans.

Speaking of Darwin Porter, I came across something a few weeks ago that really got my goat. I was researching an actress and found that her Wikipedia page was mostly filled with misinformation. There is a feature on Wiki called the "Talk" page, where people discuss the person in question, and talk about relevant information pertaining to them or problems with the page. There, I saw that the son of this actress was attempting to correct and add to her page, but Wikipedia rules would not allow it. It seems first-hand, *personal* information is a no-go on this website because it "can't be trusted." The facts have to be published elsewhere in at least one book or article for it to be valid as a source.

Then, days later, I happened across Wiki's entry on actor Ralph Graves. Reading on, there was a quote attributed to him about a sexual relationship he supposedly had with Howard Hughes. Graves died in 1977 and I was curious where and when he was interviewed. I was disgusted to find that the source of this quote was Darwin Porter's *Howard Hughes: Hell's Angel*.

It upsets me that I live in a world where Wikipedia treats dubious info as credible simply because it was published in a book, but totally disregards valuable information on a person when it is supplied by a relative who knew the person intimately. Amazing. Simply amazing.

***

"This book covers American full-length motion pictures in which boxing is central to the film's theme or the leading character is a boxer. It is comprehensive through 2003 and covers one film released in 2004."

So writes Frederick V. Romano, author of **The Boxing Filmography: American Features, 1920-2003** (McFarland), but he's only partially accurate. This is a film-by-film survey. But, obviously, the author decided that some films were not worthy of their own separate chapters. These films include some of the East Side Kids / Bowery Boys films, *Right Cross*, *The Girl from Monterrey*, *Knockout*, *Flying Fists*, *Duke from Chicago*, etc. Instead, these movies are relegated to footnotes or brief mentions in other entities; I see no point to this. There is no justification in denying us of an analysis of these films and others that are completely missing.

How many books about boxing in films are there? It's a popular sport subject on film, but it's rarely written about. Including all of them wouldn't have been a bad idea, it wouldn't have burst the seams, it would have made this volume definitive — and "comprehensive" as the author claims.

The much-written-about *Rocky* series of films, all five of them, are divided into separate chapters, but the Joe Palooka series is given just one chapter to talk about eleven films — and, even then, not all of them are covered. (Also not mentioned are the nine Palooka short subjects from 1936-37 which starred Robert Norton and Shemp Howard.) You never read anything about the Joe Palookas, and it would have been nice if the author favored *Rocky* less. I understand why he did it — *Rocky* is a boxing icon — but bandwagon-jumping has never been my style. Newer films, presumably because of their "realism," get mentioned more. In his entry about *Night and the City* (1992), with Robert De Niro, his excellent write-up is marred by neglecting to mention that it was a remake of the same-titled 1950 *wrestling* film starring Richard Widmark and Gene Tierney.

The reason I lament the loss of the missing boxing films is that Romano does well with the ones he does include. Being a boxing historian, he adds more to his entries than a normal film writer would. He examines the historical aspects of the films — this is done especially well in the chapters on *Ali* (2001) and *The Hurricane* (1999) — and the boxing techniques of the actors. This is great stuff, written well and definitely the reason boxing film fans should buy this. He also uncovers good background about the films, the real-life boxers, and the trainers who put the actors through their paces. I could have done without all the quoted reviews, but his perceptive comments have a lot of merit.

A big problem I had besides the omissions and the total lack of photos (none!) were the film fact mistakes. The author chastises the film *Rocky Marciano* (1999) for its errors, which causes "a severe impediment" for the viewer because of the "film's numerous and often factual blunders." I trust that Romano is up on his boxing facts, but, film-wise, he is seriously impaired. Warner Oland is referred to as "Oland Warner." *Sunday Punch* was 1942, not 1948, was released by MGM, not Warner Bros., and it's Dan Dailey, not "Daily," who appears in it. Director Lloyd Bacon is named Francis Bacon, for some reason. MGM's *Edison, the Man* and *Young Tom Edison* (both 1940) were not released by Warners. Jane Wyman won Best Actress for *Johnny Belinda*, not Supporting Actress. It's Marcia *Mae* Jones, not *May*. In the section on *The Killers* (1946), no mention is even made that the film added to the Hemingway short story; that the beginning of the film was where the written story ended; he makes it seem that the whole was Hemingway. Romano makes mention of Virginia Mayo's "stylized vocals" in *The Kid from Brooklyn*; she was dubbed. Poor Gordon MacRae is spelled as "MaCrae" twice. (*The Big Punch*, with Wayne Morris and MacRae, is mentioned only in a brief footnote.) He regrets that John Garfield as the Golden Boy was never realized. Maybe not on film, but Garfield did perform it much later on stage. Even a simple name such as Dick Purcell is misspelled as "Purcel." Et cetera.

A very serious lapse was in the *Gentleman Jim* (1942) chapter. I was surprised that a boxing historian like Romano would say that James L. Corbett's "origins in the fledgling film industry ... remain ... curiously unheralded." I'm surprised because McFarland published a terrific, detailed biography of the boxer/ actor in 2001 called *James J. Corbett:*

A Biography of the Heavyweight Boxing Champion and Popular Theater Headliner by Armond Fields. Romano would have done well to consult this volume. It contained much more than Romano delivered about Corbett.

I recommend this book, regardless. The boxing angle is handled expertly by the author. This should fill in the void nicely until someone else writes a more complete one. However, I do doubt anyone could match Frederick V. Romano's fine analyses of the boxing parts of the films.

***

Character Actors in Horror and Science Fiction Films, 1930-1960 by Laurence Raw (McFarland) purports to be a biographical dictionary of 96 "talented, versatile character actors" that promises to be "complete with a biography and in-depth analyses of the actor's best performances." The author, who is a teacher based in Turkey, has a distinct gift for watching scenes and finding messages that surely weren't intended by the movie's writer...or its director...or its players...or anybody else, for that matter. On the other hand, the book does have a certain dash and air of authority. Nowhere else could you find John Agar's character in *The Mole People* interpreted as a "representative of the free (American) world," which "contrasts starkly with the despotic world of the ancient Sumerian underground."

Mr. Raw promises to provide bios for each actor, but the bio info is usually contained in a few lines of easily available information, when such lines appear at all. He also says that he will examine these actors' performances, but there's little of that. Instead, we get a list of each movie character's activity within each movie, sometimes accurately described, sometimes hilariously not. In other words, we're given a film synopsis centered upon each character. Since the author has supposedly seen each of the movies he writes about, I find it more than a little odd that he gets so many plot details wrong. To make matters worse, he freely interprets simple lines and makes them sound bizarre, especially when he gives us the wrong ending for *Revenge of the Zombies*. Apparently, he was watching the special Turkish version not released in the United States. It's also very confusing when he doesn't fully explain the plot and then starts talking about a character he hasn't mentioned before. In his discussion of *Captive Wild Woman*, he tells us who plays the ape and about the mad doctor, and then: "The ape kills the mad doctor Walters, then runs over to the circus to rescue Fred from being mauled to death by a lion." You know, I would care more about Fred's sad fate if only I knew who the hell he was.

Since the book's title tells us that it is about character actors, it would be helpful if the author gave us his definition of what a character actor is. In a normal book, a character actor is defined as a supporting player who sometimes specializes in certain kinds of roles or personality types. Most of us agree that a movie's main hero or heroine is not played by a character actor, but Mr. Raw is using a much looser definition because this book includes such lead performers as John Agar, Faith Domergue, Leslie Nielsen, Jeff Morrow, Clayton Moore, Ellen Drew, Susan Cabot, Tom Conway, Kenneth Tobey, Simone Simon, Jon Hall, David Manners, Rosemary La Planche, et al. The author also seems to have a problem defining genre. The book's title tells us that it's about horror and sci-fi, so why does he include *The Racket, Sorry, Wrong Number, Fallen Angel, Phantom Lady*, and *Brute Force*? No, they aren't horror and sci-fi, but they're included here anyway.

Lawrence Raw, it says here, has "published extensively in the field of film adaptations and performances. He teaches in the Department of English at Baskent University, Ankara, Turkey." Although the author prides himself on being a primo analyzer of film and performances, I found myself utterly baffled by his comments. His writing is strange, and if you don't want to take my word for it, here are some samples:

"Although a devout Christian off-screen, Dwight Frye possessed a pair of staring eyes ..."

"Sometimes [Evelyn] Ankers was forced to play passive heroines, which suggests that Universal wanted to keep her under control, so that she would not upstage her male co-stars."

Lionel Atwill's "contribution to horror films was never particularly innovative or of great historical importance ..."

The police sergeant in *The Mad Ghoul*, according to Raw, "suspects" Turhan Bey's character "of being homosexual," although I've never noticed a hint of this in the film. Also, in regard to Bey, Raw actually recounts the plot of *The Climax* in such a way that Bey's hero is portrayed as a bad guy who will only bring his leading lady (Susanna Foster) unhappiness.

Mischa Auer's "highly accented English made him an ideal figure for playing 'foreign' roles."

Not of This Earth: "... he eventually dies in a car crash, thereby proving that aliens are as likely to die prematurely as human beings." (That's something to keep in mind, especially when driving with aliens.)

The 27th Day: "Despite his authoritative presence as he coordinates the test, [Paul] Birch's admiral turns out to be largely redundant in a world dominated by the threat of extinction."

In *Creature from the Black Lagoon*, Whit Bissell's character Thompson is "assaulted once more by the creature, whose webbed foot comes through the porthole and grabs him by the throat." Okay, the Creature was powerful, but did he had prehensile feet? Maybe Universal should have titled this film *Creature with the Choking Toes*.

I Was a Teenage Frankenstein's "violent ending makes it clear that teenagers can neither be created nor controlled by adults; they need to develop on their own."

I Was a Teenage Werewolf: "If teenagers like Tony are rebellious, they should be allowed to work out their problems for themselves, rather than seeking advice from psychoanalysts."

Regarding three of *The Leopard Man*'s female victims: "All of them are Latinas — passionate and amorous — and hence more at risk of attack, especially at night."

In *Bride of the Gorilla* one of Raymond Burr's "superhuman powers" after he transforms into a gorilla: "Identifying enemies at long distances."

Regarding Raymond Burr's relationship with his wife, played by Anne Bancroft, in *Gorilla at Large*: "They seem to be happily married, except for the fact that Cy keeps following her without saying anything, as if unable to trust her."

In *Creature from the Black Lagoon*, "director Jack Arnold includes several cheesecake shots of Reed's [Richard Carlson] muscular physique, as he embarks on several diving expeditions dressed only in a swimming costume." The term for shirtless men is beefcake; cheesecake refers to women.

In *The Valley of Gwangi*'s "final sequence, director James O'Connolly's camera shows [Richard Carlson] in close-up, stroking his chin and looking down at the floor, as if unable to look the viewer in the eye out of shame for what he has done." Oh. Come. On. The author, too, after writing this book.

Port Sinister's Paul Cavanagh "seems to be the ideal captain, except for the fact that he knows nothing about the seafaring life."

In *Teenage Monster,* Anne Gywnne is a single parent of a son who is turned into a monster. "Deprived of the stabilizing influence of a man, she cannot keep control of her son, who repeatedly escapes from his bedroom and kills his victims, even if he does not mean to." Listen, cut her a break; even Ward Cleaver couldn't control a rampaging son.

This next one belongs in the EEEK Department of reading too much into a simple scene: In *The Invisible Agent*, Jon Hall "resists the torture administrated to him by the evil Japanese scientist Ikito (Peter Lorre), which include angling hooks being placed by his nipples." (No way, except in someone's fantasies, and, actually, Lorre does not play a scientist and there is no "The" in the title for *Invisible Agent*.)

More weirdness is found in discussions of two other Jon Hall films.

Arabian Nights: "Director John Rawlins cuts to many close-ups of his bright face — aware, perhaps, of how it glistens in the film's gorgeous Technicolor palette." *Ali Baba and the Forty Thieves*: "Hall plays the title role — another fundamentally good man with a pencil-thin mustache reveling in the opportunity to wear colored clothing." (Cha-cha-cha!)

Rose Hobart, in *Dr. Jekyll and Mr. Hyde*, is improbably called a femme fatale; Mr. Raw explains that she is the "unwitting victim of Jekyll's experiments." How exactly does that make her a femme fatale? Anyone? Anyone?

Ghost Chasers (1951): "If we do believe in ghosts, the film suggests, then perhaps we will also be protected from evil."

Richard Denning, in *Creature with the Atom Brain*, is "thoroughly competent at his job; this is suggested by frequent close-ups of his face set in studious thought...."

Murder By the Clock "foreshadows *King Kong* in the way it treats [Irving] Pichel as a noble savage falling victim to a corrupt society."

Angelo Rossitto was "typecast as a dwarf." Not to be mean or anything, but he *was* a dwarf ...

The Mummy: "Perpetually in search of romantic love, Frank [David Manners] climbs on top of Helen [Zita Johann] in search of a kiss." I hope he wasn't afraid of heights.

Here's a nicely written line about the movie *The Strange Door*: "In the end it seems as if father and daughter have been condemned to a grisly fate, as they are locked in a cell with the young hero Corbeau (William Cottrell), whose walls are gradually moving towards them." What, the hero's walls are closing in on them? (And, p.s., Cottrell's Corbeau was one of the movie's villains, not its hero.)

In writing about *House of Frankenstein*, this gem shows up: "The two of them quit [sic] the room in a passionate embrace — a fitting testimony to the power of true love." I have nooo idea.

Mr. Raw overuses many phrases to the point where you cringe as they come up again and again; characters smoke pipes to seem thoughtful, wave them around to make points, clasp and unclasp hands when nervous or thinking intently, look up to the heavens to seek divine intervention, are always sidling up to something, and it seems as if everyone wears a trilby hat.

Raw also concentrates on voice inflections and how the characters say certain words. He is truly obsessed with body types, although I would disagree with what he says: John Archer is called "physically slight," while almost everyone else is "thick-set," including William Hudson, Richard Denning, and Dick Purcell, who is also called "portly." How many freakin' times can the author use the term "sang-froid"? Too many, I'd say. Instead of the correct spelling of "inhuman," he uses "in-human" — which, I would think, means something totally different.

Mistakes run rampant here. Raw calls *Mystery of the Wax Museum* a "rehash" of *Doctor X*, and then claims that Frank McHugh played Fay Wray's boyfriend in the former. His whole rendering of the plot is a mishmash, confusingly out of order.

He calls *Genius at Work*, with Lionel Atwill, a serial.

Adele Jergens is misspelled Jurgens. Alan Dinehart is spelled incorrectly as Allan.

John Archer "played in several horror and/or science fiction films between 1930 and 1960." Archer's film debut came in 1938 and his first genre credit was 1941's *King of the Zombies*.

"With the advent of talking pictures, [Richard] Arlen's career took something of a dip, and he became a reliable supporting actor rather than a star...." Maybe not a star on the level of Clark Gable, but Richard Arlen was a star of B movies and would not become a supporting player until the late 1940s.

Frankenstein was released in 1931, not 1930. *Road to Rio* is 1947, not '50.

About *The Wasp Woman*: "Janice's gradual transformation into a rodent is signaled by gestural changes ..." How he got the idea that Susan Cabot's character turns into a rat or a mouse is a mystery. Common sense tells you the movie is not called *The Rodent Woman*. It did, however, lead me to envision a scene of Cabot foraging for cheese.

Jon Hall wasn't at Universal in the 1930s. Nor did Dick Purcell get his start at the same studio; he was with Warner Bros.

Sex change: Director Jean Yarbrough is *not* a woman, except in this book where he is referred to numerous times as "she."

Tom Conway was not the younger brother of George Sanders, he was older.

In *Monkey Business*, Robert Cornthwaite "acts as a comic foil to [Marilyn] Monroe and Cary Grant." Once again (sigh), we see the common mistake of confusing the different categories used to define acting roles. Raw makes it seem that Monroe is Grant's co-star — actually, Cary's co-star was Ginger Rogers. Then, on the same page, Mr. Raw claims that Marilyn appears in a cameo. It wasn't a cameo, it was a supporting role and it was billed.

Dr. Cyclops creates a "serum that reduces people to midgets, no more than thirteen inches high." Albert Dekker (in the title role) shrinks them with the aid of a ray. Calling them "midgets," too, is questionable. There's another mistake in the Dekker entry, regarding *Among the Living*, as the author says that Dekker's John embraces Susan Hayward's Millie at the conclusion.

Lynne Roberts, in *Dr. Renault's Secret*, is referred to by Raw as "Lynne Renault."

Allan Nixon is mistaken for Robert Knapp in the plot write-up of *Mesa of Lost Women*.

The photos are a treat all by themselves. It's a good idea for all 96 actors to have their own photo, but it's too bad that not all of them are clear. Some are fuzzy long shots, some aren't even the actors in question. The photo for Turhan Bey from *The Amazing Mr. X* is actually Donald Curtis. A photo of Olin Howlin from *Little Women* (1933) with Joan Bennett is labeled *Little Women* (1949) with Elizabeth Taylor. Howlin was in both versions, but Bennett looks nothing like Taylor. Margo is wrongly ID'ed as Jean Brooks from *The Leopard Man*. Some photos are dated wrong. Beverly Garland's is not 1954, but a shot from the 1970s. Patric Knowles' photo was taken in Britain before he came to Hollywood, not 1945.

Raw actually thinks the directors have all manner of control over the screenplays, along with other mythical powers, allowing them to carry out vendettas against actresses.

In *The Monster Walks*, director Frank R. Strayer "obviously finds Krug [Mischa Auer] an intriguing personality, as he repeatedly cuts to close-ups of his scowling face." Repeatedly? No. Auer, this time in *Drums of Jeopardy*: "Director George B. Seitz seems fascinated by Auer's presence, as he cuts to frequent close-ups of the actor looking shiftily to the left of the camera, a spotlight shining on the lens of his small metal spectacles."

In *The Brute Man*, director Jean Yarbrough "makes some attempt to humanize" Rondo Hatton; "she [sic] gives him some dialogue and invents a backstory ..." For the record, *The Brute Man*'s story was written by Dwight V. Babcock, and the screenplay by George Bricker and M. Coates Webster.

There's a warped attitude directed against Roger Corman and his feelings toward leading lady Beverly Garland in *Swamp Women* and *It Conquered the World*. The author really gets on Corman's case, accusing him of deliberately abusing Garland personally for the thrill of it! In *Swamp Women*, the harpoon used to kill her on screen is "clearly a phallic symbol" and "suggests that the (male) director has reassumed control over his female star. Vera's bid for power has evaporated into nothing." Then there is this bizarre comment about Garland's death scene in *It Conquered the World*: "Corman cuts more than once to close-ups of her face contorted with fear — a typically scopophilic move giving the (male) spectator the vicarious pleasure of experiencing female suffering firsthand."

Director Edward Sloman "obviously has a soft spot" for Regis

Toomey in *Murder By the Clock*. The script "obviously" has nothing to do with it.

Tor Johnson's lack of character in *Plan 9 from Outer Space* was due to director Ed Wood's reluctance "to let the actor do anything else for fear of alienating his cult film audience." (I have no idea.)

Strangler of the Swamp's director, Frank Wisbar, "seems slightly uncomfortable with Maria's [Rosemary La Planche] strength of character; hence he has her wear a top that provocatively reveals one of her bare shoulders. The message is clear — if male members don't like the idea of her assuming control of the situation, they have a chance to ogle her good looks."

Clearly, this book is unique. Now, excuse me, while I put on my trilby hat, clasp and unclasp my hands, puff on my pipe, and turn my glistening face heavenward in search of divine guidance as I ponder the burning question of how anyone could top this turkey.

***

Charles McGraw (1914-80) is one of those actors who made an indelible mark in the 1940s and '50s. Despite his record of solid performances, he is not as well remembered today as he deserves. McGraw came to the fore in the late 1940s and early '50s with a series of film noirs—*The Killers, T-Men, The Threat, Armored Car Robbery, Roadblock*, and, most importantly, the classic *The Narrow Margin*. He was a formidable presence in these films, probably the toughest, most authentic guy in crime and noirs, with a voice to match.

How great it is, then, that finally a book has been written about him, **Charles McGraw: Biography of a Film Noir Tough Guy** by Alan K. Rode, with a foreword by Jim Steranko (McFarland). It's also great to know that Rode made the effort to find key people in McGraw's professional and personal life to give us a well-rounded portrait of the man and the working actor.

Rode obviously admires McGraw—faults and all—and doesn't

mince words when it comes to the actor's drinking problem. The author's admiration extends to the films, which are given incredibly detailed treatment. Even a movie like *Loophole* gets space, and respectable space, too, unlike the treatment given by other authors who seem to think, "Well, this wasn't a major movie, so I'll only make a condescending remark about it." It also helps that Rode has an excellent knowledge of all kinds of films.

"The actor became synonymous with blunt portrayals of hard-boiled crooks and coppers," the author writes, adding, "McGraw and noir went together like ham and eggs." That last statement could well describe Rode, whose writing fits perfectly his subject and the film noir style. What I like most about Alan Rode's writing is that he's a natural writer, with a genuine love of film. I adore his at times offbeat descriptive abilities; his use of adjectives, for instance, is almost always original.

My only quibble with the book concerns what I consider to be extraneous material. Going into detail about the feud between Louis B. Mayer and Dore Schary, just because McGraw made a movie at MGM, isn't necessary in a book about Charles McGraw. I thought the Mark Hellinger material fascinating and very well written, but it includes more than we need here. When Rode sticks to his subject, the narrative is interesting, and when it deals with things like McGraw's death and family problems, it is absolutely riveting. Rode's good judgment and writing skill shine in the part about McGraw's daughter which was very, very sad, but handled adroitly.

All in all, Alan Rode gives us very valuable insight into a neglected actor who is richly deserving of a book. And the photos are outstanding, containing a rare assortment. I highly recommend this.

***

I have long been a fan of director Richard L. Bare because of his Warner Bros. films, like *Flaxy Martin* and *The House Across the Street*, so

I was very pleased to see Scarecrow Press releasing Bare's autobiography, **Confessions of a Hollywood Director.**

Known primarily for his television work, especially for helming the popular *Green Acres* throughout its run, Richard Bare has only directed about ten films, but they were tough, sharp and they moved.

I thought there was trouble ahead when he wrote, "My name may not be a household word, but you'll see it on some of the 421 television films, 92 two-reelers, and dozen or so feature films I've directed, none of which is as interesting as the story you are about to read." And, yes, to my complete horror, none of the films I'm interested in were discussed. To my complete amazement, I was mesmerized anyhow.

Bare spends half the book trying to *get* to Hollywood! He made amateur shorts and ran various movie houses, all with a sense of humor. He recalls when actress Sally Eilers was making a film on location and stayed with his family; working on an independent Western short with Denver Dixon (*The Double Cross*) that wasn't released; shooting newsreel footage; and briefly doing, or actually attempting, odd jobs at Paramount in the 1930s. It was a long road before he was signed by Warner Bros. to write short subjects, eventually writing/ producing/directing the Joe McDoakes two-reelers with George O'Hanlon (1942-56) and wartime shorts (The Hollywood Commandos). His first feature wasn't until 1948's *Smart Girls Don't Talk*.

I could go on and on about the underrated (and devilishly handsome) Richard Bare. His book is just so diverting, packed with stories other autobiographies can only dream about. I savored every page, and you will, too, even if he isn't a "household name." After this book, he should be.

***

One of my very favorite authors is crime/film noir icon Cornell Woolrich (1903-68). Some of the classic films derived from Woolrich stories include *The Leopard Man, Phantom Lady, Deadline at Dawn, Black*

Angel, *Rear Window* and François Truffaut's *The Bride Wore Black*. Born Cornell George Hopley-Woolrich in New York City, his parents were separated when he was young; he lived briefly with his father in Mexico before returning to live with his domineering mother in New York. He attended Columbia University, but when his first novel, *Cover Charge*, was published in 1926, he did not stay to graduate.

Woolrich began writing (sometimes uncredited) for movies during the period between 1928 and 1930 (*The Haunted House, Seven Footprints to Satan, Children of the Ritz*, and *House of Horror*), and he penned short stories for the pulp magazines *Argosy, Dime Detective Magazine, Black Mask*, etc., where detective, suspense and crime became his specialty. He wrote under at least two pseudonyms, William Irish and George Hopley.

Woolrich, who was gay, was married once, in 1930, to Violet Virginia Blackton, the daughter of film producer-director J. Stuart Blackton; they separated after three months, and finally had the union annulled in 1933. Woolrich went back to living with his mother in New York City, an arrangement that lasted until her death in 1957.

Although his stint as a screenwriter in the early '30s proved unfruitful, Hollywood discovered in the 1940s that Woolrich's stories and novels were fertile ground for film, especially for film noir, and many of his works were adapted for the screen. His stories have also been tailored for radio and TV series like *Suspense, Robert Montgomery Presents, Lights Out, Playhouse 90, Lux Video Theatre, Alfred Hitchcock Presents, Thriller*, and *The Alfred Hitchcock Hour*, among many others.

"Woolrich isn't in the league of Dashiell Hammett or Raymond Chandler as a weaver of mood through the precise or voluptuous phrase," wrote *Time* magazine in 2003. But, they concluded, "You don't read Woolrich for the writing, exactly. You read it for the atmosphere, the smoky, urban settings that enshroud his helpless or conscienceless characters ... Woolrich deals in moral ambiguity on its way to becoming moral invisibility. In Woolrich, love and death — the act of love and the act of death — can be the same thing. The author's triumph is to make the subjects and stories so varied (and thus suspenseful) while the tone is constantly dark, menacing, inescapable. This world-view is so consistent, it must be personal. In his fiction, the mystery man wrote his own autobiography, one page at a time."

A perfect example of Woolrich's ability to weave a mood comes from 1943's *The Black Angel*: "Oh, it was so dark along this street. Just that hooded, half-dimmed light on the other side, too far behind me to do any good anymore. Looking downward into the little pool of its own reflection, like a discreetly retiring eye refusing to see what happened to me ... A car passed once in a while, but even that was nothing, just a swift black shape hastening along on the black tide with a glint of silver at its prow."

Woolrich's personal life was unhappy, fraught with problems, mainly issues with alcoholism and his health. In later years his leg was amputated when a foot infection spread. He became reclusive, his health worsened, and his weight dropped to 89 pounds. Woolrich was 64 when he died, and he is interred in the Ferncliff Cemetery in Hartsdale, New York. He bequeathed his estate, totaling about $850,000, to Columbia University, to endow scholarships in his mother's memory for journalism students.

At the time of his death, he was working on a novel called *The Loser*; fragments have been collected in *Tonight, Somewhere in New York* (2005). To get a more detailed look into his personal life, read *Cornell Woolrich: First You Dream, Then You Die* by Francis M. Nevins, Jr.

McFarland & Company, Inc. has an excellent book that provides in-depth analyses of Woolrich's novels and short stories made into films, **Cornell Woolrich From Pulp Fiction to Film Noir** by Thomas C. Renzi, and how his writing techniques and themes influenced the noir style as a whole. Twenty-two stories and thirty films are discussed: "The Corpse Next Door" (January 23, 1937; film, *Union City* [1979]); "Face Work" (October 1937; film, *Convicted* [1938]); "I'm Dangerous Tonight" (November 1937; film, *I'm Dangerous Tonight* [1990]); "I Wouldn't Be in Your Shoes" (March 12, 1938; film, *I Wouldn't Be in Your Shoes*

[1948]); "All at Once, No Alice" (March 20, 1940; film, *The Return of the Whistler* [1948]); "C-Jag" (October 1940; film, *Fall Guy* [1947]); *The Bride Wore Black* (1940; film, *The Bride Wore Black* [1967]); "He Looked Like Murder" (February 8, 1941; film, *The Guilty* [1947]); "Nightmare" (March 1941; films, *Fear in the Night* [1947], *Nightmare* [1956]); *The Black Curtain* (1941; film, *Street of Chance* [1942]); "Rear Window" (February 1942; films, *Rear Window* [1954], *Rear Window* [television, 1998]); *Black Alibi* (1942; film, *The Leopard Man* [1943]; "Dormant Account" (May 1942; film, *The Mark of the Whistler* [1944]); *Phantom Lady* (1942; film, *Phantom Lady* [1944]); *The Black Angel* (1943; film, *Black Angel* [1946]); *Deadline at Dawn* (1944; film, *Deadline at Dawn* [1946]); *The Black Path of Fear* (1944; film, *The Chase* [1946]); *Night Has a Thousand Eyes* (1945; film, *Night Has a Thousand Eyes* [1948]); *Waltz into Darkness* (1947; films, *Mississippi Mermaid* [1969], *Original Sin* [2001]); "The Boy Cried Murder" (March 1947; films, *The Window* [1949], *The Boy Cried Murder* [1966], *Cloak & Dagger* [1984]); *I Married a Dead Man* (1948; films, *No Man of Her Own* [1950], *J'ai epouse une ombre* [1982], *Mrs. Winterbourne* [1996], *She's No Angel* [television, 2003]); "For the Rest of Her Life" (May 1968; film, *Martha* (German television, 1973]).

Each examination starts off with the history of Woolrich's story or book and a synopsis, followed by the same for the film in question. Then, the author goes into the similarities and differences from the printed word to the screen. Renzi is adept at scrutinizing the works, comparing them with other films, and investigating thematic elements and stylistic techniques. His write-ups make for intelligent and interesting reading. Just one standout is his interpretation of *Fear in the Night*'s homosexual subtext; his attention to detail is quite good, and fascinating, especially since it was something that I did not notice; his persuasive breakdown makes perfect sense. Also handled well is his explanation of the perverse added elements put into the film *Original Sin* (2001), taken from Woolrich's 1947 novel *Waltz into Darkness*. He argues that one of the reasons "extremely outrageous things" creepily creep into some movies

— and, believe me, that is a gross understatement concerning the vile *Original Sin* — is to "satisfy the private perversions of the director." (Or, I might add, the adapter.) For a complex movie like *The Chase* (1946), Renzi gives us different ways of approaching the storyline; food for thought.

There are some very minor blips here and there, none of which should deter you. Misspellings (Onslow Stevenson, Fred Zinneman, etc.), wrong lines (The Shadow didn't say, "Who knows what evil lurks in the minds of men?"), and wrong cast (Tom Tryon didn't co-star in *Psycho*; he means John Gavin). Throughout the book he deftly references other, non-Woolrich, films if he found parallels in their stories; so I was surprised that he didn't see the similarities in Woolrich's novel *I Married a Dead Ma*n to *While You Were Sleeping* (1995), which starred Sandra Bullock. Speaking of *I Married a Dead Man*, for the first film adaptation, *No Man of Her Own* (1950), he makes this interesting comment about star Barbara Stanwyck: "As a gifted actress, Stanwyck has the incredible ability to produce a blank stare that paradoxically conveys an impressive exterior while telegraphing a dark, turbulent malevolence roiling behind the mask."

Renzi's approach here is authoritative, with several neat surprises in store for noir fans. This is a meticulous evaluation of the films and the author proves that he really knows his noir and Woolrich. Highly recommended.

***

Dana Andrews, the star of such film noir classics as *Laura* and *Where the Sidewalk Ends*, has been largely ignored by film scholars, despite his big role in the mainstream classic *The Best Years of Our Lives*. My favorite of his films, besides his noirs, have been the ones where he played against type: *Beyond a Reasonable Doubt*, *Brainstorm*, and *Madison Avenue*. There was something about Dana's controlled intensity in these films that made his bad-guy characters much more effective.

I was very surprised by the new **Dana Andrews: The Face of Noir** by James McKay (McFarland) and how evenhanded and well-done it was. Although his acting has been called "minimalist" by some, Andrews' understated acting style, says the author, "subtly projected a decent all-American guy, whose outlook was usually tempered by a susceptibility to disappointment, inner bitterness or moral dilemma. As a consequence, his characters were sometimes noted for their ambiguity and air of restrained heroism — qualities that became a hallmark throughout much of his career."

This is just a superb book. A terrific read, with a nicely written biography section, it is the product of painstaking research and also boasts some fabulous photos, both personal and film scenes. Each movie is given substantial space. While I feel that the plot synopses go on for too long, at least McKay doesn't use them as page fillers. There is much substance here, with background information, trivia, and good insight into Andrews' career. The author has done a ton of research and he seems to know Andrews inside and out.

This is definitely a must-have, probably the best of McFarland's books that go film-by-film. It's also nice to see Dana Andrews getting some recognition in print for his talent and endurance in the film industry. It's about time!

***

The late Arthur Lyons was/is a respected writer, author of numerous fiction and nonfiction books. The praise heaped on him is well-deserved. The kudos garnered for his volume **Death on the Cheap: The Lost B Movies of Film Noir!** (Da Capo Press/Perseus Books) is, to a degree, justified, though I do not think as others do that it is the definitive book on the subject. Writer Andrew Neiderman (*The Devil's Advocate*) said that Lyons "shines a bright light of insight, information, and analysis on a hitherto dark subject. Not only is it interesting material to read, it's written in a style that flows and keeps the reader comfortably swimming through facts and references that could easily have been delivered in a dry, scholarly fashion. The reader feels he or she is on a true journey of discovery."

I do like Lyons' writing style in the first seven chapters, which details the history and prevalent themes of noir. "The purpose of this book is not to repeat the same material that has appeared and reappeared in the dozens of recent books on film noir but to fill in some gaps left by that body of literature," Lyons states early on. "The first part of this book is an attempt to define in some understandable way what film noir was and is, the subject of much wrangling by film critics and authors, as well as to pinpoint its origins and association with B film production. I have expanded my investigation beyond the boundaries of noir and looked at the development of the B movie in general because it is important to understand that film noir developed as a style within the crime film genre and ultimately developed into a genre itself."

I don't think that there is anything perceptibly new or different in Lyons' text, to be perfectly honest. What he does do differently is make said history more palpable to film buffs. His breezy tone is a huge help in keeping the pages rustling by at a quick pace. The approach is jaunty and interesting, which is always nice, especially with a subject such as film noir which is often written with a heavy-handed style or with an irritatingly bogus tough-guy prose. The first sixty-six pages are the best parts of the book.

Some facts are wrong, though. Monogram was not responsible for casting Sidney Toler to replace Warner Oland; the switch happened when the series was still with 20th Century-Fox and then continued when the series was transferred to Monogram. PRC's classic low-budgeter *Detour* (1945) is given two dates by the author, the correct one, and 1946. The Technicolor process was not invented in 1935. It goes way back into the teens. The earlier version, called two-strip Technicolor, was put into effect in 1922 and used in that year's *The Toll of the Sea*. The process was upgraded in 1928 and '31. Three-strip Technicolor, utilizing all the colors, scored a breakthrough with Walt Disney's Oscar-winning *Silly Symphonies* cartoon *Flowers and Trees* (1932). The first movie to use three-strip, albeit in one sequence, was *The Cat and the Fiddle* (1934), which was followed by a couple of short subjects. *Becky Sharp* (1935) was the first feature filmed entirely in three-strip Technicolor. So on and so forth. Am I being picky? I don't think so. I think that Lyons, with this knowledge at hand, could have worded it much differently.

Later on, he says that *The Sign of the Ram* (1948) was Susan Peters' "first and only film." I'm guessing the twenty films she made before this one for Warners and, most notably, MGM (*Dr. Gillespie's New Assistant, Random Harvest, Young Ideas, Song of Russia, Keep Your Powder Dry*, etc.) do not count. She was nominated for Best Supporting Actress for her performance in *Random Harvest* (1942). Peters was involved in a tragic hunting accident in 1945 when she was shot in the spine and paralyzed from the waist down. *The Sign of the Ram*, in which she marvelously portrayed a wheelchair-bound woman manipulating her husband and stepchildren, was her last movie. She worked on the stage (*The Glass Menagerie, The Barretts of Wimpole Street*) and the short-lived television series *Martinsville, USA* (1951), in which she played, years before Raymond Burr's Ironside, an attorney in a wheelchair. She suffered from depression, developed a severe eating disorder, and was having kidney problems, all of which resulted in her early death in 1952, at the age of 31. Peters, who often played sweet-nothings on screen, had acquired a depth to her acting as a result of her devastating accident, and *The Sign of the Ram* is quite a stunning role for the actress — one that deserves much more than Lyons is able to deliver in his all-too-brief, and erroneous write-up.

In the blurb about *The Whistler* (1944), he says the Whistler would intone, "I am the Whistler, and I know many things. For I walked by night. I know the tales of many men and women who have stepped into the shadows." The correct words are: "I am the Whistler, and I know many things, for I walk by night. I know many strange tales, hidden in the hearts of men and women who have stepped into the shadows. Yes ... I know the nameless terrors of which they dare not speak." The speaking voice of the Whistler in the Columbia movie series was an uncredited Otto Forrest, a fact that Lyons could've mentioned. The only comment about the Whistler entry *Mysterious Intruder* (1946) is "It all sounds pretty silly, but all in all, this film is nicely handled and a solid entry in the series." A backhanded compliment, I must say.

The intriguing eight-film Whistler series (1944-48) is worthy of more respect. It is one of the very few movie series made during the '40s with noirish elements. Calling Richard Dix's central performances "as wooden as the walking tree in *From Hell It Came*" unfairly ignores the versatility the actor displayed in this series. The Whistler was unlike other series at the time; each film was separate unto itself, with Dix playing different characters, sometimes hero, sometimes villain. There were no connecting characters, except for the shadowy Whistler who opened the films and narrated a bit. It was a unique, entertaining series. *The Return of the Whistler* (1948) was the last of the series and the only one not to star Dix. Instead, Michael Duane was cast. The write-up mentions trivia about featured player Richard Lane later becoming a wrestling announcer, but there's nothing more written about the film.

There's some peculiar repetitive phrasing going on when Lyons refers to producer Val Lewton. First, he writes, "Val Lewton was given a great deal of autonomy because of the studio's precarious financial situation." Then: "The fact that many of the B units and directors were given a large measure of autonomy, such as the Val Lewton unit at RKO ..." The third time is the charm: ". . . but Val Lewton's B unit, given virtual autonomy by the studio, was busy . . . ." These references are grouped fairly close together in the text. It's hard to imagine why he thought it necessary to whack us over the head with the idea.

However, Lyons is capable of sprinkling the text with a number of clever expressions. I particularly favored: "Noir characters know they are one step from their final one" and "Just as film noir would be seen later by critics as an attempt to peel back the false face of society and reveal the corruption beneath, the paperbacks told of a murderous, dark, greed-filled world ruled by sex, money, and violence." To be honest, though, there are a few annoyances and things that Lyons probably thought were hilarious, but just fall kurplunk on the floor. For instance: "By the end, you wish they would all go to Mexico and stay there." He "wryly" remarks that *Murder Without Tears* (1953) is "extremely talky and made for seventy-five cents." I was also not amused by his sole comment on *Girl on the Bridge* (1951): "His suicide belatedly puts the audience out of its misery."

My guess, too, is that he has no clue about *Murder Without Tears* star Craig Stevens. Otherwise, why would he say Stevens "played supporting roles in Poverty Row films throughout the forties"? Stevens was under contract to Warners in the 1940s. He also knows zilch about Ed Tierney, the younger brother of noir star Lawrence Tierney, which is evident in the write-up about *The Hoodlum* (1951). Besides, to brush aside *The Hoodlum* as "minor" is a mistake too often made by critics. To simply call Lawrence Tierney's performance "appropriately menacing" is unjust considering the emotionally intensity he put into his part. The plot details, too, for *The Hoodlum* are muddled. Lyons moreover dismisses Tierney's *Female Jungle* (1956), deciding to spend the write-up talking about AIP and Tierney's decline and return to movie favor in the 1980s. I was exasperated that Tierney's *Born to Kill* (1947) and *The Devil Thumbs a Ride* (1947) were not included here.

The second part of the volume, as Lyons explains it, "is a filmography of B film noirs that have been neglected by most books on the genre and therefore may be considered lost, at least by the general public," although some well-known films are included. Novelist Gerald Petievich, in the book's preface, claims that Lyons has "dusted off" these B movies "and he has some fun doing it," calling Lyons' approach to the subject "entertaining" and "fresh." To an extent this is true of the book's first section, but not the so-called detailed filmography. Although author Sue Grafton asserts that Lyons' "take" on these films will "bring a grin to your face," it simply brought a grimace to mine. Here's why.

The filmography's purpose is to list the noirs and borderline-noirs, give credits (cast, director, producer, writer, cinematographer, editor, music), plotlines and Lyons' "entertaining and fresh" take on the films. Maybe I am reading a totally different book. What I see is lazy writing used to fill space with reams and reams of tedious plot exposition. Film noir is an electrifying experience for fans. Do we need to have the plots broken down in such mundane form? Lyons, 99% of the time, resorts to wearing the reader down with "This happened, then that, then that, and finally that." He even gives away the endings to some of the films, which in a few cases, results in revealing a key plot twist.

The digressions from the nominal subjects are mind-deadening. Even though we are told that *Hollywood Story* (1951) is only "loosely based on the murder of silent movie director William Desmond Taylor," that does not stop the author from taking up almost the whole of the commentary space telling us all about the real-life Taylor case. All we get about *The Houston Story* (1956) is producer Sam Katzman's career history. Yawn. The "behind-the-scenes" comment for *Behind the High Wall* (1956) is just one line about hunky star John Gavin later becoming an ambassador to Mexico.

After the plot is regurgitated and thrown in your face, your beaten-down psyche is faced with Lyons' commentary, which is supposed to consist of trivia and valuable behind-the-scenes information. Mingled in with the plots, however, are several irrelevant and ill-advised tangents and some head-scratching comments.

Most entries end after only one line. *Blonde Sinner* (1956) simply says, "This film is extremely downbeat and slow." Okay, explain why. What about this film makes it noir? Even if a film is not good overall, it's essential to discuss its good points in a book like this, but Lyons often fails to do so. For *The Big Frame* (1953): "Weak in almost all departments, this is one of the many noirs produced in England with American stars." He says that *Road to the Big House* (1947) is "extremely depressing," but, of course, he does not elaborate. *The Lady Confesses* (1945) is "extremely low budget but not bad." *The Deadliest Sin* (1956) has absolutely no personal comments; just a storyline.

Quite a few directors are disparaged within. For instance, William "One Shot" Beaudine, who, although not a filmmaking genius, got the job done competently and quickly under severe budgetary limitations. Frankly, I respect directors such as Beaudine, whose job could not have been easy. He did not have the luxuries that other, bigger directors enjoyed, so it was impressive the entertaining films he did turn out.

The above brings me to a major pet peeve of mine. Arthur Lyons is a writer whose opinions film fans and fellow authors respect and take as gospel. His takes on certain filmmakers undoubtedly will seep into other's consciousnesses and they, in turn, parrot his views, no matter how unfair they seem to those of us with open minds. In fact, I have seen, online, Lyons' statements about actor-writer-director Hugo Haas repeated as the absolute last-word. It is time, however, to correct the misinformation propagated by writers such as Lyons.

A little history first: Hugo Haas (1901-68) was born in Brno, the capital of Moravia, in Czechoslovakia. His father owned a shoe store, but he and his wife encouraged their sons Hugo and Pavel (1899-1944) to get involved with the arts at a very early age. The two studied piano, musical history, singing and drama. (Pavel later became a noted composer and would die with his father in a Nazi gas chamber during the War.) After high school, Haas enrolled in the State Conservatory of Music and Drama in Brno. A year later, he started a three-year stint with the Brno Municipal Theatre. In 1925 Haas joined the Prague State Theatre, remaining there until 1939. Also starting in 1925, he wrote, directed and/or acted in many Czech films. One in particular, the anti-

Nazi *Bila Nemoc* (1937), called *Skeleton on Horseback* when it played in the U.S. in 1940, incurred the ire of Hitler, and Haas was put on the Gestapo's blacklist. He married dancer and actress Maria Bibikoff in 1938; she was 19, he was 37. The two would have a son, Ivan. When the Nazis invaded Czechoslovakia in 1939, Haas and his wife fled to Paris. During their stay, Haas acted in *Ocean in Flames* and directed and narrated a propaganda film called *Our Cause*. From Paris, the two went to Portugal to wait for visas to enter the United States, a process which took six months. Once in the U.S., Haas worked on Broadway (*The First Crocus*) and, beginning with *Days of Glory* (1944), he became a noted, busy character actor, appearing in many Hollywood productions. (Haas was also an acting coach, teaching, among others, *Days of Glory* star Gregory Peck.) He acted, too, on the stage in such shows as *The Good Fairy, Volpone, Galileo* and in the Jules Dassin-directed Broadway musical *Magdalena* (1948). Haas had starred in films years earlier in Czechoslovakia, but now was merely a supporting player. Recalling his early days starring, writing and directing, Haas decided to undertake a bold move: He would not only direct, write and star, but also finance his own movies. His first was *Pickup* (1951), in which he used his savings and a bankroll of $20,000 from various investors. It was a sleeper, made a big profit, and led to another thirteen movies. Beverly Michaels and Cleo Moore were the standout female leads in nine of Haas' movies. (Michaels starred in two; Moore, seven.)

With the exception of *Pickup*, his films did only modestly at the box office, but he never gave in to the pressure — he made his films his way. Haas' procedure was to finance his films himself and then sell them outright to the studios so he could go on to the next movie. *Lizzie* (1957) and *Night of the Quarter Moon* (1959) were different situations, both made at MGM. The charming *Paradise Alley*, made in 1958 as *Stars in the Backyard*, was Haas' last film. It wouldn't be released until 1962. He did some television in the '50s, and only acted in three movies during this time that he did not helm, supporting roles in *King Solomon's Mines*

(1950), *Vendetta* (1950), and *The Tender Trap* (1955). In the late '50s, he wrote a play called *A Very Special Guest*, but his goal of getting it to Broadway was not realized. "The play is too clean," he told reporters. "... no drunks; no perverts. It didn't have a chance." He and his wife left New York in the early 1960s and headed to Rome, Trieste, and Vienna. He did a television comedy in 1967 in Vienna, *The Crazy Ones*. He was planning to return to Czechoslovakia when he was hospitalized for asthma. He died there, at the age of 67; his ashes were returned to Prague.

For years I avoided Haas' '50s films. I had read devastatingly awful reviews of them, and was turned off. Everyone seemed to be of the opinion that Haas was a talentless hack, unable to successfully realize his writing and directing dreams in America.

Enter my friend Jackie Jones. She had, for reasons unclear to me now, latched onto Haas' films one weekend and had a Haas-athon that left her very impressed, making her a diehard fan. You must understand that, except for a couple of his films, Hugo Haas' '50s dramas are unavailable on DVD and are not in general circulation. Jackie's zeal for these little-seen, much-maligned films had me intrigued. She graciously sent me copies of his films, and I became equally hooked, fascinated not only by his stories and technique, but his authentic acting.

While I thought Beverly Michaels was perfect in *Pickup*, I was more impressed by Cleo Moore and her ability to alternately bring a likability and ruthlessness (depending on the role) to her roles. She was the perfect foil for Haas. In *Strange Fascination* (1952) character player Mona Barrie, best known for her wittiness on screen, gave a poignant performance in perhaps her best, most multi-layered part. Alas, I have never seen anyone give credit to Barrie for this film, and it's a shame.

Now, we come to Arthur Lyons' take on Hugo Haas' films:*Pickup* (1951): "God knows why Columbia turned Haas loose to do what he wanted, but they did" is the only commentary. Columbia did no such thing. Haas sold the film to Columbia for distribution. Methinks, too, that Lyons didn't watch the movie too closely. Lyons' plotline is very vague and, unlike the others in the book, doesn't give a true representation of the actual story, which is much more involved and interesting.

Hit and Run (1957): "Haas delivers yet another stinko performance . . . [Cleo] Moore was Haas' favorite star, probably because her acting talents equaled his own." It should be noted that not only was Cleo an acceptable actress, but Hugo was also quite good. He was very unassuming, frequently touching, never hitting a false note, with his acting.

Bait (1954): "Haas, a Czech-born actor who decided to start a film career at the age of fifty, went on to become one of the world's worst writers-directors-actors and seemed intent on dedicating his entire film career to remaking bad copies of *The Postman Always Rings Twice*. In this one, he welded the plot to *Treasure of the Sierra Madre* with the usual awful results." First off, as I noted above, Haas did not just start making movies in the '50s. Also, just because his films have an older man/younger woman/younger man does not mean it follows the pattern of *The Postman Always Rings Twice*. *Pickup* and *Hit and Run* are variations of this, but they veer off in other, unrelated, fascinating directions. As for *Bait*, except for the plot device of greed brought upon by gold, it is not a clone of *Treasure of the Sierra Madre*. In fact, Haas gives a devilishly good showing here in an unsympathetic role, quite different from anything else he did.

The author's constant running down of filmmakers such as Haas is very superficial and does not teach us anything about the films. It just shows that he can be snarky.

Let's give credit where credit is due. Hugo Haas infused his distinctive '50s movies with an emotional quality and visual sense that belied the films' low budgets. He was also an excellent actor, his non-movie star looks giving the stories a realism they otherwise would have lacked. His movies were not traditionally Hollywood; they were before their time, true-to-life, sometimes depressing, but always based in a heartbreaking reality. As a director, Haas possessed a keen eye for detail and a darkness that was almost unrelenting and overwhelming. In Hugo Haas' world there were few happy endings, no easy ways out. It was this unusual blend that set his films apart from the mainstream. Unfortunately, his films' limited availability has tainted their reputation with film historians and movie fans, and this is not helped by historians such as Arthur Lyons who take delight in throwing potshots Haas' way.

Another, earlier, example of how Hugo Haas has been misunderstood by critics comes from a 1977 *Bright Lights Film Journal* article on director Douglas Sirk, "Sirk and the Critics." Jean-Loup Bourget wrote, in part: "It might be said, a little schematically, that Haas' case is diametrically opposed to Sirk's. The Czech Haas presents a more independent profile as an 'auteur' than Sirk. He, too, was surrounded by a team. It was comprised of the associate producer Robert Erlik, the designer Rudi Feld, the actress Cleo Moore . . . But Haas' work, in spite of its very personal themes, is almost entirely devoid of style. The intention is more interesting than the outcome. *Hold Back Tomorrow* is a Z picture with the pretensions of an artistic masterpiece, flourishing Haas' signature as scriptwriter, producer, and director. Sirk proves somewhat more modest and could not be considered responsible for the material he treated, some of which he detested. On screen, however, the film might be less 'personal,' but it is infinitely more meaningful than Haas' idiosyncrasies."

Of course, this is a classic example of a writer tearing down a filmmaker to make another look better. Hugo Haas' 1950s films were deep in meaning, style, and an emotional urgency that reflected the real world. If more of his films were shown today, Haas' stature would surely be elevated. To ensure bigger profits, he was urged to make purely exploitation films, but he stuck to his guns and made the films his way. Haas created shadowy stories on film, but now, ironically, his fate as an important filmmaker has been resigned to the shadows. He was a true auteur, as well as a survivor, who fought to have his stories told on film, and it is time for a serious reevaluation of Hugo Haas' films as a director and writer.

"This book is not a scholarly dissertation on film noir; there have been more than enough of those published in recent years," Lyons writes in his introduction. "I wrote it out of a passion for film noir and, indeed, B movies in general, and because tracking down these largely ignored films was akin to that excitement a paleontologist must feel dusting off a rock and discovering a dinosaur bone. I had the thrill of exploring territory others have previously explored and discovering something new in it."

To some degree he succeeds, but mostly in the first section. The filmography left me wanting much, much more. In fact, at least two key films were missing: *Night Editor* (1946) and *The Tattooed Stranger* (1950). The former, in particular, is one of the most under-appreciated noirs of all. It is highly regarded, however, by hardcore noir buffs, especially because of Janis Carter's essential performance as a sexually warped *femme fatale*.

The appendix is very useful. Lyons groups together the noirs in separate lists by year and by studio. It makes for a handy checklist.

Death on the Cheap is not a terrible book. There's much that is good here, especially in regard to noir history and evolution and he efficiently pinpoints the themes of noir. However, I dislike the way he fails to see the worth of so many films. That wouldn't be so bad if he had taken the time to explain why, but he doesn't.

Arthur Lyons passed away in 2008, but his impact on the noir world is still potent. (How noir can you get: Reviewing a book by a dead man?) Even though this book was first published in 2000, it is still in print, still regarded with esteem, and still consulted as a reference. But I question such admiration. I do not call into question Lyons' abilities; he was a terrific writer. The main text of this book flows at a captivating pace, and I had a lot of fun with it. I just would like to stress that this book should not be held up as the definitive source of noir opinions and information.

***

Diane Keaton is one of the very few contemporary actresses whose performances I always love, no matter the quality of the movie (*The Other*

Sister, Town & Country). With one Oscar to her credit (for *Annie Hall*) and three other nominations (*Reds, Marvin's Room*, and *Something's Gotta Give*), she's one of our best and most versatile actresses. Compared early on to her idol, Katharine Hepburn, she escaped being typecast as Woody Allen's longtime foil (*Play it Again, Sam, Sleeper, Love and Death, Annie Hall, Interiors, Manhattan, Radio Days*, and *Manhattan Murder Mystery*) by branching out in risk-taking roles (*Looking for Mr. Goodbar*). Unlike the nobody-actresses today, Diane is superb in a variety of roles, never letting herself be pinned down. She's no "personality actress," but instead inhabits and internalizes her roles to an amazing degree. Her range is awesome. When I see her in slapstick parts (my favorites, *Sleeper* and the underrated *Plan B*), I find it hard to believe this is the same actress who showed such veracity and guts in *Looking for Mr. Goodbar* (1977), who gave such a lovely, understated performance in *Mrs. Soffel* (1984), who went over-the-top, humorously so, in the TV movies *Northern Lights* (1997) and *Sister Mary Explains it All* (2001) and *Hanging Up* (2000), who played legend Amelia Earhart so convincingly in TNT's *Amelia Earhart: The Final Flight* (1994), and who was so touching in *Marvin's Room* (1996). Her most recent performances in *The Family Stone* (2005) and the CBS TV movie *Surrender, Dorothy* (2006) shows that she continues to amaze with her deeply-felt acting. I am particularly knocked out by the Lifetime cable movie *On Thin Ice* (2003), where she realistically portrays a mother who deals drugs and gets hooked on crystal meth. I cannot imagine someone like Gwyneth Paltrow or Angelina Jolie doing the kind of roles Diane Keaton tackles.

Unfortunately, since *Diane Keaton: Artist and Icon* was written in 2000, we don't have the pleasure of hearing Deborah C. Mitchell's takes on *Town & Country* (2001), *Sister Mary Explains It All* (2001), *Plan B* (2001), *Crossed Over* (2002), *On Thin Ice* (2003), *The Family Stone* (2005) *Surrender Dorothy* (2006), and Keaton's Oscar-nominated, Golden Globe-winning triumph in *Something's Gotta Give* (2003). (For a detailed review of *Town & Country*'s disastrous history, please read James Robert Parish's *Fiasco: A History of Hollywood's Iconic Flops* [Wiley & Sons].)

In addition to her acting, she has directed a number of excellent TV episodes (*Twin Peaks, China Beach*) and movies (*Wildflower*), as well as big-screen fare like *Heaven* (1987), the critically acclaimed *Unstrung Heroes* (1995) and *Hanging Up* (2000). She is definitely someone who deserves a good critical study of her work.

There have been two previous books about Miss Keaton: *The Diane Keaton Scrapbook* by Susan Munshower, a short photo-filled tribute, and a purported full-length biography, the tedious *Diane Keaton: The Story of the Real Annie Hall* by Jonathan Moor. At 158 pages, the latter promises to give "intimate details," but ultimately is very skimpy and shallow, with practically nothing substantial to say about Keaton's artistry.

That's where **Diane Keaton: Artist and Icon** by Deborah C. Mitchell (McFarland) comes in. Mitchell knows what she's up against, but Keaton's reluctance to talk about personal matters doesn't faze her a bit. Instead, Mitchell concentrates on the films, while artfully gleaning what personal nuggets Keaton has given out through the years to add meat to her book.

Yes, the book is shorter than I would like, 161 pages, excluding the back matter, but Mitchell more than makes up for that by packing as much as she can in that short amount of space. Her 21-page bibliography is simply amazing, and it shows me that she really did her homework. Every sentence here is equivalent to ten sentences because each is the product of a writer completely in control of her subject.

Diane Keaton: Artist and Icon is beautifully written, and Mitchell's succinct descriptions of Keaton's films and her performances in them are striking and highly readable. It was enjoyable reading descriptions of some of my favorite scenes, especially from *Love and Death* (1975) and *Baby Boom* (1987), because Mitchell has a wonderful knack of relating funny scenes, with dialogue, and keeping them funny. It's not as easy as it sounds. I've read other writers totally mangle a fun line or funny action because they couldn't express themselves properly.

Her opinions are distinctive, and completely her own. I like the fact that she doesn't always agree with the critics, as in the case of Keaton's performances in the *Godfather* movies. She doesn't see Diane's participation in the series as inconsequential. And, when a past writer compares Keaton's style to Sandy Dennis, of all people, Mitchell jumps right in and counters.

But, she's also not fawning over Diane, even though she's a fan. It can be a tricky balance to maneuver, but Mitchell succeeds. She finds the good and the bad in Keaton and her films. This is especially evident in her discussion of the much-maligned *The Lemon Sisters* (1990). Not my favorite Keaton film, I still enjoyed the author's description of some of Keaton's best moments in it. She doesn't summarily dismiss the film, as writers often do if a movie has gotten a bad rap; she, instead, makes the effort to freshly analyze it and give it some due, while also not forgetting its faults. While I don't agree wholly with her estimation of *Little Drummer Girl* (1984), one of the first Keaton films I saw by the way, I can see where she's coming from. Her judgments are strong, perceptive and intelligent, and worth considering.

Another terrific, and valuable, aspect of the book is the author's personal interview with Keaton herself. Diane Keaton is well known as an intelligent, thoughtful, and artistic person, and her comments don't disappoint the reader. Mitchell also conducted an interview with Woody Allen, and his comments are likewise insightful in understanding Keaton's work.

Deborah C. Mitchell, while lacking the usual personal tidbits that writers crave, is still able to paint a portrait of an independent, creative woman who continues to grow as an actress, and gives us an understanding of who Diane Keaton is.

Actor Denny Miller has a nice sense of humor. It's quite obvious while reading his autobiography, **Didn't You Used to Be What's His Name?** (To Health With You Publishers). It's this sense of humor that makes many of his showbiz-related stories so entertaining. However, his stories are interrupted every now and then by chapters that take on a preachy tone: Mr. Miller's take on certain issues and health-related topics. His more rabid fans will probably love this, but I found it irritating. He should have concentrated more on his movie and TV credits, less on his grandstanding, where he tends to be repetitive. I mean, honestly, how many times can he tell us that we are all unhealthy and out of shape? What do I give a damn if Denny Miller thinks I should stay away from hamburgers? What's it to him? Give me more of the career.

And Denny Miller has had a respectably diverse, if unremarkable, career in acting through these many years. He portrayed Tarzan in the 1959 MGM remake, and was a quite blond and impressive looking one at that. He did many commercials, including his long stint as Gorton's Fisherman. He was a regular on TV's *Wagon Train*, and did numerous guest shots on other shows. A very capable, handsome actor.

His meeting with Katharine Hepburn at the beach and teaching her to body surf was laugh-out-loud funny. He recounts problems on the sets with Bette Davis (*Wagon Train*) and Charles Bronson (the film *Caboblanco*), and remembers improvising with Peter Sellers and Blake Edwards on the movie *The Party*. He even makes his chapter about filming a Miller's Beer commercial fun. Did I mention he played Superman in a commercial? Another good anecdote.

The text's one real weakness, since this is an autobiography, is that when we want to know about Denny personally, we get jokes instead. His life, save for his college years and a couple of problems, is very vague. We never really know who he is. He drops little hints along the way, but his private life still remains a mystery. Of course, if he wants to stay private, I respect that. But this aspect in the book was something I noticed right away.

Don't let this dissuade you. This book is entertaining, and the photos are fabulous.

***

As I looked down at the beautiful, sunny, smiling face of Doris Day on the cover, I had no idea what was creeping up on me. I should have been on guard, but I was oh so gullible. Reading **Doris Day: The Illustrated Biography** by Michael Freeland (Andre Deutsch) is truly a bizarre experience. After reading it a while, I began to feel as if I were in quicksand, unable to extract myself from the mire.

All exaggerations aside, this 127-page volume is a head shaker. It presents itself as a biography, but, even though it follows that narrative form, it veers away into something very strange and illogical. It's as if author Freeland has found his ultimate fantasy and he does his damnedest to make us, the poor unsuspecting readers, share it with him. As I read this, I couldn't help but feel sorry for Doris Day.

We all know the standard conception of Doris as the ultimate screen virgin. Oscar Levant didn't help matters when he quipped, "I knew Doris Day before she was a virgin." This cliched notion of Doris ignores the simple fact that she rarely played a virgin on screen; it's just a myth that has grown because the joke behind it is so "funny." Unfortunately, the worst thing about the myth is that it seems to invite some disgusting fantasies.

Sex is a big theme in this book. Freeland makes quite a few odd comments about how Doris viewed sex, how she liked sex, how she looked sexually, etc. Maybe Freeland cares about how she enjoyed the "physical side of marriage," which was the "greatest thing" about her second marriage, but I don't. It's really not important enough to warrant multiple mentions.

"Oscar Levant . . . was the one who would say he remembered her well from the time before she became a virgin. That was not a statement she enjoyed hearing. 'It was such a load of junk,' she later said. 'After all, I was married with a child at the time.' But the public didn't know that. And her films didn't give the impression of a woman who knew, to quote Sammy Cahn again, what went where. Nobody, however, really thought that Levant's quip was anything but a good joke about a pretty good singer."

Okay, this quote gives us the idea that Levant said that virgin line in 1948 which is not true. And I find it rather odd that Freeland would take Cahn seriously and hint that Doris was sexually naive. Doris' early (pre-1950) Warner Bros. screen image was hipper than her girl-next-door persona of the '50s. She was bouncy and fun, less mannered in her acting. To be honest, this Doris Day remains my favorite, before she decided to become an "actress." To assert that she was virginal in these early movies is delusional.

Here is another example of the book's weirdness: "She would never have fitted into an age when girl singers dyed their hair, not just blonde, but that scary shade of blood-red, and pierced their noses with safety pins. You knew Doris Day had never seen a safety pin in her life. She was always far too refined for that."

Here's some more: "It was like those film stories again. In her movies, you just knew that both she and the man in her life would never do more than merely kiss, and be extremely content for ever after. If she had children, you knew for a fact that all those medical books and how-to sex manuals had got it wrong. In her case, no, she didn't want any nonsense about having them delivered by storks. That was quite ridiculous. No, they had to have come from underneath somebody's gooseberry bush, although probably not hers."

How about this choice bit: "She was pretty, had a little pert way of standing and, it is said, had the kind of breasts that made them drool." She had "the hips and bust that really did excite men who came to see the band at work. [Her first husband Al] Jorden thought those assets were reason to consider his child wife a whore."

During the filming of *Julie*, Doris was in a car accident. Other writers would simply recount the accident. Freeland has to mention, for some awful reason, that she had vaginal bleeding.

Don't worry, her backside is not neglected. He makes several references to it, quoting someone calling it a "wild ass." It's even suggested that someone might what to play Bridge on her rear end. (Freeland neglects to mention if it would be two-handed, or four-handed.)

Nymphomania is discussed; it's only natural in a book like this, because we must find out who was "getting beneath those sheets with her." Sex was "vitally important to her," he claims, disagreeing with her own assessment of herself as an "old-fashioned peanut-butter girl next door" type. "As noted, she was a sexy woman, a sexy woman who enjoyed sex. It was not something said very openly at the time, but sex was important to her, much more than it was to her husband, a fact that might amaze the men who gazed longingly at her on screen."

Still fixated, Freeland can't let go: "Sexual deprivation and the worries about what she was doing with her career and her investments were all having their effect. Doris and Marty separated. But not for long . . . He pleaded with her to take him back . . . So, for financial reasons, they came back together again, in public . . . As far as she was concerned, any real marriage was over. There would be no more sex, a sacrifice on her part, but it was also a fact that she no longer fancied him in bed."

The author just can't decide: Does he like her as the sweet virginal girl, or the sexy, love-starved eager mama? We find both visions here.

I thought Michael Freeland might at least prove that he knows about her movies and maybe her music, but I was wrong. He seems uninterested in most of the films, writing either snidely, uninspiringly or just plain overdoing it. In the movie *Young at Heart* (1954), was the hit song "Ready, Willing and Able"? Or, perchance, was it, more correctly, the theme song? It is also mentioned that there is no music in *Young at Heart*'s source film, *Four Daughters* (1938). While that movie was not a musical, per se, the Lane Sisters sang classical pieces which is not surprising since the movie's family was supposed to be very musical. For another musical, *The West Point Story* (1950), he calls her and Cagney "improbable teaming at the time." Freeland seems to think they were a romantic twosome in that, but they were not. Virginia Mayo got Cagney; Doris got Gordon MacRae.

Working with her first big bands in 1938-39, Doris would not be singing the song "That Old Black Magic," which was introduced in the movie *Star Spangled Rhythm* (1942). Nor would she be singing "Murder, He Said" then as well. He also calls this number "Murder SHE Said." Frances Langford never was Glenn Miller's vocalist. And Ray Eberle, who did sing with Miller, didn't spell his name "Eberlee." Twice he mentions as one of Doris's big hit songs, "Perhaps, Perhaps, Perhaps." I know this song quite well and Doris did not have the hit.

Freeland doesn't seem up on details, getting the circumstances of Doris' son Terry Melcher's problems with Charles Manson wrong. Events in Doris' life are squished together in shorter timelines, and things are eliminated. Doris was with Les Brown's orchestra on two separate occasions, there being a break in between, but not so in this book. Her importance during the '40s is misrepresented. He exaggerates her popularity; yes, "Sentimental Journey" was a hit, but it did *not* make her the leading songstress of the period. That would come later.

Forgetting the creepy sex angle, the book strangely presents an idealized Doris. Every actress (or actor) appearing with her is inferior to wonderful Doris. If Doris is doing a remake, her version is better. No one compares to little Doris. Pretty Elizabeth Fraser is here called "plump and homely," and Dorothy Malone is just "trying to look sultry" in *Young at Heart*.

I fail to understand the comment that her third husband, Marty

Melcher, was jealous of her leading men because he wasn't as good-looking as they were, "except possibly Jack Carson." And what's with the snide remark about the "other Doris Day," who acted briefly in the late '30s and early '40s? Is that necessary? Is it that actress's fault that that was her name?

The movie *The Pajama Game* is, of course, made better because of Doris. Sorry, but I believe that if Janis Paige had been allowed to reprise her Broadway role on film, it would have been just as fine, if not better. The fact that *Calamity Jane* is a rip-off of *Annie Get Your Gun* doesn't faze Freeland who thinks the songs for *Calamity* are on par with the classic Irving Berlin score for *Annie*. The Oscar-winner "Secret Love" is a good song, but is "The Black Hills of Dakota" truly a classic comparable to "The Girl That I Marry" or "My Defenses Are Down"? Just askin'.

But what's with the goofy idea that "with no Melcher controlling all her movements, she might have become a great character actress"? This comment is made during a 1955 passage. The author does not realize that Doris owes her movie fame to Marty and the comedies he set up for her at Universal, starting with *Pillow Talk*. Can anyone imagine Doris Day as a Thelma Ritter-type character actress? Marty was, ultimately, bad for her, but it would be narrow-minded not to see the whole picture; they both took from each other, good and bad.

And I wish someone would explain this line to me: "It would be nice to think that she thought it a thoroughly wonderful thing that she had broken her leg in more places than was quite decent." What the hell does that even mean?

Michael Freeland tries to invoke a casual tone, but, instead, tends to sound creepy and simplistic. (A kindergarten-age Doris wetting her pants is mentioned at least three times in these pages.) The writing seems sugar-coated and warped at the same time, and it does not make for comfortable reading. But the author seems oblivious, little realizing how the creepy-crawly details affect the reader.

In an attempt to explain what he's doing, Freeland leaves you scratching your head. He writes that the book doesn't intend to "get bogged down in the kind of detail that doesn't lend itself to this particular subject. It is not one of those biographies that wants to spellbind by words that become more the focus of attention than the details of the life they are supposed to describe. Nor is it going to want to put the subject on some kind of printed psychiatrist's couch. (The very notion of putting Doris Day on a couch would be far too unseemly in any case. It would [be] impolite and I don't intend to be that.) But, while it won't attempt a *National Enquirer* kind of expose, neither is it going to escape those unhappy moments that those old fan magazines like *Photoplay* or *Picturegoer* would eschew so vehemently."

He wrings out every emotion, being oh-so dramatic. As a teen, she was in a car accident, and she was depressed: "One day, listening to that radio, she thought she would get the better of her condition. She threw the crutches away and decided to dance. Tried to dance, more truthfully. Failed to dance, in fact. The song was 'Tea for Two' but the next cup of tea was strictly for one, in a hospital room."

The Tunnel of Love was not a success, "It didn't work. But Doris tried. How she tried!"

The photos are the book's best feature, presented vividly, on glossy stock. Some are not identified, which I guess isn't surprising. For instance, Jack Smith in *On Moonlight Bay* and Frank Lovejoy in *I'll See You in My Dreams* are not credited in their stills. The worse blunder of all is also unintentionally funny: a photo of June Allyson is identified as Doris!

"Unlike a great many entertainers, and like those films, her own story isn't merely bland and insignificant. If it had been, offering you these next pages would be to cheat." Too late, honey, you cheated us — big time.

I have some words of advice for Doris, if she's listening, and, for her sake, I hope she is. To paraphrase the tagline on the poster for *Julie*, "RUN DORIS RUN, RUN FOR YOUR LIFE!"

***

I have mixed feelings about **Evelyn Brent: The Life and Films of Hollywood's Lady Crook** (McFarland) by Lynn Kear with James King, with a foreword by Kevin Brownlow. Brent (1895-1975) is best known for the two films she made for director Josef von Sternberg, *Underworld* (1927) and *The Last Command* (1928), and for Paramount's first talkie, *Interference* (1928). Brent, even when she was doing low-budget films during her declining years, was always an intriguing actress, a performer with snap. I love the title of the book, because that was what Brent was best at: playing lady crooks, with pizzazz and a lot of moxie.

The main biography is a bit uneven. I appreciated the early effort to sort through publicity materials to get at Brent's true childhood and early years before she entered film. There were many conflicting stories, with the author recounting the various versions Brent herself told reporters.

Yet, publicity is basically used later on to tell her story — excessively so. I do realize that Brent is a tricky subject to pin down; there's only so much information available. But a little common sense, please: there are too many needless stories reported that go on far too long. Do I really care about her various articles of clothing and jewels and how she felt about them? A detailed description of her Malibu beach house? Endless quotes about how she felt about movies and her roles? Nope, sorry, no way.

There are sections that should've been pared down to insure a brisker reading pace, slicing away unnecessary information or repetitive items. There are quotes from newspapers and magazines that needed serious editing — say it once; don't hit us over the head with it multiple times. After reading this, I thought I was suffering from blunt force trauma. Sorting through the redundancy and publicity rubbish, however, we find an excellent central story about a woman with some emotional issues — Brent attempted suicide more than once — who also had problems with bankruptcy, career missteps and men. As Brent entered the 1930s, made the wrong decisions, did vaudeville and lesser movies, the narrative gets going and is at its best. The 1960s and '70s, in particular, are very well handled and interesting because of interviews and Kear's keen sense of drama. Through it all, I do think that Kear captured Brent's personality very well. She also did an outstanding job describing her relationships with first husband, producer Bernard Fineman, second husband Harry Edwards, entertainer Harry Fox and writer Dorothy Herzog. The filmography, however, is an ordeal. When trivia/behind-the-scenes info is included, all is well and good. The problem? Someone needed to do some heavy-duty editing on the miles-long plot summaries — nonstop drivel detailing every nuance of the plot, with dialogue, no less. Also included, for some unfathomable reason, were short little biographies on the other players in the movies. Why was this needed? It's a waste of time and takes up way too much space. I had my imaginary red pen in front of me crossing off whole, bulky sections of worthless text. This is a book about Evelyn Brent. I don't want to read about the other actors she worked with. As I say, when Kear sticks to basic info about the movies, that's when the filmography is interesting and of use.

On the whole, believe it or not, I liked this book. I recommend it, but with reservations. This is the first biography about Evelyn Brent, an actress (a "scowling beauty") greatly in need of reevaluation and attention. It's a well-meaning attempt at giving this under-appreciated actress her due. And Brent deserves the attention.

***

I am not generally interested in '70s films, unless one of my favorites appeared in something from that decade. But I had reason to consult **The Films of the Seventies: A Filmography of American, British and Canadian Films, 1970-1979** by Marc Sigoloff (McFarland), a very impressive and complete sounding book, when I got a video of *Fugitive Lovers*, a 1975 low-budget film that included in its cast John Russell (TV's *Lawman*), Virginia Mayo, Jeff Morrow, Doodles Weaver, and Frankie Darro.

What I found was disheartening. My question is this: If you are going to do a filmography on one particular decade, why not include every film — or at least make a good try of it? Certainly, McFarland's other volumes on the '30s, '40s, '50s and '60s were as complete as they could be. Yet, as Sigoloff mentions, in his cop-out introduction, "Some exploitation films such as sex-oriented and low-budget independent ones, and also animated films and documentaries, are excluded because they are out of the mainstream and serve no purpose here." So what exactly *is* the purpose here? It's not as if the author tries very hard with the films he does include. Besides, documenting hundreds of easily accessible mainstream films does not make a book like this valuable. What we need info on are the hard-to-find oddities, many of which feature older movie stars.

Fugitive Lovers was interesting in that it starred John Russell as a vengeful, possessive husband tracking down his runaway wife (Sondra Currie, real-life daughter of Marie Harmon) and her pool cleaner boyfriend (Steve Oliver). It was also Frankie Darro's last film before his death in 1976; a sad appearance, but worth it, I think, to his fans to see him in a small character part. (This was also Jeff Morrow's last feature; he died in 1993.) Also seen briefly is Virginia Mayo, who looks stunning as a movie star who helps the runaways. (*The Runaways* was the film's original title.) *Fugitive Lovers* is not a good film, it's very laughable in spots, but it deserves to be cataloged in a book about the seventies.

Some of the other films missing here are *Piranha, Piranha!* (1972), yet another remake of *The Most Dangerous Game*, starring William Smith as the crazed hunter; *The Astral Factor* (1976), also called *Invisible Strangler,* whose cast boasts Robert Foxworth, Stefanie Powers, Sue Lyon, Mark Slade, Leslie Parrish, and Elke Sommer, but terrible special effects (gotta be seen to be believed); and *The Brain Machine* (1977), notable because of James Best's tormented, affecting performance as a priest and for an early appearance by an unrecognizable Gerald McRaney (*Simon & Simon*). The only Ann Sothern (spelled here as Southern) movie listed is *Crazy Mama* (1975), but what about *The Killing Kind* (1973), which many consider one of her best performances? Also notable in the cast is John Savage (as her disturbed son), Ruth Roman, Cindy Williams, Luana Anders, and Peter Brocco.

Thankfully, there was more to the seventies than the often-boring mainstream films and the likes of Warren Beatty. Unfortunately, you wouldn't know that reading this book. It fails miserably to give us a complete look at the decade.

***

An unexpected surprise was **From Shock Theatre to Svengoolie: Chicago Horror Movie Shows** by Ted Okuda and Mark Yurkiw (Lake Claremont Press). The only horror hosts I've ever been familiar with are Vampira, Zacherley and Elvira, so it's not a subject I am an authority on. But I was drawn in by the book's buoyancy and verve, not to mention the great first-hand insights. This volume is "the first comprehensive look at Chicago's horror movie programs, from their inception in 1957 to the present." It presents "career profiles of the Horror Hosts who provided comedic interludes between commercial breaks" and even monster programs that didn't include a host.

As an added bonus, there is a guide to one hundred films that were broadcast on Chicago TV (each film has cast and director credits and short synopses), a detailed list of 8mm monster films (very well done) and the Shock!/Son of Shock! horror libraries that "started a TV craze."

My only issue with this book is the section devoted to the Shock! and Son of Shock! packages. Each film gets one quote from a genre-related book (or whatever). Bryan Senn, Leonard Maltin, and Don Miller are among those who should be quoted and are, but the ones who are missing and conspicuous by their absence are Gregory Mank and Tom Weaver. These two remarkable authors/interviewers are the undisputed Kings of Horror Writers. Mank has written (among others) *It's Alive!*

The Classic Cinema Saga of Frankenstein (A. S. Barnes & Company, Inc.) and, for McFarland, *Karloff and Lugosi, Hollywood Cauldron: Thirteen Horror Films from the Genre's Golden Age, Women in Horror Films, 1930s,* and *Women in Horror Films, 1940s.* Weaver has written *Poverty Row HORRORS!: Monogram, PRC and Republic Horror Films of the Forties,* and, most tellingly, *Universal Horrors: The Studio's Classic Films, 1931- 1946, 2d ed.*, with Michael Brunas and John Brunas, as well as twelve interview books (so far) covering all kinds of horror and science-fiction movies/personalities. It boggles the mind that these authoritative works were not quoted from. Yet, IMDb "experts" Arthur M. Fried, Daryl 17, cygnus58, bru-5, wiluxe-2 and moviebuffcan *are* quoted. Why should we care about them? I can understand quoting from Mark Clark's McFarland volume, *Smirk, Sneer and Scream: Great Acting in Horror Cinema*, but, honestly, he's hardly an authority for the authors to be citing him over a half-dozen times.

For once, I don't mind hearing from "real" people who watched these horror shows as kids. (And I am *not* talking about the wannabe IMDb "reviewers" above.) These comments went right into the over-all spirit of *From Shock Theatre to Svengoolie* and I actually enjoyed these little reminisces. "On the surface, our book is a history of Chicago TV monster movie shows," writes Okuda. "But it's also a remembrance of them from our perspective as humble viewers, as well as an extended thank-you note to all the producers, directors, writers, programmers, on-air talent, and behind-the-scenes staffers responsible for these shows." The information about the local horror show celebrities is one-of-a-kind and it is doubtful that these on-air hosts will get better (if any) coverage elsewhere. This is particularly true of Terry Bennett, the first, groundbreaking Chicago host. And the photos? Live on-the-set candids are always fun, and there's a slew of them, all excellent.

This is a unique report that shouldn't be missed. The authors tell an engaging story. The book's publisher, Lake Claremont Press, "fosters and celebrates what's distinctive about Chicago's history, culture, geography, spirit, and lore. Join us in preserving the past, exploring the present, and ensuring a future sense of place for our corner of the globe." It certainly does. Good job.

***

When I received **George O'Brien: A Man's Man in Hollywood** by David W. Menefee (BearManor Media), I was happy to see that finally a biography was written about one of the great western stars. He was also an under-appreciated dramatic actor, as evidenced in F.W. Murnau's classic *Sunrise*. Unlike some actors, his life is an unusually colorful and heroic one; he served valiantly in World Wars I and II, and was decorated for his bravery. So, there's a lot of material for a really outstanding full-length biography.

Author David W. Menefee has written numerous books, including *The First Female Stars: Women of the Silent Era* and *The First Male Stars: Men of the Silent Era*. Unfortunately, in writing about George O'Brien, the author has forgotten that he is not writing another multiple-actor book. It might seem logical to him to interrupt O'Brien's life story to discuss at length other stars of that era, but to me it's a big distraction. We do not need paragraphs on Janet Gaynor, Olive Borden, F.W. Murnau, and Wallace Reid, etc. And we especially do not need periodic updates on them. Same with Lou Tellegen — there's a lot about Lou here, for some reason. While I think Lou deserves to be remembered — he led an interesting life, which ended in a tragic suicide — all that would be better served in a book devoted entirely to him. And could someone please tell me *why* in the blue hell his name was always written in the book as Lou-Tellegen? What's with the hyphen?

The writing could have been much tighter. Quotes are allowed to go on and on, many of them containing frustratingly repetitive information. There is a lot of detail about O'Brien surviving the 1906 San Francisco earthquake. It's fascinating that he was involved, but too much of it made my eyes glaze over: Long-winded, overly descriptive passages that go on for page after page does not make for a good read.

What I found most disconcerting was the coverage of the period after O'Brien's last starring film, 1940's *Triple Justice*. We are told that he decided to re-enlist in the Navy, but there is some confusion when exactly this was. It sounds as if he immediately enlisted after he made this last movie, but then we are treated to a quote that tells us he signed up three days after Pearl Harbor. A weird mistake in a photo caption confused me further: "Lieutenant George O'Brien on April 28, 1942, entering the San Diego naval base three days after the attack on Pearl Harbor." Ah, yes, April 25, 1942, a date which will live in infamy. When exactly did he enlist? If it was December 10, 1941, what did he do between that time and the completion of his last movie?

Before 1940, the author's biography is pretty detailed, but after that he seems to give up, and his timeline becomes muddled. I was never sure of the order of things during the war — when O'Brien was hospitalized for injuries, what his duties were or when he did them, etc. After a while, you don't know what the heck is going on.

O'Brien's 1933 marriage to actress Marguerite Churchill ended in 1948, but you wouldn't know it by reading this book. The author has things so scrambled after awhile that it seems they divorced in the 1950s. Not only are his facts on Pearl Harbor wrong, but he has the Korean War *starting* in 1958! Ai, yi yi!! I kept shaking my head, wondering what time period I was in. After O'Brien left the service altogether in the early 1960s, the narrative simply falls to the ground, whimpering and staggering along until O'Brien died in 1985. Everything gets crammed into only a few remaining pages — the actor has a stroke in 1981, and then we're told he was confined to his bed and then ... he is dead in the next sentence. But wait! The following paragraph reprints an obit that says O'Brien had a stroke in 1979. Ugh. The paragraph after that has O'Brien being buried at sea. The end!

This biography runs roughly 174 pages. The next 149 pages of the book are dedicated to each of O'Brien's films, one by one. Frankly, I found the second section useless — time would have been better spent trying to convey the details of O'Brien's engrossing life in a clearer fashion. There is no reason why Mr. Menefee couldn't have filled in those gaps in his story and made sense of everything. I've said this before and I'll say it again: Why spend time researching a subject to death if you are going to rush through the writing process? Are these authors simply not up to the job? More likely, their *friends* have been telling them their book is wonderful and there is no need for improvement. A true friend would be honest and say, "Hey, this needs more work."

Okay, about this film section: each movie gets cast/crew listings and a (mercifully) short plot synopsis. Right upfront, Menefee tells us, "This author makes no judgment of George's work ..," instead relying on contemporary reviews. The bulk of the entries are taken up by these multiple critiques that sometimes don't even touch on O'Brien's performances. I would have preferred some critical analysis from a writer who appreciates O'Brien's work; someone who was able to see things reviewers back then overlooked. Quite a few of the assessments of his westerns are downright condescending and frivolous, telling us nothing about the movie in question. O'Brien's westerns were very popular and enjoyable for his fans, and they should be given the respect they deserve. Also, while it's important that Rita Hayworth co-starred with O'Brien in *The Renegade Ranger* (1938), does that mean that we need a mini-bio of her? I should say not.

Let me say this: There is a lot of good material here — many sources are cited — which is collected here for the first time, and the author had at least some help from O'Brien's family. Menefee just needed to organize it all better. George O'Brien was a handsome, extremely well-built man, and there are some fabulous photos, although I wish a few of them were reproduced better. This book needed a good editor, a clearer timeline of events, and a less willy-nilly presentation after 1940.

I will definitely recommend this to George O'Brien fans, but be prepared for a messy read — a hard slog, indeed.

***

Recently, a friend of mine (who shall remain nameless) recommended what he said was "The best-ever A to Z reference on film noir." He really did rave on about it and I felt, okay, this *must* be something special. Right? I took the chance and bought **A Girl and a Gun: The Complete Guide to Film Noir on Video** by David N. Meyer (Avon Books/HarperCollins). The subtitle to this "groundbreaking work" is "From *Double Indemnity* to *La Femme Nikita*, the ultimate video guide to the most celebrated classics of Film Noir." That's pretty impressive, considering that *Merriam-Webster* defines "ultimate" as "the best or most extreme of its kind" and "incapable of further analysis, division or separation."

This is a 275-page book that also purports to be "entertaining, informative and stylishly written" and "the first comprehensive listing of film noir — both classic and modern, foreign and domestic available on video. The book brings together everything there is to know about noir films and filmmaking." It also boasts "probing insights."

Film noir is one of the most intriguing of movie styles, encompassing fate, hidden psychological subtexts, irony, alienation, violence, sex, and other such goodies. They are films that overflow with "moral ambiguity," where the hero knows what he is doing is wrong, but does it anyway and suffers the consequences. Such a tough, often-uncompromising series of films deserves, I think at least, a writing style to match. Meyer's style is not stylish; it has no flair, no punch. Instead, we are treated to dull, dull plotlines and descriptions that often made me wince, such as this one for Dennis Hopper's character Ripley in *The American Friend*: "A speed freak, a hustler; a stylish, rootless hustler with the attention span of a gnat, the arrogance of a vampire, and the aggressive instincts of a wolverine." In short, I guess the guy is a hybrid of a blood-sucking, hairy insect.

Here are the films covered in this "ultimate" volume: *After Dark, Sweet, The American Friend, Angel Heart, Ascenseur Pour l'Echafaud* (*Elevator to the Gallows*), *The Asphalt Jungle, At Close Range, The Big Clock, The Big Combo, The Big Heat, The Big Knife, The Big Sleep, Black Angel, Blade Runner: The Director's Cut, Blood Simple, The Blue Dahlia, Bob le Flambeur, Body and Soul, Cape Fear* (original version), *Caught, Chinatown, City That Never Sleeps, The Conformist, The Conversation, Criss Cross, Crossfire, Cutter and Bone* (aka *Cutter's Way*), *The Dark Mirror, Dark Passage, Dead Calm, Deep Cover, Detour, Le Deuxieme Souffle* (*Second Breath*), *Les Diaboliques* (original version), *D.O.A.* (original version), *Double Indemnity, A Double Life, Le Doulos* (*The Finger Man*), *The Driver, Force of Evil, Gilda, Gun Crazy* (aka *Deadly is the Female*), *Heatwave, He Walked By Night, The Hit, Homicide, Human Desire, In a Lonely Place, Invasion of the Body Snatchers* (original version), *I Wake Up Screaming, Kansas City Confidential, The Killers, The Killing, Kiss Me Deadly, Kiss of Death* (original version), *Kiss Tomorrow Goodbye, The Lady from Shanghai, Lady in the Lake, La Femme Nikita, Laura, The Long Goodbye, M* (original version), *The Maltese Falcon, The Man I Love, Mildred Pierce, Murder, My Sweet, The Naked City, The Naked Kiss, Night and the City* (original version), *Night Moves, Notorious, On Dangerous Ground, Ossessione, Out of the Past, The Phenix City Story, Pickup on South Street, Point Blank, Police, The Postman Always Rings Twice* (original version), *Prince and the City, Raw Deal, Le Samourai* (*The Samurai*), *Scarlet Street, The Set-Up, Sorcerer/Le Salaire de la Peur* (*The Wages of Fear*), *The State of Things, The Stranger, Sunset Blvd., Sweet Smell of Success, T-Men, Taxi Driver, They Live by Night, They Won't Believe Me, Thief, The Third Man, This Gun for Hire, To Live and Die in L.A., Touch of Evil, Undercurrent, Underworld, U.S.A., Vertigo, The Woman in the Window,* and *The Wrong Man.* Yes, that's right, no *Phantom Lady* or *Born to Kill*, to name just two noir classics missing from the book.

My question to the author: How exactly is this a video guide? None of the entries includes even the basic information of what company put out the movies. Second, the entries themselves are just irritating. If I want to know about *Touch of Evil*, I don't want to read pretentious mumbo jumbo and a stringing together of the usual adjectives to fill up the page. It's confusing, very difficult to read, and, in the end, we gain no insight. I was not entertained one bit. In fact, reading the author's opinions of actors, calling Betty Grable's voice in *I Wake Up Screaming* "screechy," was just a put-off. He "cleverly" calls the script "so dumb, it could be made today." Harty har har! *He Walked By Night*'s acting, Richard Basehart's aside, "is barely discernible." How do you write about *Detour* and not talk about Ann Savage's incredible performance? Well, Meyer manages to do that, totally ignoring her pivotal contribution. Speaking of *Detour*, the write-up is mostly filled with ridicule, although he's kinda on the fence about it, calling it "unintentionally hilarious," "comically bad," "easily mocked," but "like great rock and roll, the film remains moving and expressive because of its crudeness, not in spite of it." He doesn't really make it clear whether he likes the film or not. Director Edgar G. Ulmer "has neither the time nor money to play around with metaphors," he says, but *Detour* is crammed with them and the low budget works for the film, not against it, giving it the necessary raw edge that makes it the classic it is today. And something must be wrong with the author's ears. Like Grable, Tom Neal's voice is frowned upon, referred to as "squeaky."

Each entry starts with a "Mood Guide," which "describes the emotional atmosphere of the film." So, for *Crossfire*, it says, "Well-intentioned message-making." *The Set-Up*'s mood is "Heavy-handed boxing movie." He has no idea what to call *The Blue Dahlia*, so its Mood Guide merely says, "Alan Ladd vehicle." *This Gun for Hire*? "Moody, slightly comic chase." Is any of this helpful? Each entry then lists director, cameraman, screenplay, cast, and a brief plot summary. Now, the brief plot paragraph, totaling just a few sentences, is a good idea, but, then, in the main written section he goes into *boring* detail about the plot. Not needed. Also not needed are the weird, badly-drawn icons that come with each movie to "indicate the key noir elements that each film contains." The most laughable is the single eye and eyebrow (?)

that signifies "Deadly self-delusion." Does that icon belong next to the author's name on the cover?

This book needed a good editor to trim the author's posturing. It also needs to include many more older films, an objective slant, a more readable writing style, more background info, and a better informed point of view. Meyer might think he's clever when attacking actors like Victor Mature and movies like *The Set-Up*, but he's gonna be alienating a lot of film noir fans if they attempt to read this. He'd be a lot better off if noir fans skim it, then toss it, and forget all about it.

***

The usual response from film fans when they hear that a son or daughter has written a book about one of their famous movie star parents is, "Oh, no, not another *Mommie Dearest* ..." Christina Crawford and Gary Crosby have famously told of the horrors of living with a star. While that's all well and good, these books are hardly balanced accounts, not giving the whole picture. That's why I was pleasantly surprised by **Glenn Ford: A Life** (University of Wisconsin Press), written by his son Peter. The author has a lot to complain about — his life with father wasn't exactly a walk in the park, but he tempers this with a good appreciation of his father's career while also sharing some of the good times. You think this is easy? Hell no, Glenn Ford was a complicated personality.

On screen Glenn Ford (1916-2006) had an everyman quality about him that made audiences identify with him, and he did this in a variety of genres. The natural ease and low-key approach seen in his performances would make him a sought-after star, but it also worked against him in the long run. Let's face it, Ford was a big star, starring in such classics as *Gilda* (1946), *The Big Heat* (1953), *Blackboard Jungle* (1955), *3:10 to Yuma* (1957), and others. He paired memorably with actresses like Rita Hayworth, Gloria Grahame, Gene Tierney, Barbara Stanwyck, Bette Davis, Ida Lupino, Eleanor Parker, etc. Yet, for all his many performances, he was never nominated for an Oscar or given an honorary one. He's a criminally under-appreciated actor.

Two of my favorite Ford performances are *The Man from Colorado* (1948) and *The Gazebo* (1959). These two roles are polar opposites, but are first-rate examples of Ford's fine acting. The first was an atypical part for him — here, he's actually the bad guy, plainly off his rocker, and the seething intensity Ford radiates is a wonder to behold. He doesn't chew the scenery, but, instead, simply puts a disturbing twist on his usual low-key demeanor. *The Gazebo* is an underrated black comedy that Glenn drives along with his deft comedic touch. Managing to make himself likable while his character is muttering off-hand comments as he tries to dispose of a dead body is further proof of his talent and star quality.

Peter Ford's book could have concentrated solely on his father's personal life, but instead he achieves a fine balance of career and the personal. It could not have been easy for a son to be writing about his father's numerous affairs, especially ones that happened during Glenn's marriage to Peter's mother, dancer Eleanor Powell. He includes a strange, yet touching encounter with Marilyn Monroe; Glenn's difficult long-time affair/friendship with Rita Hayworth; his complicated relationship with actress Hope Lange; and many on-set dalliances with co-stars. The whole section about Glenn's third wife, Cynthia Hayward, and a person who took advantage of his frail health is just heartbreaking. It's really an appalling story, and you truly feel sorry for poor Glenn.

There is a refreshing honesty found in this book, as Peter delves into thorny aspects of Glenn's life. But the very fact that a person so close to the subject is willing to share his unique insights, is extremely valuable for the reader. Another writer attempting Ford's life wouldn't have been able to uncover some of the stories found here. On the other hand, a family member might be inclined to grind his personal axe; as painful as some of the events of his childhood must have been, however, Peter maintains his balance as an intelligent, perceptive biographer.

I was especially taken by his comments about Powell, who comes across as a warm-hearted person. Her marriage to Ford was not an easy one, and I cannot imagine having the task of writing about one's own parents and the breakdown of their relationship. There's a lot of good, solid info about Powell's life herein as well. I did laugh out loud when he quoted his mother making an "uncharacteristically bawdy remark," about Merle Oberon.

The information about the films is masterful. Peter went the extra mile to interview people associated with his father and because he knows many of them personally, he was able to get some candid stuff about Glenn. There are good behind-the-scenes tidbits, and you get a feeling that Peter is a real fan of his father's work.

He was helped greatly by his own interviews with Glenn and passages from his father's diary. There are nice anecdotes about his lifelong friendship with William Holden, especially a story about them smoking pot together. We learn that Glenn turned down or lost roles in *From Here to Eternity, All the King's Men, A Song to Remember,* and *Born Yesterday.* A very intriguing story turns up later on about Lon Chaney losing out on his scheduled role in *Day of the Evil Gun* (1968).

Many biographies I read are flat and lifeless, but the opposite is true of *Glenn Ford: A Life.* Not only did Glenn live quite a life, but his story is told in an engaging, interesting, and affecting manner by his son. I never would have thought that an actor as unassuming as Ford would have had such a dishy life. This is a must-read book — a page-turner filled with terrific behind-the-scenes stories.

***

Gossip or Fact?

I have become interested lately about Hollywood gossip and some of the things we take for granted as being *true*. How do we know the things we accept as facts about Hollywood actually are factual? I was watching a "newer" movie recently called, appropriately enough, *Gossip* (2000). It wasn't a particularly good film — surprise, surprise — but the premise was intriguing: for a class project, three college students decide to start a rumor and track the results. Their simple rumor changes and gets built upon as it travels from person to person. The end result is a totally distorted, and much worse, version of the rumor.

Could this not happen with Hollywood history and the off-screen escapades of its stars? Authors blindly reference books without questioning, "How did this start?" and "How do I know this is true?" As the years pass and the stories are told over and over, the stories are subject to numerous distortions.

Authors need to be more cautious and skeptical of what they see in print these days. Especially suspicious stories that sound too much like other popular or trendy stories. When you see stories made to fit predictable patterns, you know that the author might be falling into the trap of giving a story more sales appeal by making it conform to a popular trend. Unfortunately, a lot of people want to believe these stories, and as the years pass truth gets buried under a mountain of fictions and fantasies. I guess it's easier to print the legend. Just a thought ....

***

Growing Up on the Set: Interviews with 39 Former Child Actors of Classic Film and Television by Tom Goldrup and Jim Goldrup (McFarland) is an amazing collection of interviews with child actors. Even if some who should be here aren't (Jackie Butch Jenkins, Sybil Jason, Margaret O'Brien), you can't fault those that *are* included: Lee Aaker, Phillip Alford, Baby Peggy (who wrote the foreword), Mary Badham, Sonny Bupp, Michael Chapin, Ted Donaldson, George Ernest, Richard Eyer, Edith Fellows, Billy Gray, Gary Gray, Jimmy Hawkins, Billy Hughes, Jimmy Hunt, Teddy Infuhr, Tommy Ivo, Eilene Janssen, Claude Jarman, Jr., Marcia Mae Jones, Mickey Kuhn, Gordon Lee, Sammy

McKim, Shirley Mills, Roger Mobley, Larry Olsen, Gigi Perreau, Jon Provost, Gene Reynolds, Bryan Russell, Jeanne Russell, Mickey Sholdar, Frankie Thomas, Leon Tyler, Beverly Washburn, Bobs Watson, Delmar Watson, Johnny Whitaker, and Jane Withers. A great mixture, spanning several decades.

Baby Peggy (Diana Serra Cary) recalls the harrowing early days of moviemaking when children weren't as protected from harmful situations. Her hair-raising escapade during a movie, where she was wired to a goat because she had to do her own stunt, was pretty amazing. Marcia Mae Jones laughingly recalls director Michael Curtiz calling her "Garcia" on the set of *Mountain Justice*. Edith Fellows discloses the practical jokes she and Gene Autry shared (hint: horse manure). In one of the better stories on what it was like appearing on early TV, Gene Reynolds remembers the "big hysterical pep talk before you went on, and everybody went on like they were just kicked in the shins." Cary Grant gets a very moving tribute from his *Once Upon a Time* co-star, Ted Donaldson. The best quote about on-set schooling comes from Sonny Bupp: "What was school like being a child actor? A pain in the ass." Then there's the weird connection between Beverly Washburn and Van Heflin's toupee.

While the anecdotes are wonderful, someone like Teddy Infuhr, who made more films than the average kid actor (or adults, for that matter), comes up with zilch — and he's featured on the cover. Billy Gray says nothing about one of his best-known movies, *On Moonlight Bay* (1951), and it happens to be one of his best performances. Also, memories, especially so for children, can be faulty, and there are some mistakes in regard to dates and names. (Mickey Kuhn says that Arlene Dahl played Tess Trueheart in *Dick Tracy*. It was Anne Jeffreys.) The authors could have cleaned these and some of the other more obvious mistakes up (*The Bride Goes Wild* is called *The Bride Goes West* — twice).

Despite this, the book is a terrific, entertaining, often moving look into the lives of child actors — their struggles to cope with growing up on and off screen, and how they maintained their occasionally difficult lives through the years. The Goldrups have added a great deal to our knowledge of these actors, some of whom haven't been interviewed this extensively before. I was intrigued by what Gordon Lee, Porky of Our Gang, had to say, since I knew practically nothing about him, and that Larry Olsen (*Who Killed Doc Robbin?*) is Susan Olsen's (Cindy of TV's *The Brady Bunch*) brother. I urge all to get this.

***

Actress Zita Johann (1904-93) is best known for her role in director Karl Freund's *The Mummy* (1932), co-starring with Boris Karloff. She was born Elisabeth Johann in Deutschbentschek, Hungary/Romania, and she moved with her family to the United States when she was six. Johann made her Broadway debut in 1924 and her first film was D. W. Griffith's *The Struggle* (1931). Besides *The Mummy*, Johann appeared in the films *Tiger Shark* (1932), *The Sin of Nora Moran* (1933), *The Man Who Dared* (1933), *Luxury Liner* (1933), and *Grand Canary* (1934). After her brief film career, she returned to the theater, where she worked with first husband John Houseman and Orson Welles, among others. In later years she taught acting. In 1986, she returned for one last film, *Raiders of the Living Dead*.

Since there have been no books about Johann, I keenly anticipated **Guest Parking: Zita Johann** by Rick Atkins (BearManor Media). I thought it boded well for this biography that Atkins had a nineteen-year friendship with Johann. (The afterword claimed they were friends for eleven years ... but who's counting?)

I was wrong.

Atkins has attempted a personalized biography, interspersing his friendship with her with the facts of her life and career, but he's not a good enough writer to make it work. Unfortunately, there are numerous awkwardly constructed sentences, and passages that seem like gibberish. A big problem is his penchant for transcribing Miss Johann verbatim, not bothering to edit comments for clarity or repetition. What comes across is an occasionally incoherent stream of consciousness that quickly becomes irritating. Honestly, how many times does the text have to repeat the phrases "Do you see?" and "You see"?

There is also an inept handling of the specifics of her career. While never a big name in the business, Johann once was well known and newspapers of the day ran stories on her. Mr. Atkins could have given us a lot more than plot retellings of her plays and movies. Some intelligent commentary, please. *The Mummy* alone has enough backstory to make for an interesting few pages at least. Atkins is not even good about writing about her performances, which also could've brightened up the text. As for her personal life, he unwisely brushes off an incident in 1933 when she was a passenger in a car driven by the often-intoxicated John Huston, with whom she was involved with at the time. When Huston hit a tree, Johann went through the windshield, cut her face and broke her hips. We get very little in the way of detail here.

His sources are slight and he relies mostly on her ramblings, which would be fine if they were structured better. He should have used some common sense in paring things down. For instance, in a quote about D.W. Griffith and her film debut in *The Struggle*, Atkins actually leaves in Johann's following comment: "You may look at some of my publicity photos over there. They're from the picture." Whaaat? Why exactly is this necessary to include in the middle of a quote? But, wait, it gets worse. She then adds: "Where is that book? Let me find it. I feel that it sums things up pretty well. Here it is. I'll read this to you." Talking about the play *Waltz in Fire*, he writes, "Zita said, 'It became a legal disaster. You can read it for yourself in this article, if you please.' After the article was read, Zita said, 'That was just another of the many struggles that go on in this business.'" UGH! It was at this point that I just wanted to throw this book out the window. Likely somebody outside would have thrown it back at me, though.

It's a shame because there is some good info sprinkled about. Atkins clears up some previous inaccuracies about her life, and Johann, from time to time, has some intriguing and revealing things to say (particularly about her family). What this interview needed was better writing and organizing, not to mention more substance and a better use of sources. Notice I said interview and not interview*s*. Basically, many of the personal quotes within come from his one actual meeting with her and her letters to him, and not a whole series of talks. He said they talked on the phone many times, too, but I did not get a sense that the quotes emanated from these conversations. Also, considering that they were buds for nineteen (or eleven) years, there should be much, much more here in the way of her recollections.

There is also something odd about the text. Near the beginning, Atkins writes, "The mild evening Florida air was welcomed. I was in full view of the evening sky. As I gazed at the bright stars, suddenly off to the right, I saw my first shooting star! Grinning, I said aloud, 'Zita's here!'"

More flowery chatter: "Being awakened at five a.m. by the sound of wind whistling through my bedroom window was a start. This was immediately followed by the sound of breaking glass! Soon, I discovered that a picture frame that hung on the opposite side of my room had fallen off the wall and shattered. The picture in the frame was that of Zita Johann. Fortunately, the photo remained intact. After the cleanup and a light breakfast, I walked out to my back porch. Clear skies and lovely breezes were welcome. The weather was identical to another Sunday long ago remembered, the day that Zita Johann and I met. An inner prompting led me to church that August morning." What follows is Atkins going to church, praying and worrying that he had forsaken Johann since her death. I commend Atkins for his spiritual beliefs, but how should the reader react to all this, directed toward an actress he corresponded with and met only once? Passages like these sound self-conscious and out of place.

I know many of you are wondering about the title of the book: Guest Parking. Atkins explains: "My friend [Zita] and I had once agreed that life is so precious yet temporary. It was something that we referred to as Guest Parking. When one stops to think about it, we really are only guests, alluding of course to our very temporal mortal existence here on earth." Frankly, this awful title won't connect with Johann's core audience of horror fans. Also dreadful is the blurry cover photo. While it shows off a pensive Johann, it is just too bland and fails to capture her unique beauty. Since she is best known for *The Mummy*, it would have been wise (from a marketing standpoint) to place on the cover a striking, provocative portrait from that horror classic.

There is, however, a special treat for Johann's fans. Reprinted from pg. 145 to pg. 294 is an unpublished play she wrote during the late '30s-mid-'40s called *And Then It Was Morning*. This is fairly interesting, and it shows what a talented and intelligent woman Johann was.

The photos, from Johann's personal collection, are excellent and very rare, although quite a few are not reproduced well. I laughed out loud at one caption of her and Boris Karloff: "Another scene from *The Mummy*, in which Zita Johann said that she 'was Egyptian.'" There is a fabulous quote attached to a pose from *The Struggle*, where Zita is clutching a wall: "Oh that? That's how I felt about motion pictures, you see ... hemmed against a wall most of the time."

I felt similarly hemmed against the wall reading this mess of a book, and yet I recommend this to her fans. After all, when are we ever going to get another book about Zita Johann? Just don't expect much from this one. The best I can say about this book is that amid the disorder we really do get a sense of what Johann was like as a person. Atkins succeeds in transmitting her character, ramblings and all, on these pages, and I admired her honesty about her life and career. It's always a difficult task capturing what an actress is really like off camera, but he somehow manages it.

For a very well-written write-up on Johann, I could point you to Gregory Mank's chapter on her in *Women in Horror Films, 1930s*

(McFarland). Come to think of it, where's Gregory Mank when you need him?

Miranda Seymour's narrative approach in **Chaplin's Girl: The Life and Loves of Virginia Cherrill** (Simon & Schuster) is similar to Atkins' book, but handled much better. True, Seymour is not a movie fan or very knowledgeable about films, but she makes no bones about it and tries to fill us in as best she can. (I was annoyed that a photo with Cherrill and Cary Grant had two men with them listed as "unidentified." The two in question are Jack La Rue and Johnny Mack Brown. Nobody at Simon & Schuster knew this? Oh, that's right, big publishers often are clueless about film history and rarely seem to employ anyone as fact-checkers. My bad.)

Actress Virginia Cherrill (1908-96) is even more obscure than Zita Johann, even though film buffs will immediately recall her as the blind flower girl in Charlie Chaplin's classic *City Lights* (1931) and for being Cary Grant's first wife (1934-35). To be honest, Cherrill's brief film career, except for the Chaplin movie, was largely forgettable, so you really can't blame the author for not concentrating on this aspect of her life. That said, the section on *City Lights* and the problems they had making it, including Chaplin's strained relationship with Cherrill, is superb.

And what a life Virginia Cherrill had. What is truly remarkable is that Seymour was given taped recordings of Cherrill talking about her life to a friend and neighbor, Teresa MacWilliams. These reminisces are wonderful and absolutely fascinating. She also had access to Cherrill's scrapbooks, letters and candid photos. This is a lady who mingled with high society, traveled the world, was married to a pre-stardom Cary Grant and an English earl, and hung around with the likes of Bea Lillie, Oscar Levant, the Maharaja of Jaipur, David Niven, James Mason, Marion Davies, and so many others. The text is littered with an amazing assortment of famous people with whom she remained friends for years.

It's an understatement when the author says Cherrill was "lucky in her fortuitous connections."

A highlight, and laugh-out-loud moment, was a story about Dame Judith Anderson. Seymour's account of Cherrill's marriage to Cary Grant is harrowing and insightful. Cherrill also talks a bit about his friendship with Randolph Scott, whom she also knew. Finally! Someone who can talk about them with authority because she was actually there. And I can't even print here what she says about Loretta Young — hoo, boy!

The book relies heavily on the taped recordings, which are a treasure trove, but Seymour does not stop there. She adds much to what she was given, describing people Cherrill knew, giving interesting backstories, setting up situations, talking about different countries' customs, etc., all in an effort to educate the reader about the time in which Cherrill lived in. It's all very captivating and comprehensive.

Seymour's one fault is her reading into photographs. She thinks she can guess what the people in photos are thinking and feeling based on their body language. One, in particular, with Cherrill and Cary Grant, she says shows tension between them, but when I look at the picture, I see nothing of the sort.

The book's format is unique as Seymour takes the reader on a personal journey through Cherrill's life. She is continually going back to Cherrill, in bed and talking to her friend who is tape recording the conversations. It's a charming way to do a biography and it works — and is not at all confusing. The combination of Seymour's and Cherrill's voices is magical. The style is partly informal and it only adds to the enjoyment of Cherrill's unique story. My only problem is that Seymour frequently refers to Cherrill as "the old woman" when she quotes from the interviews.

Commenting on a photo of Cherrill in 1939, Seymour writes, "She looks like what, in essence, she always remained: an uncomplicated young woman from a simple background. It's apparent, glimpsing her like this, why she always maintained such an easy friendship with the people who worked for her; she asserted — for she felt — no lines of division." Cherrill's persona literally leaps off these pages and we come to genuinely like her and agree that she had an "incorruptible integrity of spirit."

This book covers a lot of ground, encompassing not only Hollywood but also international celebrities, giving us a rare peek into the world of the rich and famous. I am thrilled there is a book about her, even more thrilled that it is a creditable one with many remarkable stories. Virginia Cherrill's first-hand memories are priceless. Excellent, absorbing reading, not to be missed.

***

Don't be put-off by the knotty title. **Harold Lloyd: Magic in a Pair of Horn-Rimmed Glasses and Other Turning Points in the Life and Career of a Comedy Legend** by Annette D'Agostino Lloyd (BearManor Media) is another fine volume on classic comedian Harold Lloyd (1893-1971) by the dedicated writer/researcher Ms. Lloyd (no relation). Annette is the author of McFarland's *The Harold Lloyd Encyclopedia*, another must-have volume.

Turning Points is unusual. One would think it is a biography and it *is*, in a way, but Annette has turned the standard biography on its ear with this one. She groups related topics together, mixing things up, yet deftly keeping his life and career in chronological order. It's an extraordinary feat that is successful simply because Annette is an authority and because she's just a marvelous writer. Her style flows with a beautiful rhythm. The reader gets caught up with her story, her enthusiasm and her vast insight and knowledge. Simply put, Annette knows just about everything on Harold Lloyd and I found myself marveling at the passion with which she wrote. She loves his comedy, his movies, and she ably conveys this. She's a very clever writer, too, and her choice of words was something I noticed immediately. The vivid use of an adjective is harder than you think, especially when writing about movies. The right word in the right place truly transforms a sentence, elevating it and, in Annette's case, making situations funnier. Hers is a sprightly style, and I liked it.

In his Paul Bern book, E.J. Fleming (q.v.) talked about details and how "biographers search for that one tiny detail that will answer a question, fill in a gap, or help bring a person to life." While he mishandled this in his Bern book, Annette fulfills the concept. Her attention to details does bring Harold Lloyd to life. She knows him backwards and forwards and she fills in many a gap left open by other historians. But she does it in an entertaining way and you do believe that she has a firm hold on the life and career of her subject. She stays focused on her target and aces it.

While plots are retold, they are told in a way not to induce sleep. Annette D'Agostino Lloyd loves these movies and her discussion of them is lively, smart and very informative, especially the section about *The Cat's-Paw*. We learn about their makings, of how gags were invented often on-set. How did Harold Lloyd devise his comedy? What led to his invention of his famous "Glasses Character"? What were the motivations in his life? These are answered thoughtfully and fully by a terrific author who has conducted many interviews and who actually has an opinion. I love authors who can express themselves and tell us *why* they like so-and-so and why they like or dislike a movie. The turning points idea is a good one because she is able to weave all the important parts of this great comic's life and career into a well-planned narrative. It is novel and entertaining and I'm grateful to an author taking the time to get it right. I urge you to buy this book; it's a real winner, written by a highly intelligent lady. I wish she would write more books.

***

"The point of a good book is to crowd as much into it as possible without making it cluttered," Davis Grubb says in **Heaven & Hell to Play With: The Filming of The Night of the Hunter** by Preston Neal

Jones (Limelight Editions). He could very well be describing this excellent volume. Jones crams as much information as he can into this 400-page wonder, but it never seems too much. In fact, this is one of the best "Making of" books out there — and very few have the credentials or the foresight this one has. Jones has done an amazing amount of research, conducting interviews with author Davis Grubb (who wrote the original book the movie was based on), Louis Grubb (his brother), producer Paul Gregory, stars Robert Mitchum and Lillian Gish, actor Don Beddoe, art director Hilyard Brown, cinematographer Stanley Cortez, editor Robert Golden, Sonya Goodman (widow of composer Walter Schumann), second-unit director Terry Sanders, and actor/Laughton pal William Phipps. Shelley Winters is not newly interviewed, which seems strange because of her closeness with the film's director, Charles Laughton, but still an incredible representation of the original film, you must admit.

The Night of the Hunter, which has become a cult classic, is a haunting fairytale-like film that was unlike anything onscreen in the fifties or since. It was also Charles Laughton's only directorial effort for the screen. I always wondered why he never continued in the director's chair, but reading this book, the reasons become clear.

"It was Mother Goose with goose bumps," the author writes in his introduction. "A tale of terror told from a child's point of view, [*The Night of the Hunter*] was the only film directed by the late actor Charles Laughton. Underrated by many critics, ignored by most of the public, this 1955 film nevertheless had a vision and a vitality which today mark it as a major achievement, while other, more successful pictures of its period have been largely forgotten."

The book is driven mostly by its heavy amount of quotes, with Jones letting the principals involved with the movie speak for the movie, which is a perfect situation rarely afforded an author. When Jones does interrupt the quote flow, it is to add choice material and to sort through the conflicting stories. The research is extensive and detailed. One marvelous addition to the book: Jones had access to outtakes and raw film footage. This rare, previously undocumented material is presented as research for the first time. It shows Laughton at work, the way he coaxed performances out of the children (Billy Chapin and Sally Jane Bruce), and the effect he had on his other actors and the technicians around him.

Pre-production, production, post-production, and "the morning after," are all addressed. The film's lighting, scoring, writing — an excellent analysis of the original book — all the blood and sweat that went into making this difficult film, is all chronicled in detail. Jones' comprehension of the unique visualization that Laughton and Cortez brought to the film is incisive. Photos are terrific: sketches, behind-the-scenes snaps, stills, sheet music, publicity, etc.

Not only is this a complete study of the film, but this book also gives us a great understanding of Charles Laughton's motivations and demons. The author's personal portrait of Laughton is sharp and, at times, brutally honest. There's a strange story of Phipps, Mitchum and Laughton smoking pot that is very atypical in regard to Laughton.

I wish a bit more was said about the mishandled remake with Richard Chamberlain for television in 1991 (the date is not given in the book). The remake's major flaw (amid so many) was the casting of Chamberlain. His heavy makeup, to make him look evil, was all wrong. Much of Mitchum's effectiveness in his role was his attractiveness. Laughton, according to Mitchum, "wanted the preacher to be sensuous, so that he would make his evil more convincing — in the sense that people would, quite naturally, have been taken in by him." That was completely lost in the remake.

Laughton was a driving force in *The Night of the Hunter*'s style and form, this book literally taking the reader step-by-step in the creative process. *Heaven & Hell to Play With* is significant and required reading. I'll never look at the film in the same way again.

***

I had such high hopes for **Hiding in Plain Sight: The Secret Life of Raymond Burr** by Michael Seth Starr (Applause). The book has a neat title, but don't let it mislead you. Given its content, its title should have been: *Fat Gay Liar: The Secret Life of Raymond Burr.* Are you disgusted by my substitute title? Does it make you angry? If it does, I don't blame you. You should be disgusted, and you should be angry. Sadly, this book is just a waste of time that adds up to little more than an insult to the life's work of a very talented and charismatic performer.

Burr (1917-1993), the beloved star of TV's *Perry Mason* (1957-66) and *Ironside* (1967-75), is the perfect candidate for a good, solidly researched biography. It was revealed after his death that Burr made up certain facts in his life, including stories about two wives and a son who died tragically young. Burr, in fact, was lying about his private life, and, in actuality, led a secret gay life, all to protect his privacy and preserve his career. He was complex and not very consistent, making up confusing and conflicting stories over the years. This complexity could have made for a fascinating character study, but Starr drops the ball with a resounding thud.

What we find here is an obsession with Burr's "paranoia" and his fluctuating weight. This latter aspect of the book particularly angered me. Burr was a good actor and by all accounts a fine, generous man. The author, for some unfathomable reason, picks on Burr's weight, referring to his "lard" and his "morbid" obesity continually, claiming that the actor was tortured not only by his sexuality but also by his disgusting girth. Frankly, I was offended by these repeated references. The issue of rudeness aside, I've been watching Burr for many years and I never thought he looked repulsive. Never. In addition to his wonderful voice, Burr could be an attractive presence in front of a camera. When I see Burr belittled because of his weight, and turned into a grotesque caricature, I feel such disgust.

Wisely, the author never mocks Burr's homosexuality, even though he goes overboard on this issue. But Starr does have other problems. As you read the book, you feel as if Burr's life and career are taking a backseat to the author's fixations. Over and over you read about Burr's weight, his sexual orientation, and his phony cover stories, and you lose focus on any deeper understanding of Burr's substantial accomplishments. You wish the author had focused more on how this skilled actor who convincingly portrayed a creepy character like Lars Thorwald in *Rear Window*, then could go on to create an attractive and appealing character like his Perry Mason and earn the devoted following of millions of fans.

If Starr has a deep knowledge of films and TV, he does a good job hiding it. It's as if Starr went to IMDb, looked at Burr's list of films, and then with little interest or knowledge of Burr's work, he bangs out a book. The long, detailed, and intimate acquaintance that a good celebrity biographer has with the work of his subject is missing here. As a substitute, there are plots galore, especially cumbersome, torturous ones for *Raw Deal* and *Rear Window*.

Another telltale sign of Starr's limited perspective is that he doesn't understand that just because Burr was in *Adventures of Don Juan* with Errol Flynn you should not say that Burr "co-starred" with Flynn. This is an amateur's mistake, and one Starr makes often. Predictably, he complements this faux pas by overplaying Burr's early years in Hollywood as a rising "star."

Yet another sign of his limited perspective is his total omission of a true starring role for Burr in *Bride of the Gorilla*. Those who lack a deep knowledge of the industry routinely ignore films like this. True, this is not a movie an actor would list proudly on his resume, but it gave Burr a lead nonetheless, and he did a good job in it. Omitting it means that the author is not going to give us an accurate impression of the progress of Burr's career. (For detailed information on that movie, read *Kiss Tomorrow Goodbye: The Barbara Payton Story* by John O'Dowd [q.v.]) Adding to this superficial interest in movies and lack of movie knowledge are the factual errors and name misspellings (e.g. Sheila Graham, Edmund O'Brien).

Despite the author's skill as a writer, he ends up with an irritating narrative. Burr was a wonderful actor whose career deserves more understanding and whose character deserves more respect. What a disappointment.

***

Not the most pleasant subject, but excellently done, **The Hitler Filmography: Worldwide Feature Film and Television Miniseries Portrayals, 1940 through 2000** (McFarland) establishes once and for all author Charles P. Mitchell's mastery of film criticism. His knowledge of history, literature, and film comes together to make his commentary erudite, lively and interesting. No mean feat, considering this is about Adolph Hitler.

Around one hundred films featuring (lead, cameo) an actor (no newsreel footage or voice-overs of the real Fuehrer) portraying Hitler are covered. No cartoon images (which needs its own book), documentaries or short subjects, but TV movies and miniseries are included. There's a separate appendix of series TV depictions.

Each film is discussed thoroughly, containing an annotated cast list, crew, synopsis, Mitchell's appraisal of the movie and the actor playing Hitler, and quotes. Every film gets extensive coverage (missing this time is Mitchell's usual star rating system), but what I admired most was the author's impressive check of historical accuracy. He compares real-life with the scripted events, while also analyzing different screen versions of the same incidents (the movies dealing with Hitler's last days, etc.). Another fine touch is the few biographical notes on the actors playing Hitler, a distinguished group for such a despicable man: Bobby Watson, Richard Basehart, Anthony Hopkins, Heinz Schubert (who is also depicted on the book's eerie cover), Gilbert Gottfried (not distinguished, perhaps, just an odd choice), Alec Guinness, Luther Adler, Ian McKellan, Scott Henderson (doing that hysterical "Hitler on Ice" from Mel Brooks'

History of the World — Part One), Ludwig Donath, Robert Vaughn, Tom Dugan, and others.

The appendix features a fascinating story about MGM's "Aborted Hitler Western," which Dore Schary had been planning in 1943; Louis B. Mayer pulled the plug on the filmed project. It was developed as a parable, placing Hitler, his allies and enemies in a 1870s "range war." Schary and Sinclair Lewis' before-its-time screenplay was eventually published in book form in 1963, titled *Storm in the West*. Interestingly, another appendix focuses on "Possible Hitler Film Projects," novels that Mitchell feels would make good/unusual material for future filmmakers.

In his entertaining way, Mitchell urges the reader to seek out some of the distinctive movies included in his filmography. Three, in particular, sound interesting: the spoof *That's Adequate*, Veronica Lake's campy *Flesh Feast*, and the oddball *The Magic Face*, with Luther Adler.

Even if you don't think Hitler is the best subject for a book, you still cannot deny Charles P. Mitchell's astute examination. McFarland should put him to work on another right away, if on a more cheery topic. Last year, Mitchell gave us *The Devil on Screen*, this year Hitler. I suggest something much lighter in tone, but otherwise this is an excellent reference for film fans.

***

Hollywood's Child: Dancing Through Oz (BearManor Media) is an engrossing biography by dancer/actress Caren Marsh-Doll, who, as per the title, also acted as Judy Garland's stand-in in *The Wizard of Oz* (1939). Doll did numerous dancing bits (*Rosalie, Best Foot Forward, That Night in Rio,* etc.) and feature and lead parts (Bob Steele's leading lady in *The Navajo Kid*, 1945) during the 1930s and '40s, without ever having achieved stardom. But, unlike some from that time period who write books, seeking their belated fifteen minutes of fame, Doll actually has a story to tell — an inspiring one, it turns out.

Hollywood's Child fully and charmingly captures Doll's wide-eyed innocence when she first came to Hollywood in 1937. Most vivid is her first day at MGM, an expressive section that is unlike anything I've read. Doll takes the reader into that time period, her writing putting us in her shoes as she deals with the filmmaking process for the first time. *Wizard of Oz* readers will revel in her recollections of Judy Garland and her on-set experiences. It's very hard, at this late date, to hear anything new about this 1939 classic, but Doll provides. The book's one flaw, but part of its charm, is its disregard for a proper chronological order. She skips a period of several years in a flash, acting as if it was a natural thing to do, even though her organization doesn't quite make sense. Some references, like songs, are also not in the proper order, but these can be overlooked, considering the enthusiasm and delight that Doll takes in telling us her story.

Doll's private life has been less than ideal, and her candor in this area makes her story more interesting. Her story switches to gutsy, although still optimistic, prose as she deals with a devastating plane crash, in which she was one of the few survivors, and a marriage to an alcoholic. She gains much sympathy with her honesty and her spunky perseverance in the face of problems and setbacks. You can't help but like Caren Marsh-Doll. And, undoubtedly, you will like her book. It's a good read — and the pictures are terrific. One boo-boo: no filmography. Considering all her unbilled dancing bits, a film list should have been mandatory.

***

In Tom Weaver's archives there must be long rows of file cabinets that he regularly packs with material on vintage horror and sci-fi films; and I picture these overfilled cabinets beginning to vibrate and rattle and rumble whenever the build-up of never-published production information and photos becomes too great. The quaking grows in intensity until the only way to ease the pressure and avoid explosion is for him to release some of this material via a new book or two.

BearManor Media may have recently saved us from a detonation when *in one day* they debuted two new Weaver books, one about the 1959 sci-fi movie *The Hideous Sun Demon* (q.v.). The other is **The Horror Hits of Richard Gordon**, a book-length interview with the English-born, New York-based producer of the made-in-England fright favorites *The Haunted Stranger* (1958) and *Corridors of Blood* (1962) with Boris Karloff, *Fiend Without a Face* (1958) with Marshall Thompson, *Island of Terror* (1966) with Peter Cushing, *Horror Hospital* (1973) with Michael Gough, as well as *First Man Into Space* (1959), *Devil Doll* (1964), *Curse of the Voodoo* (1965), *The Projected Man* (1966), *Naked Evil* (1966), *Secrets of Sex* (1970), *Tower of Evil* (1972), *The Cat and the Canary* (1978), and *Inseminoid* (1981).

Gordon actually wrote the first chapter, a six-page reminiscence about his beginning days as a producer in the mid-1950s when he specialized in low-cost crime movies, starring the likes of Pat O'Brien, Zachary Scott, Wayne Morris, Keefe Brasselle, Richard Denning, Faith Domergue and other imported American actors. There are also contributions by Frederick E. Smith, the writer of the short story on which *Devil Doll* was based, and Norman Warren, director of *Inseminoid*, and a humorous intro by Robin Askwith, a supporting player in Gordon's *Tower of Evil* and the star of his *Horror Hospital*.

Not only does the book provide the history of Gordon's horror movies, it also makes the reader fully aware of what a producer's job *is*: With his hands-on approach to moviemaking, Gordon is in a position to give us a fly-on-the-wall view of the start-to-finish process for each picture: It begins with him securing the rights to existing story material (*Fiend Without a Face, Devil Doll, The Cat and the Canary*, etc.) or supervising the writing of original scripts, then moves on to financing, casting, lining up locations, serving as on-set peacemaker, all the way to scoring, dealing with censors, promotion, theatrical distribution and sometimes even the movie's decades-later home-video release.

Gordon even talks about some of "the ones that got away" — movies he'd hoped to make but, for one reason or another, couldn't; they include a remake of Karloff's 1933 *The Ghoul*, new versions of *Dracula* (with Karloff) and *The Most Dangerous Game* (with Bryant Haliday), a Karloff-starring filmization of Poe's "The Facts in the Case of M. Valdemar," and more.

Gordon is sharp, his memory a thing of wonder; he describes everything thoroughly and often with some humor. Tom has his humorous moments, too, of course, although they're not always in the best of taste. For instance, when Gordon mentions that Karloff made his home in the NYC apartment house The Dakota where *Rosemary's Baby* (1968) was shot, Weaver merrily chimes in, "And where John Lennon was *also* shot!"

This is definitely not a biography — it's strictly about Gordon's movies, and almost reads as though Gordon's first day on this Earth was the day he started producing his first picture. I assume, since the autobiographies that Tom co-wrote with Robert Clarke and Paul Picerni describe those actors' childhoods, that for this book, the decision to avoid the early years was Gordon's. However, Tom does find sneaky ways to get Gordon to talk about his boyhood: He asks him questions about the movies he saw as a kid, the way they were ballyhooed in England, etc. And thank goodness he does, because raconteur Gordon spins some amusing tales: risking his teenage neck by going into London's seedy Limehouse section once a week for 15 weeks to see the serial *The Amazing Exploits of the Clutching Hand* in the only local theater running it; trying to find ways to get into theaters showing the Karloff and Lugosi horror classics (rated "For Adults Only" in England at the time); insisting that a theater manager run *Busman's Honeymoon* (aka *Haunted Honeymoon*, 1940) with Robert Montgomery at its scheduled late-night showtime even though he and his brother Alex were the only two people in the theater, etc. He even describes the experience of attending plays starring Tod Slaughter.

Even though Gordon has been featured in several of Tom's McFarland interview books, I don't believe there's much duplication. In a few spots, the reader is advised (via a parenthetical Editor's Note) to read the Gordon interview in a particular McFarland-Weaver book for further discussion of movies on which Gordon was involved but not as producer; for example, *Mother Riley Meets the Vampire* (1952) with Bela Lugosi and *Svengali* (1955) with Hildegarde Neff.

Tom often has more information than he can comfortably squeeze into the text, so here, as in his other books, some of it gets re-routed into the photo captions, which often give us biographical tidbits about the person pictured, the location, additional production information, etc.

Gordon gives a lot of insight into both Boris Karloff and Bela Lugosi — separately and the way they interacted with each other. In particular, I found Gordon's comments regarding the way Bela was depicted in *Ed Wood* (1994) enlightening.

However, my favorite this time around is in the *Corridors of Blood* chapter: a piece of 19th-century artwork depicting Horace Wells, the real-life dentist and anesthesia pioneer upon whom (Tom opines in the caption) Karloff's Jekyll-and-Hyde character in that movie is based. In the captions, Tom also indulges in his usual subtle, sometimes easy-to-miss wordplay; for example, a photo of Gordon in a relaxed pose on the *Tower of Evil* set next to the large stone statue of a pagan god is called "an idol moment." A *Cat and the Canary* shot of Carol Lynley in the grip of the monstrous Cat, who wants to steal her inheritance, is described as "a bad heir day." There's lots of pictures, some familiar, others behind-the-scenes and probably never-before-published.

In addition to being superbly written, this is definitely the best looking book BearManor has ever put out. It is presented in a larger format, the picture quality is stellar, and the layout is classy. A must-must-read.

***

I have waited years for a good biography on the magnificent Joan Blondell, and it's finally here. **Joan Blondell: A Life Between Takes** by Matthew Kennedy (University Press of Mississippi) is the excellently researched, yet not completely satisfying, result.

Matthew Kennedy, author of biographies on Marie Dressler (McFarland) and director Edmund Goulding (University of Wisconsin), is a good writer. His narrative is clean, highly readable, straight to the point, and nicely researched. But there's a lack of warmth in Kennedy's writing, which can be off-putting. While this was no real detriment to his other biographies, it seems wrong for the warm and easygoing Blondell. Her on-screen life is snappy, fun, and attractive. Would it be too much to ask that her biographer try to capture this? Reading this, I felt little of the enjoyment I feel watching even the most average Blondell movie.

Blondell's movies help define the 1930s. Rarely out of work, especially during those heady days of the pre-Coders when she was at her peak, she gave Depression-era audiences someone to identify with in her struggles to get ahead. (Is there anything better than Blondell, as Blondie Johnson, elevating herself in the rackets?)

In this book, good coverage is given to her critically acclaimed films, such as *The Public Enemy*, *A Tree Grows in Brooklyn* and *Nightmare Alley*, but I wanted to read more about her other films. I just couldn't believe that the author disliked, and brushed aside, Joan's last film under contract to Warners, *The Kid from Kokomo* (1938). True, it's been panned elsewhere, but a better look at this neglected gem is much needed. Seriously, I can't be the only one who likes *The Famous Ferguson Case* (1932, with its great jaded dialogue and pre-Code sensibilities), *Miss Pinkerton* (1932), *Goodbye Again* (1933), *Miss Pacific Fleet* (1935), *Stage Struck* (1936, hilariously hamming it up), and *The Corpse Came C.O.D.* (1947). Most of Blondell's movies were wholly dependent on her brash, wisecracking ability to transcend the material. If you love Blondell, there is much to like in her performances, even in such movies as *Good Girls Go to Paris* (1939). The author is right, however, in the respect that these movies did not do anything for her career. As with other status-conscious writers, Kennedy's disregard for her routine films gives us a good idea of her career momentum, but as a film buff, I'm looking for a healthy respect for all of her films. Those who watch Blondell's films on TCM don't care if *Central Park* (1932) or *Three Men on a Horse* (1936) did anything for her career or status. We watch them and value them because we love Blondell.

Even when Kennedy attempts to be critical and/or appreciative of a film, the results are at times overly dramatic, and overdone. Take for example, *The Blue Veil*, a Jane Wyman weepy that the author accurately pegs as "quite an eyewash." It was the only film in which Joan was nominated for an Oscar (supporting), albeit for an appearance that barely lasted ten minutes. "She invested her downward-spiraling character with a barely contained panic and fear," he writes, as I wonder why.

(Kennedy could have used another University Press of Mississippi book as a model for walking that very fine line between critic and appreciator, *No More Little White Lies: The Life of Dick Haymes* by Ruth Prigozy.)

Despite my different point of view, I like this book. The title, I think, says it all: "A Life Between Takes." And that is what Kennedy concentrates on, and excels with — her life. The detail and insight he was able to draw from her family in interviews is remarkable. The reason you should buy this book is Kennedy's understanding of Joan's personal life, and he doesn't pull any punches. She led a hard life, not helped by her destructive relationships with husbands George Barnes (who forced her to have abortions) and the abusive Mike Todd. Dick Powell, her second husband, comes across better, but, even then, it is clear that Joan was not good at picking husbands.

I was greatly interested in her life, which, despite her autobiographical novel *Center Door Fancy*, hasn't been well documented. Kennedy handled it all objectively, and with great thoroughness. The author seemed to be in-tune with Blondell as a person, genuinely liking her.

Joan Blondell is one of my favorite actresses. I wrote about her in *Killer Tomatoes: Fifteen Tough Film Dames* (with Ray Hagen, McFarland), so, of course, I have always concentrated on her performances. Don't let my criticisms of Kennedy's handling of her films sway you from buying this book. *Joan Blondell: A Life Between Takes* is worth buying for its deep insight into its subject. Here, Joan comes across as a funny, gutsy woman, who went through hell with husbands, money, and her health. Matthew Kennedy succeeds fully in capturing this.

***

John Gilbert: The Last of the Silent Film Stars (University Press of Kentucky) by Eve Golden has been criticized for not being a typical biography, that the author's style is opinionated and unconventional. To that, I say: Thank goodness. Too often I read biographies from writers who are so lazy that they parrot other writers' opinions. Or, they are so in love with their subjects that they take his every word as gospel. How refreshing, then, to have an author who not only has a handle on her subject, but also questions existing legends.

The legend that is John Gilbert is one of the saddest in film history. One of the top stars of the silent era because of movies like *The Big Parade* and his pairings with Greta Garbo, "talkies" ruined his career — and ultimately his life. Gossip tells us that MGM's Louis B. Mayer vowed to ruin him, and succeeded. How many books repeat this story and the basic "facts" that we all "know" about Gilbert? Supposedly, he had a high, squeaky, effeminate speaking voice. Ultimately, what this has done is obscure Gilbert the actor, and has lessened his standing in film history.

Here, Eve uses common sense and debunks the "legends." We need more historians like her — those who look objectively and care enough to set the record straight. Gilbert's famous relationship with Greta Garbo is explored in depth; I believe this is the first time that a sensible assessment of that pairing has been presented in print. Also, the way Eve deconstructs the oft-told story of the Gilbert-Mayer "famous" fistfight really makes you think.

The writing is lively — the Golden touch is felt throughout. GIbert's life was not a happy one, as he was a self-doubting alcoholic. Eve doesn't dwell too much on this, but she presents it honestly, as she does his womanizing. Plus, because of all the fibs he told, it had to be tough untangling the truth from the lies, but Eve does an excellent job sorting things out. Gilbert had a habit of stretching the facts of his life, but Eve relentlessly brings us closer to the truth about Gilbert, and the others in his story.

The tone is informal and breezy, while being alternatively clever, sympathetic, and even skeptical when needed. Review quotes are chosen wisely, and Eve's opinions of existing films are fun to read, and very informed. The author's word choices are unique. When was the last time you heard someone being called "slumberous-eyed"? Or, this, about a writer: "With prose as purple as a three-day bruise..." Or this favorite: "Besides having a good script and accommodating director, Jack also had a beautiful, unmarried leading lady to fall in love with, which always cheered him: Jack was on her like a lion on a wildebeest."

One of my favorite sections concerns the life that Gilbert's father, mother, and stepfather led as actors. Eve paints a vivid picture of early traveling performers with fascinating tidbits thrown in, especially the one about actress Clara Bloodgood. These nuggets about Gilbert co-workers are so good they never seem to interrupt the main narrative, but add to it. This also includes a tally of scandals in Hollywood, pre-Codes, and the other actors who had trouble adapting to sound.

While there is one other book about Gilbert, *Dark Star*, written by his daughter Leatrice Gilbert Fountain, this book paints a fuller, more objective portrait of a sometimes tormented man. Plus, we have Eve's lively commentary about the films. Gilbert's strengths and weakness, whether on or off screen, are explored with candor, wit, and common sense. The narrative is detailed, with some very dramatic passages.

We can only hope this book will lead to a John Gilbert revival, where he will again be recognized for his achievements, and not just his supposedly weak speaking voice. This book gives us a sense of what Gilbert was like as a person, while discussing in detail his film work. This is a thoroughly enjoyable read. More than 60 photos, including a *very* handsome and striking cover shot. (Oooh, mama.)

***

I wish I could rave about **The John Wayne Filmography** by Fred Landesman (McFarland), but I was very disappointed with it. The format itself is irritating — all of Wayne's films are arranged alphabetically, instead of being put more sensibly in chronological order.

Then there is the all-important question of content. As with all Films Of-type volumes, we get date, studio, running time, an extensive credit/crew listing, reviews (too much), synopsis, and notes. The problems turn up in the "notes" section.

Commendably, the author has written quite a bit for each film, but do we learn much about them? No. Undeniably, there's some good material in the entries, although the heavy reliance on players' salaries gets tiresome from one film to the other. The bulk of the entries is taken up with co-star bios. There is endless prattle about feature players, character actors, bit players and extras, and even stuntmen — and on and on. With that said, and if that's what the author wants to do, why are so few of Wayne's leading ladies even mentioned in their respective films? Ann Dvorak (*College Coach* and *Flame of Barbary Coast*), Joan Blondell (*Lady for a Night*), Ann Rutherford (*The Lonely Trail*), Marie Windsor (*The Fighting Kentuckian, Trouble Along the Way, Cahill U.S. Marshal*), etc., are not given bios — the stuntmen are obviously more deserving. I was particularly puzzled at the omission of Dvorak, who played the title role in *Flame of Barbary Coast*; her character dominated the whole production, the plot revolving around her. Instead, the author chooses to highlight Virginia Grey, an actress I like very much, but her part was very small in the movie.

Another minus for the book is Landesman's lack of personal commentary. He has no thoughts about the films or Wayne's performances. His entries are geared to be nonobjective, lacking in any type of criticism — save for the heavy paragraphs containing other people's reviews of the films. An analysis of Wayne's work is something you never see. Don't worry. You still haven't.

Some of the info is good, but there's just not enough. The good stuff sits amid a clutter of unneeded material — and it's a shame. A proper *Films of John Wayne* has not been written; this book could have filled a major gap. The photos (120) are okay, but some aren't even of Wayne, which is a strange decision. Even if he had only a bit part, either find one of him in a crowd or don't use one at all; Wayne made 169 films — there are enough images to choose from.

The best part of the book is located in "Appendix B" — "Unrealized Films with John Wayne as Star," a list, arranged year-by-year. Here we learn that producers wanted Wayne for such diverse projects as *Knute Rockne All-American* (as The Gipper), *The Tom Mix Story* (never filmed), *Rawhide, All the King's Men, High Noon, The Sun Also Rises* (Tyrone Power's role), *Heaven Knows, Mr. Allison, Dirty Harry*, and quite a few others, including an odd-sounding *Duel in the Sun* with Wayne and Hedy Lamarr, and *Annie Get Your Gun*, a proposed 1965 remake with Doris Day. (To paraphrase Irving Berlin, "No, he *can't*!") This section is the most intriguing (and entertaining) in the book.

If you're a John Wayne fan, maybe, just maybe, you'll find some gold here. Like I said, the entries have some good facts, if you can find them amid the rubble.

***

I'm not gonna sit here and say that **Journey Without a Map: A Memoir** by Gardner McKay (BearManor Media) is the best written autobiography I've ever read. It's not. The writing style is, at times, rough, disjointed and confusing, and that might put off some readers. That said: I don't think I've ever enjoyed myself more. Rough, disjointed and confusing are actually strong points here, not to mention McKay's insight, thirst for adventure, and refreshing candor and self-deprecating humor. The very strangeness of the narrative fascinated me as he shared his unique perspective on life and Hollywood. "What was I doing there? I was being taken for somebody I wasn't," McKay writes. "It must have been a mistake. I was on some sort of interesting list. I had been telephoned by 20th Century-Fox. In the background, I had heard the bottom of the barrel being scraped." He admits, "While I was there at 20th Century-Fox, I did nothing. Ample quantities of nothing. It was like being kept by a distant benefactor who didn't give you much to live on and never asked anything of you. Treading water in a lukewarm pool. Avoiding film, giving lines away. The effort was not to be seen in a bit part."

The gorgeous McKay (1932-2001) was best known for his role as adventurer Adam Troy on the popular television show *Adventures in Paradise* (1959-62). Until this book, however, I didn't realize how much the real McKay resembled this fictional character; McKay had a wanderlust and interest in art and exploration that took precedence over TV and movie work and he regularly turned down acting jobs to pick up, move on and travel.

This book details just some of his Hollywood activities (including fun stories about TV's *Boots and Saddles*), or, to put it more precisely, his disdain for the phoniness of Hollywood and his lack of interest in the ambitions others had that he didn't. "I had no ambitions, no future.

Admittedly, it was odd not to want anything but the next woman, and live that way for years. No planning, no staff, agents, managers, PR, publishers. Never to befriend a producer, director, writer, but to drop my script as I left the studio and not see it again until the predawn of the following day."

The bulk of the text centers on his travels at sea, through jungles and uncharted territories. It's a captivating ride, especially when he talks of his hardships — you can vividly feel his pain. This is when his writing comes most alive for the reader; his descriptions of his adventures are colorfully told, with some quirky humor thrown in. "We arrived in Albina under a half moon, a little damp, pleasantly ravenous. The dogs filled the street with their sleeping. I ate, then carried a beer through the streets, looking for a place to relieve my bowels. I went off into the shadows, pulled my pants to my knees, squatted and fell sound asleep. A dog was looking hard at me in the gloom when I woke. I stood up and noticed that I had chosen the town square."

Some of the best, nay craziest, passages have to do with sex. "Including the Grand Canyon, the most beautiful void is the absence of a penis on a woman," he writes at one point, totally out of nowhere. For someone so obviously good looking, McKay was hardly vain and had few illusions about himself. Several times he makes fun of his sex symbol image. But he does admit that he was a ladies man; the way he writes about it, however, you can't help liking him for his honesty and unconventional way of looking at things: "Men with women overshadows all. It is a dangerous subject. A careful one if you must write about women. A womanizer. While other men were off conquering worlds of stocks and money, spinning in and out of offices and cars and freeways, doing families, I was raising animals and entertaining women. If this is to be a proper confessional, it must include a brief word on the pattern of life in this zone. It was different then. The trick was not to get an erection . . . Sperm was leaving my body at an alarmingly high rate. As fast as I could manufacture it, sometimes faster." He finally did settle down and get married, happily, and he writes sweetly about his wife. "She works too hard and worries too much, it threatens her beauty, but it does not succeed and she remains as always, beautiful and, though I am bored by much, I am never with her. I age like a tree while she ages like a rare bird, invisibly behind her plumage ... And we are well married, not because we are the same but because we are not. Not cogs meeting nicely in the name of unison. No, we are wheel and triangle. She picks out my clothes and I pick her books ... We will always be married. Our marriage is no less natural than water that flows freely, flowers growing between rocks, dogs that snooze in the shade, seasons ... And I sleep beside her as a blind sailor who remembers the sea and dream of her, a deer living in fear of the woods. And I remarry her each morning when I first see her, when the sun is new and each day becomes our anniversary."

Gardner McKay switched to writing novels and plays after his acting career ended voluntarily, but, he notes here, "No matter what you do, they cannot forget. It is not possible. Like any convicted child molester, a notice hangs over your door. You were once a Hollywood Television Star. Don't you forget it. For four years. You have served your time. The Old Italian tells Evita Peron that he will always be an admiral and she will always be known as a whore. The crime of starring in television will taint me for the rest of my life. My writing, no matter the years, the depth, the fineness, the beauty of it; I will always be someone who had done that. I won grants and awards, but, still, all I was was someone who wasn't in TV anymore. Nothing could change that. The actual fact [was] that I had for four years in my life done something completely different, adventurous, ill-suited to me and then quit was unforgivable ... The printed word. That is my definition. I am defined clearly by those years. I tried to do something audacious, different, outlandish, go to an area I did not belong and be despised. But they cannot forget and you mustn't either. When you commit a crime and serve your time, you are an ex-con. But I have read too many reviews of my plays that say I have turned from acting to writing. The implication being that of an unbeatable has-been has. That acting is the desired profession, writing is not. I am not drawn to writing because it is the most difficult of all the arts, I am drawn to it because of the language I love to use and America has compiled the best dictionary on earth."

After awhile his short sentences take on a marvelous rhythm. I loved this book, reveled in its beauty, humor, depth, skewed sensibilities, and overall fascination factor. It's not dull, not by a long shot, and there is much to be gained by following the path he took through life. I enjoyed getting to know the man through his writings. *Journey Without a Map* was complied by McKay during the final year of his life, as he consulted the notebooks he kept. "I'd be writing these things anyway with or without publishing them," he said, not knowing then the publishing status of this book. "I feel it's good to write these things as well as I can, as honestly. If more than a few people read this, I'll be surprised, if anyone learns anything much, except by certain errors I've made, I'll be amazed. We are all unique." Gardner McKay was certainly unique and this book is perfect testament to that.

***

I was very curious about **J.P. McGowan: Biography of a Hollywood Pioneer** by John J. McGowan (McFarland), a book centering on a man who is all but forgotten in histories of film, because I knew absolutely zero about him. I am pleased that this new volume has remedied that situation, putting McGowan back into the limelight for his groundbreaking achievements. Although the biography section is a little too short for my tastes (124 pages), what's here is a very important document, and it should be welcomed by silent movie fans and serial enthusiasts.

Australian-born John Paterson McGowan (1880-1952) was known in Hollywood as "The Railroad Man," because he specialized in films that involved trains. It was he, says the author, who "made common the image of the terrified beauty tied to a track." This beauty was exemplified by his first wife, Helen Holmes, whom he directed in the silent series *The Hazards of Helen*. He not only directed more than 600 films in his 30-year career, but he also was an actor, screenwriter, producer, and he served as executive secretary of the Screen Directors Guild from 1938 on.

Before he got into film in 1909, with the Kalem Company, he was a stage actor. I wish more space was devoted to this potentially intriguing period in his life. He did a season in *The Squaw Man* and appeared in *Paid in Full* in 1908. Four years of stage work are brushed aside in about two pages.

Movie-wise, however, the author does an exceptional job. Not only does he acknowledge and set forth J.P. McGowan's role in early moviemaking, but he puts a spotlight on the movie company Kalem, and their early, often-neglected trailblazing. The author's coverage of Kalem was very interesting, detailing why their success with and handling of *From the Manger to the Cross* (1912), one of the very first full-length American features, led to the company's demise. McGowan acted in this pioneering film, and the author's discussion of the making of this epic is very well done.

Along with his history of Kalem, two people who worked closely with McGowan at this studio are also given some credit: director Sidney Olcott, regarded as the first American director to specialize in location filming, and the surprisingly versatile actress/screenwriter Gene Gauntier.

J.P. McGowan's films include a ton of B Westerns, serials (notably John Wayne's *The Hurricane Express*, 1932, for Mascot), a Tarzan adventure (*Tarzan and the Golden Lion*, 1927, with James Pierce), and acting roles into the thirties, including one of my all-time favorite movie titles: *She Had to Eat*. (Did she?!)

The photos are great, and the filmography, all 80 pages of it, is ingeniously laid out with all the pertinent details.

The author is a distant relative of the actor/director, but he never really tells us how. A little inside family information would have been desirable. No biggie. At least, finally, J.P. McGowan's story is in print, no more a mere shadowy figure in film history, but a living, breathing person of importance.

***

Forget everything you've previously read about actress and party girl Barbara Payton. Throw aside your preconceived notions about her personality and motives. After reading John O'Dowd's dramatic, fair and insightful **Kiss Tomorrow Goodbye: The Barbara Payton Story,** with a foreword by Barbara's son, John Lee Payton (BearManor Media), you will have to do some serious rethinking.

This could not have been an easy task for Mr. O'Dowd. Today, Barbara Payton (1927-67) is not remembered for her accomplished performances in *Trapped* (1949) and Cagney's *Kiss Tomorrow Goodbye* (1950), or her camp classic *Bride of the Gorilla* (1951), or, even, that she acted alongside Gregory Peck (*Only the Valiant*, 1951). No, as good as Payton was in these films, her reputation rests on two things: the Franchot Tone/Tom Neal brawl for her affections, and her outrageous 1960s memoir, *I Am Not Ashamed*, where it was revealed that she became a prostitute when her movie days ended.

But to base your judgment of Payton on these two things would be too close-minded, too simplistic. She wasn't evil, as many have made her out to be. She was human. She made mistakes. But I only partially agree with the author that Hollywood was mostly to blame. The town didn't exactly chew her up and spit her out. Hollywood was brutal, and never forgave her, but her mistakes were of her own making. O'Dowd knows her faults and the wrong decisions she made and is unflinching about them, but the urge to make Hollywood an "evil town" springs up more than once. ("First, Hollywood takes your body. Then, it takes your soul. Once it has both of those things, it has no use for you anymore.") Yes, Hollywood contributed to her downfall, but it wasn't the cause.

Be that as it may, one can't help but feel sorry for Barbara Payton, and in this book O'Dowd has done a truly remarkable thing. Other authors have taken the standard, accusatory stance, defining her character by focusing on her scandals. O'Dowd, on the other hand, seems to see into her soul, bringing out the good side so seldom (if ever) mentioned. This insight is sadly missing in other profiles of Payton. O'Dowd makes us care for this lady, so that when her downfall comes so early in her life, you feel compassion for her. Even during all the problems with the law, our sympathy is still with her. Payton is shown to be hopelessly stuck, unable to escape the life she made for herself.

O'Dowd's ability to make us see Payton as a human being is impressive. To do this, he not only had to break out of the stereotypical mold used by others, but also he had to go that extra mile in his research and writing. His extra effort pays off big time, elevating his text far above the tabloid-style writing that dominates too many celebrity bios.

A big, big plus is the collection of interviews the author conducted in the nearly ten years he researched this book. He interviewed family members, co-workers, and acquaintances, resulting in an almost astonishing day-by-day record of what Payton was doing. I know from experience that people close to controversial subjects tend to clam up. In this day and age of sensationalized biographies, who's to know how an author will handle the information he is given? It's a credit to John O'Dowd's skills as a writer, coupled with his personal sensitivity, that he was trusted with the inside stories he gets here. It says a lot that Barbara's son, who has remained silent all these years, decided to not only be interviewed, but also wrote the touching foreword.

O'Dowd strikes a balance that is very rare, especially considering the alcohol, sex, drugs, hot tempers, suicide attempts, "frantic" searches for attention, and crime that make up much of this book. Remarkably, you never feel as if O'Dowd is exploiting Barbara. Here it is, he says, this is what happened, but, wait, here are the reasons why. It all adds up to a real page-turner, but one that is a thought-provoking, cautionary tale. This is quite a feat for a nearly 500-page book.

As good as it is, however, there's some repetition, especially near the end. After she passes away, O'Dowd goes on for almost thirty more pages so everyone who knows her can again tell us their opinions about her. It doesn't seriously hamper the text, but it was too much for me. However, O'Dowd is a good writer, and although I found this part superfluous, it was all very well written.

The photos, over 200 of them, many never before published, are simply magnificent. I especially enjoyed the photos of some of the places (bars, motels, etc.) where Barbara hung out. I recall someone complaining online that Barbara wasn't in these shots. However, I found the often-dirty-looking places eerily atmospheric and fascinating.

I couldn't have predicted my reaction to this book. All I've ever known about Barbara was what others knew: She was a bad girl. After all, didn't she destroy both Franchot Tone's and Tom Neal's lives? Didn't that "vixen" play the two against each other? After reading this, however, I finally saw the whole picture. And, I must say, I saw Barbara not as the one-dimensional figure the newspapers painted her as, but as a directionless person who just made those wrong decisions. No other book or article has managed this on Payton. Especially with her sad, heart-wrenching relationship with her son, you understand what was happening with her.

With a life like Barbara's, a biographer could have been tempted to gloss over her work. After all, her career was not that important even to her in the beginning. But, O'Dowd discusses each film, with the right amount of details (no excessive plots, thank goodness): *Silver Butte* (1949), *Pecos Pistol* (1949), *Once More, My Darling* (1949), *Trapped* (1949), *Kiss Tomorrow Goodbye* (1950), *Dallas* (1950), *Only the Valiant* (1950), *Drums in the Deep South* (1951), *Bride of the Gorilla* (1951), *Four Sided Triangle* (1952), *Bad Blonde* (1952), *Run for the Hills* (1953), *The Great Jesse James Raid* (1953), and *Murder Is My Beat* (1955). I like the way he handled the films, especially in regard to her performances. I disagreed with his assessment of *Bad Blonde*, but reveled in his lively report on the campy *Run for the Hills*.

Another indication of the intelligence of O'Dowd's writing is seen in his fairness to the people in Barbara's life. Onetime husband Franchot Tone and boyfriend Tom Neal are not pitted against each other here. While others depict Neal as a bad force in her life, O'Dowd treats him impartially, giving us both the good and the bad. Tone, too, could have come across as a stodgy obstacle between the love Payton and Neal shared for each other. Frankly, this is how these two men are always portrayed by other writers. For insight into Neal, O'Dowd interviewed his nephew who stayed with Neal and Payton at their home. For Tone, O'Dowd had the good fortune to be assisted by his official biographer, Lisa Burks. I was greatly impressed by the insight that both the nephew and Lisa possess.

Barbara Payton had plenty of troubles in her life. She does not need more criticism from unfeeling enemies who routinely condemn her. One author even calls Barbara "a monster" and has the audacity to compare her to Hitler! Clearly, she needs a champion, and she gets a good one in John O'Dowd.

Then you have the heartfelt words of her son, who well remembers the loving mother who was taken away from him. I am not embarrassed to say that I got choked up reading his foreword and his memories of his loving mother. "I think about her in some way, every single day," John Lee Payton says. "In my mind there is little notice today of the tortured movie star, or the ruin visited upon her. There is only the simple love a child feels for his mother, a kind of awe and wonder, and a yearning to return once more to that sweet embrace, to feel her happy kiss and the secure certainty of being held safe within her arms. These are the feelings I have for my mother, and nothing, or no one, can touch them." Another family member says, "No matter how short her fame, and no matter how short her life, Barbara has had a long lasting effect on the people who really knew her." This is the enduring message here. The beauty of this book is found in the way the author allows her family's love to shine through the horrors of her life. I respect and admire John O'Dowd for finding the light in the darkness. Barbara Payton's emotionally-draining life finally makes sense.

***

I was looking forward to **Lew Ayres: Hollywood's Conscientious Objector** by Lesley L. Coffin, with a foreword by Marya E. Gates (University Press of Mississippi). Ayres (1908-1996), best known for his role in *All Quiet on the Western Front* and for playing Dr. Kildare in an MGM series, has been largely misunderstood because very little has been written about this thoughtful actor. Much of what's out there is wrong or has concentrated solely on his status as a conscientious objector during World War II. Even there, the facts have been iffy, so I was hoping to read a book that set the record straight. And I got it in Ms. Coffin's book — more or less.

First, the good points. Ms. Coffin had access to personal letters, oral histories, and interviews with those who knew Ayres personally. The actor's son let Coffin reference his father's unpublished autobiography. There is a lot of clearing up of mistakes that were widely circulated by publicity, especially in regards to Ayres' childhood and educational background. His experiences during World War II are fully recounted for the first time, with the valuable help of letters he wrote to friends.

Ayres was a very complex man, who had conflicted feelings toward Hollywood and religion. The author does a tremendous job giving the readers an understanding of Ayres' personality. While Coffin goes on far too long with some of Ayres' ideological and religious quotes — to the point of making him come across as a rambler — at least it gives the reader some understanding of him.

A few of the movie analyses are quite good, such as the discussions of

All Quiet on the Western Front and his character in *Holiday* (1938). Coffin is particularly perceptive about what made Ayres tick, and does a nice job explaining how his movie characters sometimes merged with the real Ayres. The reasons Universal didn't properly exploit him in the crucial early stages of his career are well explained by the author. There's also an interesting tidbit about Ayres wanting to be cast in the role that David Manners eventually got in *Dracula* (1931). More should have been made, however, of Ayres' decision to go with Republic after a stint with Fox. Although Republic gave him a chance to direct a movie, 1936's *Hearts in Bondage*, it was a mistake on Ayres' part.

The research the author put into this book is excellent and obviously took a lot of time. Then, why, pray tell, isn't the writing better? I will never understand an author who takes the time and energy, sometimes years, to research a book to get all the details correct, and then falls down in the writing aspect. Coffin is not a bad writer and much of what is written is readable, but the writing style is often sloppy and repetitive, and there were quite a few poorly constructed sentences that made me cringe. It's pretty bad when you find the same words used multiple times in a sentence. The phrase "keenly aware" was used in two successive sentences. Redundancy is the book's big problem. Some sentences run on too long, and there are too many oddly-placed commas. Where was an editor here?

I am "keenly aware" that Lew Ayres was a good man and a thoughtful, self-taught idealist and intellectual. I know because the book rams it into your head. Along the way, I got the feeling that the author was reluctant to deal with negative aspects of her subject. Buried in a footnote in the back of the book was a quick mention of a head-on car collision involving Ayres. This was definitely something that needed to be put in the main biography, and explained. I've read news reports of his divorce from Lola Lane where she accused him of calling her a "dumb cluck." Sorry, but as a fellow biographer, I find that sort of information to be gold and quite worthy of inclusion — no matter how it makes your subject look.

I don't want to say that the author is enamored of Ayres and his ideals, but ... okay, I'll say it. I see this in many biographies, where the author has trouble distancing himself from the subject. Coffin isn't icky like some of these so-called biographers, but she does fall in the trap of not liking a movie just because Ayres didn't like it. For instance, *The Unfaithful* (1947), one of his better films and performances. I was a little perturbed that Coffin did not even bother to use Doug McClelland's *interview* with Ayres from the book *Forties Film Talk*. Instead, Coffin relied on an obit that partly quoted from the interview. Doug's interview with Ayres delved into the productions of both *Johnny Belinda* and *The Unfaithful*, and what the obit did not quote would have been useful in this biography. I am thinking specifically of Ayres' strained off-screen relationship with Ann Sheridan in *The Unfaithful*, which tells a lot about how Ayres viewed his fellow actors and how overly pious and judgmental he could be. This would seem to be another example of the author's avoidance of the negative side of Ayres' personality.

The Unfaithful section was much too short, as was the write-up on *The Dark Mirror* (1946). Considering the minor films he made after the war, these are important movies and needed to be discussed at length. Coffin pays special attention to the Dr. Kildares and some of his other pre-war films, but I felt his later films got slighted. There weren't that many films to contend with in this later period, so it wouldn't have taken that much space to handle them. It seemed that when Ayres lost interest in film, the author did as well. The best Coffin can do is call *No Escape* and *Donovan's Brain* low-budget B movies.

I am in favor of looking objectively at all films, no matter if it's an A or B. If you are writing about an actor you like, you can find something to enjoy in any of their films, no matter if it's a good film or bad, a major release or a second feature. To dismiss a film offhand also does the reader a disservice. And I found it uncalled for to chastise the Dr. Gillespie series just because Ayres had left. It's okay to favor the earlier Dr. Kildares, but don't slam the Gillespie films just because Ayres isn't in them. The Dr. Gillespies should be judged on their own merits.

I caught on DVD a 2001 documentary called *The Omen Legacy*, which covered the making of the horror trilogy. Ayres had a supporting part in *Damien: Omen II* (1978), and Lee Grant had a little anecdote about Ayres wanting to do his own stunt, getting into the icy water to shoot a scene, while Grant tried to talk him out of it. There is no mention of that in this book, and that's a pity because it showed what a true professional Ayres was. (While Coffin talks about a few TV appearances, I wish my favorite Ayres performance was mentioned: his 1964 guest shot on *Ben Casey* with Lee Grant, "For a Just Man Falleth Seven Times." Their May-December romantic pairing was very poignant. If you have not seen it, do yourself a favor and seek it out.)

On the book's jacket, it says that Lesley L. Coffin is an "independent scholar," but I'm guessing that the author is not focused on film history. What attracted Coffin to Ayres were his beliefs and curious nature, which makes the personal angle in the biography shine. There are quite a few mistakes in movie facts, however.

Lola Lane's real name was Dorothy Mullican not Dorothy Edwards.

Holiday was produced by Columbia not MGM, and Hepburn wasn't under contract to Metro until 1940.

Actress Phyllis Fraser was Ginger Rogers' cousin not her sister.

In talking about Ayres turning down the male lead in the remake of *Magnificent Obsession* (1954), Coffin says he also rejected the "impressive salary" of $250 a week. It's hard to believe a film historian would call that impressive pay for Ayres in the '50s.

Laraine Day, who appeared in the Dr. Kildare films as Nurse Mary Lamont, had previously done a small role (under her real name of Laraine Johnson) in *Scandal Street* (1938). When Day was cast in her first Dr. Kildare film, Coffin writes about her working "with her *Scandal Street* costar Lew Ayres once again." His costar in that film was Louise Campbell. (There is a difference between a costar and a featured player.)

Ayres appeared as a regular on the 1985 television series *Lime Street*.

While the show is discussed, *not once* was the name given in the text. How very strange.

At 5'8" Ayres was the "perfect height" to play romantic characters??

"Lily" Damita's first name should be spelled Lili, and it's hard to imagine why the author refers to Louis Wolheim as "John" Wolheim.

Night World (1932) is a lost film? Gad! Although I've never seen it, my friend Jackie Jones has it in her collection and tells me that it's quite a good movie. Pity the author didn't take the trouble to locate it.

In *Holiday*, "popular character actor Henry Kolker was cast as Hepburn's difficult but wealthy father." He made a lot of films before his death in 1947, but it is misleading to call him popular.

Photo caption problems: Joyce Compton goes uncredited in a still from *Spring Madness* (1938). Henry Travers is identified as Charles Butterworth in a photo from *My Weakness* (1933). For a scene still from *The Lottery Lover* (1935) — which is missing the crucial "The" and called a 1934 release — actors Sterling Holloway, Eddie Nugent, and Alan Dinehart all go unidentified. I almost split my sides when Victor Varconi was ID'ed as Alison Skipworth in a pic from *King of the Newsboys* (1938) — despite his mustache!

Ayres was married three times, to actresses Lola Lane and Ginger Rogers, and in 1964 to former flight attendant Diana Hall; that union produced his only child, a son Justin. There should have been more information on Hall and their son Justin, especially since Justin helped the author. There are also no photos of Diana or Justin.

While I have misgivings about this book, it does have redeeming qualities. The information on his war years is new, fresh and enlightening. The author had a lot to sort through, and organized it very well, including some extras located in the appendix. Coffin clears up misconceptions and outright mistakes relating to his war service and status as a conscientious objector, and his childhood and stint with musical groups in the 1920s. Also handled well was Ayres' work and obsession with his documentaries, *Altars of the East* and *Altars of the World*. Ayres was a loner, a sensitive actor, writer, director, and producer, who spent his life being eternally curious about the world around him. You come away from this book feeling this and respecting him as a person. The author's handling of some of the movies could have been managed better, but as a document of his life the book excels, despite the typos and poorly written passages. Coffin's book would have been much easier to read if it had been gone over by an editor and proofreader.

***

Thelma Todd (1906-35) was a beautiful blonde actress who rose to fame during the first half of the 1930s, especially in comedies. She's probably best known for her roles in the Marx Brothers' *Horse Feathers* and *Monkey Business*, and for her work at Roach, in particular her short subjects with ZaSu Pitts and Patsy Kelly. All of this sometimes gets overshadowed by the circumstances of her mysterious death at the age of 29.

There's only been (to my knowledge) one major book about Todd, *Hot Toddy: The True Story of Hollywood's Most Sensational Murder* by Andy Edmonds, released in 1989. The words "true story" in the title are disputable since, in my opinion, Edmonds pretty much let her imagination run wild with what sounds to me like invented dialogue and imaginary incidents. (No sources, no attempt to let us in on how she knows what was said in private conversations decades ago.)

Now, McFarland has published **The Life and Death of Thelma Todd** by William Donati. I was absolutely looking forward to reading a better take on Todd's life, career and death. At first, however, I was not entirely pleased, but, fortunately, I gave the book a chance and kept reading. In the end, Donati proves himself and gives us an important book with a fresh, new look at an oft-told, much-abused legend.

First, it should be noted that the writing is excellent with a very readable style, and the research covers a great deal of ground. My problem is Donati's tendency to go off on other subjects. While these tangents do relate to Thelma Todd, they often go on for pages. (The hardships of actors getting a break in movies make for intriguing reading, but this just doesn't pertain to Todd and how she entered the biz. Likewise, the unnecessary stuff about Charlie Chaplin, Rudolph Valentino and Pola Negri could have been omitted.) This is especially glaring during his sections about Todd's lover, director Roland West, and his wife Jewel Carmen. I recognize that background information is essential in gaining knowledge about the intertwined relationships, but a great deal of the content had little to do with our subject. The pages devoted to Carmen and her court trials — while very fascinating — just doesn't have any bearing on Todd. Same for West's business and personal dealings with other people. Too much of them, not enough of Thelma Todd. It does make you wish that Donati had written a whole separate book on West and Carmen; he has plenty of material that would be of interest to movie fans.

Interestingly, however, the author accomplishes something valuable with this by giving us a comprehensive, clear-eyed picture of Roland West, the artist and the man. While others, without a shred of proof, have painted West as a shady, abusive character, Donati gives us a more reasonable portrait, based on interviews and correspondence.

Bogging down the narrative early on was Donati's quoting of dubious fan magazine publicity; I simply didn't care to read about Todd's observations on beauty, acting and relationships since these words probably weren't even hers in the first place. Fortunately, this is offset and supplemented by the author's priceless personal interviews with (among others) William Bakewell, Lina Basquette, Anita Garvin, Ida Lupino, Will Fowler, and Thelma's cousins, William Todd and Edna Todd. There is also some marvelous, in-depth research done about her hometown of Lawrence, Massachusetts. Also, since Donati wrote a book about Lucky Luciano, the mobster supposedly implicated in Todd's death, he is able to give us valuable information he has gleaned from thousands of FBI documents. (McFarland published his *Lucky Luciano: The Rise and Fall of a Mob Boss* in 2010.)

The book really gets going when poor Todd is found dead in her car, the victim of carbon monoxide poisoning. The *Hot Toddy* book fanned the flames of controversy, adding a lot of nonsense about the mystery. Next, film fans, doubling as armchair detectives, further muddied the waters. Instead of taking the facts brought out at the Coroners' Inquest, Edmonds relied heavily on rumors and heresy and built on from there. Everyone loves a good conspiracy theory — and I certainly would be willing to believe that Thelma Todd was killed, if the facts supported this.

Donati starts things off with the whole transcript of the Coroners' Inquest, more than seventy pages of testimony. As he points out afterwards, Edmonds' allegations that Todd was severely beaten when she was found dead are not true. Nowhere is a beating mentioned in the testimony; in fact, just the opposite was noted. The Inquest is an eye-opener, and reading it makes the real situation painfully obvious: A tired Todd, unable to get into the house, and not wanting to wake Roland West, made her way that cold night to the garage, which was quite a walk. Unaware of the dangers of carbon monoxide, she started the car motor and was overcome in the small confined space and died.

As for the Luciano angle, Donati proves that the mobster wasn't even in the state when Todd died — more importantly, he couldn't find any kind of connection between the two. *Hot Toddy* contains conversations that sound as if they were recorded and then printed verbatim in order to establish a Luciano-Todd "relationship" that turned sour and then deadly. By contrast, *The Life and Death of Thelma Todd* sticks to documented facts. Donati uses common sense in approaching the mystery, discrediting each rumor, point by point, in such a way that you can't help seeing how completely "ordinary" Todd's death was. (Very damaging to a more realistic understanding of the incident were Ida Lupino's comments about her conversation with Todd that night. What is never mentioned in conjunction with this is that her father, also there, told a different, less sensational, story. Donati has a complete understanding of Lupino's personality and her propensity to exaggerate and dramatize events when he recounts her comments at the Inquest and to him.)

I'm sure a lot of people will be disappointed by Donati's demolition of the murder theory, but we've got to be realistic. I was confronted by someone on Facebook just recently, who breathlessly mentioned the rumor that Roland West confessed to Todd's murder on his deathbed. First, this is highly unlikely. Second, I am positive, relative to the events laid out in the book, that West did, indeed, hold himself personally responsible for her death. His guilt feelings through the years were perfectly natural. After all, he was in love with Todd, and felt that if he had been up that night and let her into the house, she never would have died.

I highly recommend *The Life and Death of Thelma Todd*. Donati had access to previously unseen letters, photographs, and other materials in family scrapbooks, and he is able to bring the "characters" of his story to life with his straightforward writing. To be sure, there are a few flowery passages here and there: "By twilight, Thelma Todd's Sidewalk Café was bathed in a reddish glow as the sun faded into the Pacific Ocean. As the December dusk fell, lights twinkled along the coast, and a chill wind blew over the steep palisades." And yet, he never, ever approaches the overheated, overly-dramatic prose of Andy Edmonds, which is a blessing. If you can overlook, or skim past, the detours into other people's lives and the occasional name misspellings (Wallace Beery as "Berry" a few times is particularly exasperating), you will be rewarded with an essential biography.

***

McFarland has a book about another comic Lloyd, Lloyd Hamilton. Anthony Balducci's **Lloyd Hamilton: Poor Boy Comedian of Silent Cinema** is mostly very good, and gets much better as it goes along.

Hamilton (1891-1935), once greatly admired and ranked alongside Chaplin, Harold Lloyd and Keaton, is now pretty much forgotten except by diehard silent movie fans. He was a large, baby-faced comic, known for his distinctive duck walk, but his inability to successfully graduate to feature films led to his tragic downfall and early death. Before reading this provocative volume, I only knew that he was one half of a comedy team, Ham and Bud, with Bud Duncan, and appeared in a comedy series of shorts (1914-17).

The author has been working on this project since the 1970s and I can understand that there is little information available about Hamilton. This book is precisely important because it is the only book about this neglected comic and I recommend it very highly. The author has the enthusiasm and love for his subject and when he sticks to Hamilton, he is interesting and can hold attention. There are times, however, when Balducci goes off into other directions, as he recounts the history of film companies, actors, directors and the like. Balducci knows quite a bit about silent comedy and I liked a lot of these discussions, but it was, at times, too much. Sometimes the payoff of these asides gave a better understanding of Hamilton, other times, it did not.

The author is a good writer, at his best covering Hamilton's alcohol problems, money issues and mishaps. He brings Hamilton alive to the reader. You really feel bad for the down-on-his-luck actor. The account of his untimely death is very moving. Likewise, Ham's early beginnings are handled adroitly, as the author shows how family and religious beliefs shaped his future life and motivated him.

Balducci is marvelous discussing Hamilton's comic appeal. These sections of analysis are very successful and key in understanding this long-ago star. Very commendable, vividly giving Hamilton a needed 21st-century appraisal. There are moments of real insight in these pages and I hope that the minor criticisms that I had about this book do not dissuade any reader from buying. This is a valuable book. If you are a silent movie fan, buy this, especially if you know little about Lloyd Hamilton.

The comedian deserves to be remembered in a book by a caring film historian who took the time to uncover a long-forgotten life. This is the sort of book we all should cherish.

***

Julie Adams — think of her and immediately the image comes to mind of a girl in a white bathing suit being pursued by the Creature from the Black Lagoon. Starring in that 1954 classic brought Adams fame, but there was much more to this talented actress' career. Now, we get her story in her newly released autobiography, **The Lucky Southern Star: Reflections from the Black Lagoon** (Hollywood Adventures Publishing), written with her son Mitchell Danton.

Julie started her film career in 1949 by co-starring in a series of Westerns, billed as Betty Adams, with James Ellison. A move to Universal-International in 1951 was propitious, and she starred or was featured throughout the 1950s, mostly as good girls, but at her best as a bad girl, in films like *Bend of the River* (1952), *Horizons West* (1952), *The Lawless Breed* (1953), *The Private War of Major Benson* (1955), *Away All Boats* (1956), etc.

Adams was an appealing actress, beautiful to the eye, but not a lot was expected of her during this time. It took a move to television, where she was an extremely busy actress, to show what she was made of artistically. Based on the TV roles I've seen her in, I believe she was under-appreciated. Her skillful handling of a variety of roles belies the claim she was just a pretty face. Adams had the chops! I distinctly remember her in a *Police Woman* episode from the 1970s. It was a small part, just a couple of small scenes, and then a larger appearance near the conclusion. The intensity and thoughtfulness that Adams put into her character was stunning, her emotional playing bringing the episode to a breathtaking conclusion. Another performance I greatly admired was her stylish queen to the Pharaoh on a *Greatest Heroes of the Bible* episode in the late '70s.

Unfortunately, television acting engenders little respect in the industry, but if you go to the trouble to look up old episodes from her TV series work, you will love and appreciate her more than ever. Fortunately, she has been working steadily on TV for decades, and has continued working into the 2000s.

I knew little of Adams' life before this book, and was surprised when reading of her difficult childhood. You've got to commend Miss Adams for her unwavering faith in her abilities and for her guts and determination to succeed, no matter what. What comes across vividly in these pages is what a truly nice person she is — no ego or phoniness on display. She handles sticky situations she writes about with discretion, but with honesty.

And she loves to act. There are paragraphs where she simply talks about the movies she worked on, her co-stars, and her characters and how she played them. This is a lady serious about improving her acting, and broadening her range. Her analyses of her movies should give her fans insight into not only her favorite films, but also her approach to her craft. Of course, there's a whole chapter devoted to *Creature from the Black Lagoon*, and she doesn't disappoint on details. There are loads of swell behind-the-scenes photos from the movie, too. Her reminisces about Ben Chapman, one of the actors in the Creature suit, are very special and sweet.

Speaking of photos — my God, there are close to 200 here! Being a photo collector myself, I was overjoyed by the fabulous shots. On page 51 there's one from *The Stand at Apache River* (1953), showing her with a flaming arrow in her shoulder. In the text, Adams remarks, "If you ever watch the film, take note that the terror in my eyes as the flaming arrow hits was not all acting." The story about this particular scene (and how the effect was achieved) is harrowing. In fact, Adams went through more than one dicey incident on camera. The story of a candle setting fire to the curtains in *One Desire* (1955) is a doozy; the soundstage almost went up in flames. Even better was an episode of *The Big Valley*, where she fights with Barbara Stanwyck as a fire rages around them. "The moment I remember clearly," Adams writes, "was that in the midst of the struggle with Barbara, the stage seemed to be ablaze all around us; it was getting really hot and I was ready to get out of there. Then I saw Barbara head back in toward the heat of the fire and I thought to myself, 'If Barbara Stanwyck's going back in there, so am I!' I rushed back toward her and the flames and we mixed it up pretty good."

Many of the photos reflect the anecdotes Adams tells, which is good. For instance, she writes at length about working with James Stewart on *Bend of the River* and the intimate scene they played by a wagon, and there, on the page, is the photo of that same scene. Making the photos stand out even more is the use of glossy, high-quality paper. It boasts a very attractive page layout as well.

Miss Adams covers a lot of ground in her memoirs, detailing stories about working with the likes of Elvis Presley, Robert Ryan, Tyrone Power, Joel McCrea, John Wayne, and Raymond Burr; recounting her trip to Peru to act with Dennis Hopper in *The Last Movie* (1971); and discussing a little-known aspect of her career — her work in the theater. Here is an actress actually concerned with what her fans want to read. I was surprised by the amount of television she dealt with in the text. How many autobiographies have you read where the star goes into any detail about individual TV episodes? It helps greatly that Miss Adams is a film fan. Her love of movies is transmitted to these pages, and her love of the craft of acting — the way she describes the process she went through to communicate to audiences — helps the reader to understand her better. The fun she conveys when discussing, say, her regular part on TV's *Capitol*, is infectious.

I absolutely adore *The Lucky Southern Star*, my only complaint is that it was so readable that it went by much too fast. Julie Adams has written an entertaining, intelligent, uplifting and perceptive book. Film fans will love it. While supplies last, you get a free commemorative CD of the *Creature from the Black Lagoon* soundtrack with the purchase of the book.

Adams' husband for many years was actor Ray Danton. There are a few things here and there within her book, including the afterword by her son, Mitchell Danton, that indicate Ray's complex nature. He is not an actor who has ever been written up extensively in book form, but he's someone I've always appreciated. Adams writes in her book, "Ray rarely played the good guy ... The interesting thing about Ray's screen persona was that, although he generally played immoral characters, he was dashing and charming in their portrayal, allowing his fans to root for him as the anti-hero in many of the films and television shows he acted in."

Ray Danton (1931-92) was born Raymond Kaplan in New York City, and started his career as a child actor on radio programs such as *Let's Pretend* in the early 1940s. Attending the University of Pittsburgh and Carnegie Technical School, he also worked on the stage. His most notable theater experience during this time was the 1950 London production of *Mister Roberts* starring Tyrone Power. He started out doing some TV in 1951 before entering the United States Army Infantry during the Korean War, serving from 1951 to 1954. Making his film debut in 1955's *Chief Crazy Horse* as a Native American, he was put under contract to Universal-International. His strong, smooth manner and his tall (6'), dark, and dangerous good looks typecast him early in villainous parts, which, in the long run, hindered any chances he might've had for real stardom.

After U-I let him go, he acted on various television programs. A move to Warner Bros. proved lucky, as he was cast in *The Rise and Fall of Legs Diamond* (1960); he would play the gangster again in *Portrait of a Mobster* (1961). This was followed by his portrayal of actor George Raft in the mostly fictional screen biopic *The George Raft Story* (1961). Danton did a substantial amount of work on television, a very much in-demand, busy performer, and he was a regular on *The Alaskans* (1959-60) as the appropriately named Nifty Cronin. By the early 1960s, Danton was dividing his time between the U.S. and Europe, doing mostly television over here and spy and Sandokan films over there.

He formed his own production company in Barcelona and started to produce and direct, a way of trying to jumpstart, but mostly supplement, his lagging acting career. He was rarely able to break free of his "smooth operator" screen persona, although he was a proficient actor, always turning in good performances. He continued to act on television into the '70s, his last acting role coming in a 1977 episode of *Barnaby Jones*. The 1970s subsequently saw him becoming a prolific television director, regularly helming such popular series as *Quincy M.E.*, *The Incredible Hulk*, *Fame*, *Magnum, P.I.* and *Cagney & Lacey*, among others. His final directorial job was for the television series *The New Mike Hammer* in 1989. A 60-year-old Danton died of complications from a kidney ailment in Los Angeles.

So, it was with high hopes that I read **The Epitome of Cool: The Films of Ray Danton** (BearManor Media) by Joseph Fusco. My hopes were dashed, however, by the information supplied within. Although the book was not meant as a biography, there should have been some kind of short section chronicling his life. There is simply an introduction, which is taken up with nonsense about Danton's screen persona and the characters he played and how they compare to each other. Then there is the main body of the book which focuses on the films. After reading all this, we have only a sketchy idea of the events in Danton's life, with only a bit of vital information such as birthplace, etc.

I understand that Danton is a difficult research subject; even his son says he didn't know him too well because of his complex nature. *But*, since Danton worked for so many years, there's a wealth of material to be found in the interviews he did. Fusco could have brought together a number of sources and given us so much more, but, in my opinion, he simply didn't want to go the extra mile.

The author's main concern was his movies. Okay, I'm good with that. The book is basically a film-by-film rundown in which Fusco discusses each movie. Ah, but here, too, I was bitterly disappointed. What Fusco fails to comprehend is that you shouldn't tell us the plots in excruciating detail and then fail to give us behind-the-scenes coverage.

Fusco's odd writing style doesn't help, either. He seems to be madly in love with adjectives and scatters them across the pages. Believe me, if adjectives were candied cherries, this book would be a fruitcake. He tries so hard to sound trendy and hip — it's as if he were hoping to write in a style that reflected Danton's screen persona. Here's an example: "Ray Danton's heyday was the Hollywood of slick hair, cigarette smoking, hard drinking and two-fisted negotiations. His sharp-edged baritone matched dark-chiseled features, making him a natural for his roles as suave heroes or venal hustlers. He had the look of a sly fox and the smooth moves of a dancing thief. His confident attitude, switchblade movements, serpentine stares, and silver-tongued voice gave his characters a tough menace and panache." (A dancing thief? Is he kidding?) Even worse is this line: "Eating people as if they were candies, he never flinches at the candy wrappers that are really former friends and foes."

He describes Danton as steely-eyed, icy-nerved, fast-moving, smooth-talking, shifty, ruthless, wisecracking with authority, a brooding thinker, cunning and arrogant, reptilian, cruel and cold to the touch, forceful and warlike, ferocious to a fault, poised and relaxed, and ... well, you get the idea, it just goes on and on, ad absurdum. Someone needs to slap that Thesaurus out of the author's hands and make him do some real writing.

Each film is given the same, standard, boring write-up that becomes irritating after awhile. Each is a tedious rehash of the plot with descriptions of Danton and all the other major actors and their contributions. Reading these, I felt I was learning absolutely nothing about the films.

On the other hand, most of the photos are good, although some aren't reproduced well. What I cannot fathom, however, is why the author would choose to run photos without Danton in them. Even if the photos are from Danton's movies, it's puzzling and disappointing to a reader when he has to look and look for Danton in a photo and not find him.

It's good that, finally, we have a book on Ray Danton — he deserves some kind of acknowledgment after being relegated to the shadows for so long. He was a talented man. I just wish Joseph Fusco had written more substantially about the films and had not relied on his dubious commentary. Edited-down versions of his opinions, mixed together with intelligent observations, behind-the-scenes stories, and a biography in the beginning, might have amounted to a good book. As it stands, the book is pretty pitiful. Cool front and back covers, though ...

***

The University Press of Kentucky has just published a biography on one of my favorite actresses, Maureen O'Hara. I have always admired her tenacity and feisty spirit on screen and off. An amazing woman, the still-going-strong O'Hara has led a fascinating life and has many great and near-great movies to her credit.

Since O'Hara has always been very high-profile and has given tons of interviews through the years, I am surprised more books have not been written about her. In 2005, she wrote '*Tis Herself: An Autobiography* (q.v.), a very entertaining and revealing memoir, which filled in many gaps regarding her personal life. Yet, with the exception of a 2002 German-language biography by Peter Kranzpiller (Eppe GmbH) — unreadable for those of us not fluent in German — there has never been a major biography or critical analysis of O'Hara and her work.

Maureen O'Hara: The Biography by Aubrey Malone endeavors to give us both. Unfortunately, one of the author's main problems is that many of his film discussions rely heavily on plot, and long, drawn-out story regurgitations are not my idea of fun. It is possible to write a creative and interesting plot recap, but it's rare, perhaps because those who write these regurgitations usually put little effort into them. In most cases, a star bio filled with long plot recaps is the sign of a writer taking the easy way out.

O'Hara's movie resume is strikingly impressive. Her list of classics and significant projects include *The Hunchback of Notre Dame, Jamaica Inn, How Green Was My Valley, Miracle on 34th Street, The Quiet Man*, and *The Parent Trap*. She worked with directors of the stature of Alfred Hitchcock and John Ford, and had long-running screen partnerships with John Payne and especially John Wayne. The actress' tenure at Fox in the 1940s brought about several gems, in particular the swashbuckler *The Black Swan*, co-starring Tyrone Power — one that I count as a personal favorite. O'Hara has also appeared in movies that, while entertaining, were far from classics, e.g. *War Arrow, Bagdad* (another personal favorite), *At Sword's Point*, etc. If you love O'Hara, chances are you enjoy these and her other lesser efforts. One of her most popular movies was 1946's *Sentimental Journey*; critics have been unduly harsh with this tearjerker, but movie fans just eat this one up.

I have noticed a very bad tendency among some film writers: If a movie is not considered noteworthy in the annals of film history, or if an actress has expressed her dislike of a film, then an author will react accordingly. New outlooks? Reevaluations? Bucking popular opinion? Proving you have your own mind? Those are things that can be hard to find in many books. I've always believed in forming my own opinions, which can sometimes get me in trouble such as when I talk about a film like *A Clockwork Orange* — pretentious, and definitely not for me, and I'm not afraid to say so. My late mentor, Doug McClelland, was adamant on this point: It's easy to repeat other writers' opinions, but it takes guts and ingenuity to go into another direction with your criticism. Conformity and orthodoxy makes too many film books dull, dull, dull.

It's very easy to love and praise *The Quiet Man* and *The Hunchback of Notre Dame*, but it takes stronger stuff to discover and discuss the values of a movie like *Lady Godiva*. As minor as this film is, I cannot believe that I am the only one who enjoys it. My thought is this: When you are writing on someone like Maureen O'Hara, you need to realize that the people buying your book are most likely those who love her and her movies. These readers are people who can find some value in most of what she did, and they want books that expand their appreciation of her films, not diminish it. These readers will be disgusted by mindless rehashes of opinions held by people who don't really care for their favorite star. It's such a shame that more writers can't free themselves of stale opinions and find new and interesting ways to look at an actor's career.

There's good and bad in every movie, and both sides should be addressed. This attitude has guided me well, and I find that I come away from every movie I watch feeling I have discovered something worthwhile. There are a few instances in Mr. Malone's O'Hara bio where he *does* find something nice to say, but then he seems to feel guilty doing so, and reverts back to something like, "But still, this movie is minor and not worth the effort."

Malone spends a lot of time, and rightfully so, on movies such as *The Quiet Man*; his section on this classic is excellent and the best part of the book. Yet — think about it — over the past several decades, *The Quiet Man* has been covered over and over elsewhere. A film like *They Met in Argentina*, however, is obscure but worthy of attention to the sort of person willing to buy a book like this. Many of these potential buyers are dying to read interesting discussions of her minor films, but unfortunately they won't find a lot of that in this book.

Frankly, I found many opinions hard to stomach. He brushes aside *The Redhead from Wyoming* because he feels she was trying to replicate her *Quiet Man* character, momentarily forgetting, perhaps, that that fiery red-headed and red-blooded Irish woman *was* the Maureen O'Hara screen persona. Does the writer really believe that her fans would have enjoyed going to see an O'Hara film featuring a woman who looked like O'Hara but acted like someone else? Malone also notes that *Redhead* is "only seventy-six minutes long." He adds, "Such slightness slots it firmly in the 'filler' bracket." I guess it's easy to belittle the movie for its lack of prestige, retell the plot, and mention that O'Hara herself thought it was a "stinkeroo" instead of adding anything original. How I wish he, instead, could have written something original. *Comanche Territory*, another good western, is clocked, too, at the unforgivable seventy-seven minutes, and is tossed aside with the ridiculous remark that it was "hardly *Bury My Heart at Wounded Knee*." What a foolish standard to use in evaluating a film! Does Malone think that everyone who ever made a western in the last 100 years should have it conform to the standard of one western that the author happens to admire?

Oddly, when speaking about one B given a bad review in the 1950s, Malone writes, "By now, criticism from these self-styled arbiters of taste had developed a familiar pattern: the Technicolor sop, followed by a putdown based not so much on O'Hara's acting ability as on the scripts she was being offered." The author could very well be talking about himself here.

Malone inexplicably calls *The Foxes of Harrow* a "cardboard *Gone With the Wind*." The only reason I can see for this odd comparison is that it gives the author a chance to "cleverly" say, "Frankly, my dear, nobody really gave a damn about her upper-crust pretensions." Oh, come on, please — talk about pretensions! Too many of the author's attempted witticisms failed to amuse.

What did amuse and delight me were the various words he uses to substitute "said." While it's good to mix up your words a bit to avoid repetition, there is something comical about it here. In this biography, O'Hara "pines," "gleaned," "snorted," "propounded," "pronounced," etc. The biggest laugh, however — one of the biggest ever in any book I've read — comes when the author says that one of the reasons close friends O'Hara and John Wayne did not have an affair was that both "of them were married and took their vows seriously." Someone should sit the author down and explain the facts of movie star life. If he had called Wayne a lifelong teetotaler, it could not have been funnier.

Fire Over Africa is called a "poor man's *Casablanca*, with [Macdonald] Carey and O'Hara as second-string versions of Bogie and Bacall." Again, I do not see similarities between these two films, so why compare them? And isn't it odd that he mentions Bogie and Bacall when she is not even in *Casablanca*? (*Casablanca* features Bogie and Bergman, in case he doesn't know.)

I love writers who act as if we can see an actor's personal turmoil and troubles in their performances. Naturally, this is pure conjecture. Here, we are supposed to believe that O'Hara's performance in *War Arrow* is compromised by outside diversions. I think not. The author resorts to another overused film book cliché, writing that an actress manages to say a certain silly line "with a straight face." For cryin' out loud, of course actors speak the screenplay's lines with a straight face! What are they supposed to do — laugh into the camera and tell the viewers the film is garbage and they should demand a refund at the box office?

About the few spankings O'Hara endured in various movies: "This was a curiously masochistic aspect of O'Hara's persona. She didn't view these scenes as demeaning, just good fun. In fact, she wished she had a dollar for every time she had her bottom smacked in a movie. If she did, she would have a 'healthy bank balance.' She even featured photographs of both spankings [in *Spencer's Mountain* and *The Quiet Man*] in her autobiography." Please, let's not make something out of nothing.

The Parent Trap: "Trick photography wasn't as sophisticated back then (no computer-generated special effects), so it was quite an achievement to pull it off." Yes, in those olden days of 1961 making it seem as if the same actress was playing twins on screen was a newfangled and glorious thing. Amazing.

Talking about various films O'Hara missed out on, Malone wonders why she would be upset losing a "lightweight comedy" such as *The Paleface*. Um, maybe because it was a huge hit? If indeed she was up for

It's a Wonderful Life, I seriously doubt it would have been a "potentially career-changing role" if she had been cast. This reminds me of the two "authors" who recently claimed that the rejection by Carole Landis of the B mystery *The Spider* was earth-shattering as the role could have elevated her to the top of Hollywood. Misinformed comments such as these make me laugh. Where is common sense nowadays? Bunched in with all the 1940s might-have-beens: *The King and I*, the Rodgers and Hammerstein Broadway musical that was adapted by Fox in 1956.

Malone claims that Lauren Bacall was never nominated for an Oscar. Yes, she was, for 1996's *The Mirror Has Two Faces*. She received an honorary one in 2010. It's Josef von Sternberg *not* Erich von Sternberg who directed *The Blue Angel*.

"Reviews for O'Hara's performance in *Hunchback* were generally positive, with an occasional exception. One critic opined, 'Esmeralda could be as vibrant as Hayworth's Gilda but is almost wholly eclipsed by Laughton's dominant discourse of fleshing out Quasimodo beyond the rubber mask ambitions of Chaney into a fusion of his own personal anxieties and obsessions." First of all, this "review" is from a 1993 magazine called *Film Dope*, and does not speak for the initial viewing of O'Hara's performance in 1939. Second, this is just another bizarre example of the comparisons the author uses throughout the book. Who in the world equates Gilda and Esmeralda? More drivel via *Film Dope*: Malone quotes a "critic" who claims that her films *The Black Swan, Sinbad, The Spanish Main, Bagdad*, and *Against All Flags* were "punishments."

There's some confusion in regard to Kathryn Grayson: "Grayson, like O'Hara, was married to a man named Price." O'Hara was married to Will Price and during the time of the story Malone is referring to, Grayson was married to actor John Shelton. It took me a while before I remembered that Shelton's real name was Edward Sheppard Price. Of course, this is not mentioned in the text. Speaking of RKO's contract players in 1940, Malone refers to "farceuse" Lucille Ball. According to *Merriam-Webster*, a farceuse is "a woman who is a farceur; esp: an actress skilled in playing farce." Before *I Love Lucy* Ball had a film career with a variety of roles, but Malone seems unaware of this.

Malone is not a bad writer. His sections on *How Green Was My Valley* and *The Quiet Man* are very well done, although he falls into the trap of underestimating Walter Pidgeon's performance in the former. (That *annoys* me.) My biggest problems with this new book is the author's reliance on O'Hara's autobiography. If she had not written it, Malone would not have had much of a book, so liberally does he quote and take from it. He tries to be ingenious by contrasting her "storybook" marriage to Will Price in the fan magazines to the harsh realities that she presented in her book. At first, this was interesting, but overuse made it tiresome. At one point, for some reason, the author decided to quote "Prayer for My Daughter" from *Silver Screen*, June 1945, which was movie mag pap directed to her daughter Bronwyn, who was born the previous year.

We do not need an interpretation of O'Hara's autobiography with added details. If the author's film criticism had been topnotch, I could forgive his heavy dependence on *'Tis Herself.* If you're an O'Hara fan, your best bet, frankly, is to stick with her autobio. The photos here are pretty, but if you are looking for a substantial biography or a sharp, lively critique of her work, you will have to wait until someone like Eve Golden decides to write one. It's a shame, because I love O'Hara and I feel she merits so much more than this.

Very rare are actors or actresses writing autobiographies who take into account the feelings of their fans. Many choose to ignore their films in favor of their personal lives, while others show a total ignorance of the people they worked with or what was going on around them. Facts about others are often wrong; that is, if they even care about these incidental people. That's why I was so thrilled with Maureen O'Hara's **'Tis Herself: A Memoir**, written with John Nicoletti (Simon & Schuster).

Here is a book with a perceptive look at Hollywood, a book that takes the time to talk about films, co-stars and directors, doing it in an intelligent, lively, sometimes affecting fashion. O'Hara was undeniably observant, and her sharp commentaries about John Ford, Alfred Hitchcock and Charles Laughton alone are worth it for film fans.

I have been a fan of Miss O'Hara's ever since I saw her in *The Black Swan* (1942) with Tyrone Power, a film that is still one of my favorites. The mixture of fiery redheaded beauty, femininity and toughness — she could out-fence anyone, in my opinion — endeared her not only to movie fans, but also to John Ford and John Wayne, who loved working with her; she was one of the very few actresses who could stand up to Wayne, and make it believable. She effortlessly switched from soaps (*Sentimental Journey*) to westerns (*Rio Grande*) to comedies (*Sitting Pretty*) to whimsy (*Miracle on 34th Street*) to swashbucklers (*Against All Flags*) and to dramas (*How Green Was My Valley*). Her film list has further well-known titles: *The Hunchback of Notre Dame, The Foxes of Harrow, The Quiet Man, The Parent Trap, Jamaica Inn, Ten Gentlemen from West Point, This Land is Mine, The Spanish Main, Sinbad the Sailor, Dance Girl Dance, The Long Gray Line,* etc. It is definitely an enviable career. The lengthy write-up about the making of *The Quiet Man* is extremely important, and she clears up many misunderstandings and false reports that have circulated.

This is not a tell-all, she isn't here to kiss-and-tell, which is fine by me, but O'Hara more than makes up for any lost sensationalism about herself with her gutsy prose. What I like most, perhaps, is that here is a woman who is clearly proud of her Irish heritage and fortitude, but isn't afraid to admit that she's not perfect, that, especially when it came to two of her three husbands, she was also very fallible. Maureen O'Hara succeeds in humanizing herself to the reader. I liked her even more after reading what she went through during her career and with her marriages. I've talked to two people since reading this who have the same issue with this book. And some readers might wonder, too, why, if she was as tough and salty as she claims, did she get involved with the wrong men (excluding her last husband) and why did she put up with an abusive alcoholic (her second spouse) as long as she did? O'Hara makes no bones about her weakness here. Why does *any* woman stay with a man like that? O'Hara never presents herself as anything but human, she realizes the mistakes she made; things happen. Just because she's a star doesn't make her immune to such things, it probably only made things worse.

It helps immeasurably that this is well-written, that even though there's a nice aura about this, it's never dull or sappy. O'Hara (and obviously Mr. Nicoletti) has such a spellbinding way, there's such a tone of gentleness about the text, that I found myself just savoring every word. I feel like an idiot saying so, but read the book and you'll see what I mean. Maureen O'Hara had me in the palm of her hand.

There are some surprises in here, however, not the least of which was how her second husband treated her. The whole story about making the movie *Kangaroo* in Australia was a real eye-opener — shocking, in fact. Also, her love-hate relationship (professionally and personally) with John Ford was strange, and very disturbing. This book probably includes more insights into his psyche than any ten full biographies about the man. He was complex, we know that — but *this* complex? I had no idea. "Ford's passing began a long period of confusion for me," she writes, "and I have wrestled with my thoughts about him ever since. I set out to contribute to a deeper understanding of him in this book. I wanted to come to terms with my feelings about this incredibly complex man who had played such an important role in my life and in the life of my family." She succeeds admirably.

She's clearly a lady, but it's also nice to find that she has a sense of humor about herself. My favorite quote in the book involves the movie *At Sword's Point*. She had been taking fencing lessons and was faced with a director, Lewis Allen, who doubted her competence in this skill. She was ready to prove herself. "When Lewis called, 'Action,' and that [horse-driven] coach rounded the corner, I leaped out and started fencing like a son of a bitch." Also fun is the story of a misbehaving Tim Hovey on

Everything But the Truth. For Errol Flynn fans, there's a terrific story about him at a war bond function in Texas. Did you know that Hitchcock wanted her for *Rebecca* or that the war prevented her and Laughton from doing a version of *The Admirable Crichton*? I doubt anyone will keep a dry eye when she recounts John Wayne's final days; her memories of her frequent, most well-known, co-star do the man justice. But don't get the idea that she liked everybody. It's a nice book, but it's also an honest one. This is a volume with many memorable moments. All I can say is that after reading this, I declared it one of the best autobiographies I've ever read. It's fabulous. Alas, for someone with such an impressive resume, there is no filmography. The color cover photo of Maureen is stunning.

***

McFarland's recent volume about Mercedes McCambridge, imaginatively titled **Mercedes McCambridge**, is a fact-filled but uneven biography of the Oscar-winning actress whose personal life was as fiercely intense as any role she ever played. At a mere 181 pages (30 of which are devoted to an exhaustive listing of all her radio, theater, TV and film credits), author Ron Lackmann manages to squeeze in an impressive amount of information about McCambridge's turbulent life and unique career. He seems to genuinely admire her work and his research is admirable, but his lack of basic writing skills makes for a hard slog. Put simply, this writer is no match for his electric and eclectic subject. A vivid personality needs more than a pedestrian, if earnest, biographer.

One major annoyance in this book is that digressions abound. Whenever a celebrated figure enters McCambridge's life, Lackmann feels the need to clumsily interrupt his narrative to deliver a biography of each one. Do we need capsule bios of such towering figures as Marlene Dietrich, Adlai Stevenson, Orson Welles, James Dean and Billy Rose, from birth? Considering that their fame was greater than

McCambridge's, it's hard to imagine that anyone reading a book about Mercedes McCambridge would need to be given all these life stories. And do we really need a two-page history of Joliet, Illinois, just because Mercedes was born there? Or the entire life story of her father, page after page? Perhaps Lackmann just needed a heftier word count, but padding is okay only if it's cleverly disguised.

A definite plus is the wealth of rare photos from McCambridge's early days as a radio and stage actress in the 1930s and '40s, including a number of leggy cheesecake shots that will surprise those who know her only as a stern-faced character actress. But the captions are often inaccurate. One photo of Mercedes in costume for her 1949 debut film, *All the King's Men*, is described as being a 1946 portrait she used when trying to get stage work in London. Another, captioned as a photo from her days on radio in 1947, was actually taken at Warners in 1950 while she was filming *Lightning Strikes Twice*. And a still identified as being from her 1961 film *Angel Baby* was actually from *Cages*, an off-Broadway play she did two years later.

A major gripe, for me, is Lackmann's neglect in crediting other authors whose work he uses as sources. For example, my friend (and *Killer Tomatoes* co-writer) Ray Hagen did an extensive interview with McCambridge in 1963 for *Films in Review*, and Lackmann quotes liberally from this interview throughout the entire book, mentioning only the name of the magazine. Ray's name is nowhere to be found, not even in the bibliography. *Films in Review* didn't interview Mercedes McCambridge, Ray Hagen did, and giving other writers their due credit is, at the very least, a basic literary courtesy. (Ray incorporated his McCambridge interview in his chapter on the actress in our book, *Killer Tomatoes: Fifteen Tough Film Dames*, also from McFarland.)

McCambridge's 1981 autobiography, *The Quality of Mercy*, is a riveting and brilliantly written memoir, an absolute must for any of her fans. But Ron Lackmann's biography will serve as a useful companion volume if only for the wealth of data about her subsequent life and achievements, his invaluable compilation of her multi-media acting credits, and all those gorgeous photos. Who knew she had great gams?

***

Crime writer Mickey Spillane (1918-2006), best known for creating the popular detective Mike Hammer, has always been one of my favorite writers. He began writing professionally for comic books in the 1940s. In need of extra cash after the war, Spillane wrote his first novel, *I, the Jury*, in nineteen days in 1947. The book, which was a huge success, introduced the character of Mike Hammer.

I, the Jury was also the first movie adapted from a Spillane novel. The 1953 film starred Biff Elliot as the hard-boiled detective. Elliott, however, was no match for Ralph Meeker's portrayal of Hammer in the classic *Kiss Me Deadly* (1955). Other actors who played Mike Hammer include Robert Bray (*My Gun Is Quick*), Kevin Dobson (*Margin For Murder*), and Armand Assante (1982's *I, the Jury*). Darren McGavin was the first actor to play Hammer on TV, in the 1950s. In recent years, Stacy Keach has become most identified in the role due to a series of television movies and the TV series *The New Mike Hammer*.

According to *The Washington Times*, Mickey Spillane "was a quintessential Cold War writer, an unconditional believer in good and evil and a rare political conservative in the book world. Communists were villains in his work and liberals took some hits as well. In a manner similar to Clint Eastwood's Dirty Harry, Hammer was a cynical loner contemptuous of the 'tedious process' of trials, choosing instead to enforce the law on his own terms." (Hammer says in *One Lonely Night*, "I lived only to kill the scum and the lice that wanted to kill themselves. I lived to kill so that others could live. I lived to kill because my soul was a hardened thing that reveled in the thought of taking the blood of the bastards who made murder their business.")

Spillane was a celebrity in his own right, often appearing on television as himself. As an actor, he appeared in *Ring of Fear* (1954), which was co-produced by John Wayne; Spillane also co-wrote the film without credit. Save for the dreary Clyde Beatty circus footage, *Ring of Fear* was a pretty good murder-mystery, boasting an excellent performance from Sean McClory as a silky-smooth psychotic and a fascinating Spillane as himself, a writer-detective investigating freak accidents at the circus. He would play his creation, Mike Hammer, in *The Girl Hunters* (1963), which was filmed in England. Spillane also appeared in Miller Lite beer commercials in the 1970s and '80s.

As a writer Spillane was often criticized for his heated prose, his "artless plots, his reliance on unlikely coincidence and a simplistic understanding of the law" (*New York Times*), while others had difficulty with the extreme violence and sexual content. Even Ogden Nash got into the act when he wrote, "The Marquis de Sade/Wasn't always mad/ What addled his brain/Was Mickey Spillane." Spillane, himself, called his own writing "the chewing gum of American literature." He dismissed his critics, remarking, "I'm not writing for the critics. I'm writing for the public." He described himself as a "money writer," in that "I write when I need money. I have no fans. You know what I got? Customers. And customers are your friends." And there was no denying that he was a very popular, influential, and hard-hitting writer.

Spillane died at the age of 88. After his death, his friend and literary executor Max Allan Collins edited and completed several of Spillane's unpublished typescripts.

"I snapped the side of the rod across his jaw and laid the flesh open to the bone," Spillane wrote in *The Big Kill*. "I pounded his teeth back into his mouth with the end of the barrel ... and I took my own damn time about kicking him in the face. He smashed into the door and lay there bubbling. So I kicked him again and he stopped bubbling." How can you not love that? Whew.

The aforementioned Max Allan Collins and James L. Traylor have written a terrific new book called **Mickey Spillane on Screen: A**

Complete Study of the Television and Film Adaptations (McFarland). We get chapters on: Spillane At The Movies: *I, the Jury* (1953), *The Long Wait* (1954), *Ring of Fear* (1954), *Kiss Me Deadly* (1955), *My Gun Is Quick* (1957), *The Girl Hunters* (1963), *The Delta Factor* (1970), *I, the Jury* (1982). Spillane On TV: *Mike Hammer* TV Pilot (1954), *Mickey Spillane's Mike Hammer* (1958-59), *Mickey Spillane's Mike Hammer in Margin for Murder* (1981), *Mickey Spillane's Mike Hammer: Murder Me, Murder You* (1983), *Mickey Spillane's Mike Hammer: More Than Murder* (1984), *Mickey Spillane's Mike Hammer* (1984-85), *Return of Mickey Spillane's Mike Hammer* (1986), *The New Mike Hammer* (1986-87), *Mickey Spillane's Mike Hammer: Murder Takes All* (1989), *Come Die with Me: A Mickey Spillane's Mike Hammer Mystery* (1994), *Tomorrow I Die* (*Fallen Angels*, 1995), *Mickey Spillane's Mike Hammer, Private Eye* (1997-98). Appendices: A. The Hammer (Film) Code, B. The Girl Hunt Ballet (*The Band Wagon*, 1953), C. Who's Who of Spillane on Film, D. Stars of the Hammer Film Universe, E. Mickey Spillane in His Own Words.

Each movie gets a thorough analysis, a detailed plot summary (with pertinent dialogue and comments), historical background, trivia, and the authors' opinion of how Spillane's works are adapted, how the characters are handled, opinions on performances, etc. The commentary is fair and balanced, and in a few instances very funny. I was especially tickled by the chapter on *Come Die with Me*, a simply dreadful sounding "updating" of Mike Hammer starring Rob Estes and Pamela Anderson. The plot recapping is simply mind-boggling, just amazing sounding, and the authors' insertion of humor is welcome. This was a pilot made with absolutely no understanding of the Hammer character, especially when they have the tough private eye get on a skateboard. I laughed out loud when they wrote, "It has come to this: Mike Hammer on a skateboard." The whole thing is just so surreal.

It has been acknowledged that the quintessential Mike Hammer has always been Ralph Meeker in the classic *Kiss Me Deadly*—and rightly so.

But, the authors make strong cases for Biff Elliot, Armand Assante, and, of course, Spillane himself as portrayers of Hammer.

I have a personal liking for the 1953 version of *I, the Jury*, a brutal, very under-appreciated film noir. I always thought poor Biff Elliot has been given a raw deal, by fans and critics alike. He's been knocked for his short stature, for his suits with padded shoulders, and for his overall look and speaking voice, but I enjoyed his performance very much. Biff was hot-tempered, quick with his fists, and had an edge to him, which I thought perfect for the role—critics, be damned. I'm glad that Collins and Traylor feel as strongly as I do that Biff should be better remembered. The movie is not shown often, but it's worth seeing. Another reassessment comes for the '80s' *I, the Jury* with Armand Assante. The authors make it sound like a must-see, and I must confess that before this I hadn't wanted to see it, but I do now. I judged before seeing the movie, something you should never do with films. Assante seems an odd choice for Hammer, but if the authors say he does a good job, then he should be given a chance. This is another film not in circulation.

The separate Mike Hammer television series starring Darren McGavin and Stacy Keach have neatly organized chapters. It isn't feasible to talk about every episode, naturally, but by concentrating on select episodes and summing up others, and discussing recurring themes, etc., they give us an excellent flavor of the series' runs. This is harder than it looks, but the authors make it seem effortless. Good writing, all around. Complete episode guides are included.

Their very persuasive write-ups pinpoint all of the films' strengths and weaknesses with good analyses and some clever wording. I was very glad, since we are talking about some film noirs within, that the authors did not resort to phony "noir writing." You know what I'm talking about. We've all read books about noirs where the authors think they have to write "tough," in the so-called style of noir. It only comes across as irritating. Thankfully, that is missing here, and we instead get good, solid writing.

You love Spillane? This is the book to get. A better discussion of the films adapted from his work you will not find. Nor are there authors more knowledgeable than Collins and Traylor. Plus, there's an interesting Q&A with Spillane conducted by co-author Collins at the book's conclusion.

Photos are terrific, with some behind-the-scenes shots that were new to me.

***

Alvin H. Marill's **Movies Made for Television: 1964-2004** (Scarecrow Press), with a foreword by Leonard Maltin, is an incredible (hardcover) five-volume set that lists 5,400 TV movies and mini-series. Entries include brief summaries, production and cast credits (extensive, with character names), airdates, and length. Some entries include notes. There are no photos.

Volume One covers 1964 to 1979, the golden age, as far as I'm concerned, of television films. Here you will find Barbara Stanwcyk in *A Taste of Evil* (1971); Cliff Robertson, Diane Baker and Pamelyn Ferdin in *A Tree Grows in Brooklyn* (1974); Katharine Hepburn in *The Corn is Green* (1979); Richard Chamberlain, Tony Curtis, Trevor Howard, Louis Jourdan, Donald Pleasence and Taryn Power (Tyrone's daughter) in *The Count of Monte Cristo* (1975); Arthur Kennedy, Warren Oates, Tom Selleck and Jeff Corey in *The Movie Murderer* (1970), where an arsonist burns up movie film, with investigator Kennedy "hot" on his trail; Fred MacMurray searching for love ones in *Beyond the Bermuda Triangle* (1975); and two of my favorite TV movies, the tremendous Eleanor Parker in *Home for the Holiday*s (1972) and the intriguing *The Girl on the Late, Late Show* (1974) with Gloria Grahame. Volume Two goes into the less inspiring 1980-1989 period, although there are quite a few gems there, more so than in Volume Three (1990 to 1999) and Volume Four, which goes from 2000 to 2004. Volume Five is the index. All in all, this is an incredible, much-needed endeavor by Marill.

In case you haven't noticed, television films were havens (in the early days, at least) for veteran movie stars. Besides those mentioned, Burt Lancaster, Walter Pidgeon, Eddie Albert, Van Johnson, June Allyson, Viveca Lindfors, Jane Wyman, Ricardo Montalban, Robert Taylor, Dorothy McGuire, Olivia de Havilland, Jackie Cooper, Ida Lupino, Richard Basehart, Henry Fonda, Eva Marie Saint, Bette Davis, Cornel Wilde, Lloyd Bridges, James Whitmore, Susan Hayward, etc., all found work in tele-films, and with good roles, too. TV gave them a chance, where the big screen often let them down.

Another interesting aspect is the remake. There were a few interesting television remakes of big screen classics: *From Here to Eternity* (1979, Natalie Wood, William Devane, Steve Railsback, Joe Pantoliano, Kim Basinger); *Double Indemnity* (1973, Richard Crenna, Lee. J. Cobb, Samantha Eggar); *Miracle on 34th Street* (1973, Jane Alexander, David Hartman, Roddy McDowall, Sebastian Cabot); *Friendly Persuasion* (1975, Richard Kiley, Shirley Knight); *Dark Victory* (1976, Elizabeth Montgomery, Anthony Hopkins, Michele Lee); *Cat on a Hot Tin Roof* (1976, Natalie Wood, Robert Wagner, Laurence Olivier); *Captains Courageous* (1977, Karl Malden); *Come Back, Little Sheba* (1977, Laurence Olivier, Joanne Woodward); *Dial M for Murder* (1981, Angie Dickinson, Christopher Plummer); *Johnny Belinda* (1982, Rosanna Arquette, Richard Thomas, Dennis Quaid); *I Want to Live* (1983, Lindsay Wagner); *Samson and Delilah* (1984, Antony Hamilton and Victor Mature as Samson's father); *Dark Mirror* (1984, Jane Seymour, Stephen Collins); *The Defiant Ones* (1986, Robert Urich, Carl Weathers); *Sorry, Wrong Number* (1989, Loni Anderson); *Dinner at Eight* (1989, Lauren Bacall); *This Gun for Hire* (1991, Robert Wagner); and *The Shaggy Dog* (1994, Ed Begley, Jr.), among others.

Then there are the classic original films and mini-series produced for TV: *Duel* (1971), *Brian's Song* (1971), *The Night Stalker* (1972), *The Execution of Private Slovik* (1974), *Trilogy of Terror* (1975); *Rich Man, Poor Man* (1976); *The Boy in the Plastic Bubble* (1976); *Sybil* (1976); *Roots*

(1977); *Jesus of Nazareth* (1977); *Salem's Lot* (1979); *Shogun* (1980); *The Winds of War* (1983); *The Thorn Birds* (1983), etc.

This is one serious set and is priced that way: $300. Is it worth it? Undoubtedly. There's nothing like it and, judging by the massive scope, which also includes Cable, there will never be one like it again. The brave Marill has put together an amazing research tool 5,498 films spanning forty years.

On a less grander scale, but still very, very entertaining, is **The ABC Movie of the Week Companion: A Loving Tribute to the Classic Series** by Michael Karol, with a foreword by actress Denise Nickerson (iUniverse), a 100-page look at some of the best TV movies produced between 1969 and 1975. "Few series have become cultural touchstones in a way that The ABC Movie of the Week has," writes the author. "Its lengthy run and ambitious goal (to present an original film every week to a demanding audience, one that was much larger than the typical audience of today) were partly the reason, but mostly it's because these short films — most running about 77 minutes to fill a 90-minute time slot — were funny, sad, real, horrific, and yes, cheesy. Memorably so."

And Karol does a commendable job, covering 243 films with humor and sass, while also giving some fun trivia related to the movies, in a short amount of space. His concise, colorful reviews will inspire many to go out and look for these gems and not-so-gems. I know it prompted me to get the DVD of *Moon of the Wolf* (1972), starring David Janssen, Barbara Rush and Bradford Dillman. It also encouraged me to rewatch *Home for the Holidays* (1972) and *Scream of the Wolf* (1974, with Peter Graves and a weirdly compelling Clint Walker), and to lament that I don't have a copy of the frightening *Trilogy of Terror* (1975) with Karen Black, a film that scared the heck out of me when I first saw it many years ago. The author's dedication to "all those obsessed enough to know what a Zuni fetish doll is ...," sent chills down my spine. See *Trilogy of Terror* and you'll know ... if you dare.

While the book is not substantial, for TV junkies it is worthwhile and essential. Karol is such a good writer that he makes the short page count work. I had fun reading it. And, if you like these films too, you'll have fun as well. Michael Karol has a website, www.Sitcomboy.com. Also, visit www.TVTidbits.com for more information about this and other books.

***

Growing up, I absolutely loved the TV show *The Munsters* (1964-66, and in constant reruns ever since), especially Al "Grandpa" Lewis, far and away my favorite character on the show. (I will never forget going to a movie theater in 1988 to see *Married to the Mob*, starring Michelle Pfeiffer. It wasn't particularly enjoyable, but then Al Lewis showed up in one scene. Suddenly, the movie theater erupted with hoots, hollers, clapping and stomping of feet. Everyone chanted, "Grandpa! Grandpa! Grandpa!" and I was right there with them. The commotion didn't die down until well into the next scene. I'm sure that, for most people there, it was the highlight of the movie. This was not an isolated incident; I've heard from others who tell me the same thing happened at their theaters as well. Such is the affection people, to this day, have for Lewis and *The Munsters*.)

That's why I greatly enjoyed **The Munsters: A Trip Down Mockingbird Lane** by the prolific TV expert Stephen Cox, foreword by Yvonne De Carlo and an afterword by Butch Patrick (Back Stage Books/Watson-Guptill), a gorgeous, colorful tribute to the cult series. The show starred Fred Gwynne (as Herman Munster), Yvonne De Carlo (as Lily, his wife), Al Lewis (as the wacky Grandpa, Lily's father), Butch Patrick (as Eddie, Herman & Lily's son) and Beverley Owen (and then Pat Priest) (as Herman & Lily's "normal-looking" daughter, Marilyn).

This is a reissue, of sorts, of Cox's 1989 book, but with added material (interviews and updated bios) and never-before-seen photos.

This volume is a textual and visual treat. Trivia maniacs will revel in the tidbits Cox uncovers. (Casting notes: Bert Lahr was first considered for Grandpa and John Carradine for Herman.) And I love the quotes sprinkled throughout:

Grandpa: "My father and I were very close. He used to give me such wonderful advice. I remember one day he said to me, 'Son, as you go through life, bury your mistakes.' You see, my father never believed in divorce."

Herman: "I just don't understand what went wrong with my child psychology; it always worked on *Leave It to Beaver*."

Grandpa, after putting Herman in a trance: "I learned it from Svengali when the poor fella was down and out. I got it from him for a cup of coffee and a sweet roll."

Herman, after the family tells him how much they love him: "Now look what you've gone and made me do! I haven't cried like this since they canceled *Kukla, Fran & Ollie*!"

Herman: "Aren't you going to wish me luck, Grandpa?"
Grandpa: "Drop Dead."

The presentation is spiffily designed by Jay Anning of Thumb Print, with real imagination. The book is filled with rare color photos, over 300, all on glossy paper stock. It's a *Munster* fan's dream. Cox is, of course, an authority on the show, giving us behind-the-scenes stories and trivia. A complete episode guide is included. (My favorite episode has always been "Lily Munster, Girl Model," a Yvonne De Carlo comedy tour de force.)

"Hopefully," writes the author, "I have assembled a fun representation of the show, a retrospective in which the *Munsters* will unmask before your eyes. Trick or treat?" Definitely treat.

***

I was saddened to learn recently of the passing of former child actress Sybil Jason on August 23, 2011; she was 83. Signed by Warner Bros. as a rival to Shirley Temple in 1935, Sybil made a series of movies and shorts that followed the standard Temple formula. Years before Peggy Ann Garner and Margaret O'Brien, Sybil was one of the most deeply affecting child actresses on film. As Warner Bros.' first child star, she made six movies under contract (*Little Big Shot, I Found Stella Parish, The Singing Kid, The Captain's Kid, The Great O'Malley, Comet Over Broadway*), some shorts, and a few more films for other studios (*Woman Doctor* and, most famously, *The Little Princess* and *The Blue Bird*, both with Shirley Temple).

The Little Princess, justly, contains Miss Jason's most notable role, that of Becky, the cockney scullery maid, who befriends Shirley's character. It's very hard, still today, to watch this gem of a performance and not be profoundly moved. Sybil's subtle emotional intensity is a wonder; you can't help but feel for her. It's interesting to note that Temple is at her most effective reacting to Sybil. In fact, Temple is at her most real, less mawkish, in their scenes together.

Even better, for me at least, is her heartbreaking, underrated performance as Bogart's crippled daughter in *The Great O'Malley*. Her singing and dancing with Al Jolson in *The Singing Kid* just proved her versatility. As talented as Sybil was, however, many felt she was capable of much more. While she never reached the popularity of Temple, Sybil was a natural performer and I've always actually preferred her to Temple's cuteness.

For BearManor Media, Sybil wrote three autobiographies, *My Fifteen Minutes, Five Minutes More,* and *What's It All About, Sybil?*

I first heard from Sybil in 2002, when I wrote her asking for her memories of Ann Sheridan and *The Great O'Malley*. She promptly wrote back and was gracious and helpful. She also told me that she was in the process of writing her autobiography, but was discouraged about the possibility of getting it published. Concerned about her non-scandalous memoirs, she was afraid of the fast-paced publishing world and any insistence that she spice up her book to help it sell. In 2004, she asked me if I could point her in the right direction, publisher-wise. Very often I am asked by fellow writers and friends for publishing suggestions. Depending on the book, author and subject matter, I send them to McFarland, University of Mississippi, University Press of Kentucky, and so forth. With Sybil, I knew that BearManor Media would be the best fit—and I turned out to be correct. Publisher Ben Ohmart's hands-on, personal approach and disregard for gossipy (and sometimes questionable) tell-alls was just what Sybil needed. So, in 2005, **My Fifteen Minutes: An Autobiography of a Child Star of the Golden Era of Hollywood** came out. One of the neatest, and certainly most enjoyable, autobiographies I've ever read, Sybil supplied stories, and lots of them, about all the famous people she worked with and knew. It wasn't a mudslinging tell-all; this ex-child star was—surprisingly and refreshingly—not bitter. She led a very colorful life, and shared it with her readers.

Shirley Temple fans should be delighted by Sybil's remembrances. There's a great deal in here about their friendship and sporadic meetings later when Sybil was retired and married. I was pleased to hear, for once, nice things said about Jack Warner, and I was shocked to hear even more praise heaped on the much-maligned Al Jolson. Yes, Sybil concedes, he had an ego, but his personality wasn't all dark as portrayed by others. The stories are knockouts: Rehearsing with Jolson, palling around with Lana Turner (of all people), sharing some moments with Judy Garland, having Eliot Ness for a bodyguard, some fun (and not so much fun) memories of Errol Flynn, defending Kay Francis, watching Bogart acting up in front of the camera, and revealing a fascinating tidbit about Marilyn Monroe.

The chapter on *The Great O'Malley* (my favorite) was extremely interesting. The tensions on the set and the antics of Ann Sheridan were heaven-sent first-hand information that movie fans crave. My favorite story, I think, is in regard to Jack Warner. Being a normal child, Sybil decided she was going to set up a flower-selling stand in front of her house. The following happened one Saturday morning: "I got up extra early ... on our front lawn I placed two cardboard boxes together, covered them with one of our best damask tablecloths, and then went about carefully choosing an assortment of our prettiest flowers from our garden and fashioned them into bouquets. I proudly got ready to sell them. I couldn't believe my luck that so many people stopped to buy my flowers. I couldn't understand why they asked me to sign a receipt for their purchases, but I gladly did so and was determined that I would pursue this activity every weekend that I had free.

"Midmorning, with not too many bouquets left to sell, I noticed a beautiful limousine slowly drive by. They had barely just passed my stand when the car came to a screeching halt and backed up. The rear door swung open and out stepped Mr. Jack Warner who didn't say a word to me, but just took me by the arm and led us to my front door and started pounding on it. When my poor sister heard all this noise, she was frightened out of her wits and was further startled when she peered into the angry face of Mr. Warner, who demanded, 'Don't we pay this child enough money that she doesn't have to sell flowers on the street?!' Needless to say, my entrepreneur career had come to a swift end!"

Jason's writing style is breezy, infectious and articulate. She goes from one story to the other, throwing us some personal data about her life, but sticking mostly to the people she worked with. This isn't an ego-trip, but a fun recollection of a Hollywood we no longer see. She takes us to the movie sets and shares the wonders she felt, as just a little girl, coming to Hollywood from her home in South Africa. The photos, from films and shorts, publicity and candids, number at least a hundred. I can't stress enough the importance of this volume or the entertainment you'll derive from reveling in its good humor. I loved it.

Her follow-up in 2007 was the cleverly-titled **Five Minutes More**. As with her first effort, I loved this one, too. What's not to love? Sybil herself was a person who was very lovable and she was able to transmit her gentle personality to these pages. She writes with affection about Allen Jenkins, Joe Sawyer, Linda Darnell, Glenda Farrell, Dickie Jones, Delmar Watson, Cesar Romero, Joan Leslie, Ward Bond, Joe Weber and Lew Fields, Jackie Coogan, Marion Davies, Jack La Rue, Ann Rutherford, Edward Everett Horton, Minta Durfee Arbuckle, Charlie Chaplin, Carole Lombard, Pat O'Brien, Kay Francis, etc., without sounding syrupy. I must admit that some of her stories were quite touching. The anecdote about Glenda Farrell, on the set of *Little Big Shot*, was very sweet and really shows what a genuine human being Farrell was. Sybil's brief reunion with Allen Jenkins, that wonderful character actor, was both sad and charming. The whole Joan Blondell/Dick Powell account was adorable, as little five-year-old Sybil, with a crush on Powell, knitted him a scarf. Her remembrances of Kay Francis were very welcome. Kay, says Sybil, was "a very motherly and protective woman toward me." It was a fine tribute to the lady. She sets the record straight on several accounts and relates the kindnesses that Kay displayed to her fellow co-workers. I particularly loved the section where Sybil refutes some negative comments made by an author about a supposedly unprofessional Kay on two movie sets. Since Sybil was on both the sets in question, she can say with authority that the statements were not true. With so many made-up statements about our Golden Age stars, it's nice that Sybil took the time to set the record straight.

Dancer Eleanor Powell is also well represented here, with some lovely inside stories about their friendship. No chance this material can be gotten anywhere else. A fun story revolved around Sybil's lunch date with Carole Lombard, eating picnic-style on the floor of Lombard's dressing room and teaching her how to play jacks. Not so fun, but very interesting, was Sybil's story about Harold Lloyd and his daughter. Another emotional moment was her learning of Pat O'Brien's passing. Her recounting of her friendship with O'Brien really showed off his sparkling personality and humor.

It's revealing, first-hand stories like these that make Sybil Jason's memoirs so valuable. She not only was there, she was paying attention. Her writing is very descriptive and the narrative flows naturally. It was an easy read, over much too soon, but completely satisfying. She is able to communicate what these stars were really like—and that is always a beautiful thing. The photos are plentiful and exceptional.

The last in Sybil's autobiographical trilogy, **What's It All About, Sybil?**, doesn't disappoint. She continues her journey through her career, relating stories about Ian Hunter, Guy Kibbee, May Robson, Rudy Vallee, Jane Wyman, Johnny Green, Beverly Roberts, Henry Fonda, Patrick Swayze, and Frieda Inescort, among others. Most of this material within came from newsletters from The International Sybil Jason Fan Club, greatly expanded by Miss Jason for this book.

The chapter on the under-appreciated Inescort is my favorite. Sybil relates some personal information about her life that she got firsthand from Inescort. I had no idea what a rough life the actress led until I read this chapter. Her three-dimensional portrait is a fine tribute to a skillful actress and a courageous woman.

The chapter on stand-ins was highly interesting, giving these largely unsung individuals their due. Sybil also devotes a whole chapter to her directors: Michael Curtiz, Mervyn LeRoy, Busby Berkeley, Sidney Salkow, Nick Grinde, William Keighley, Walter Lang, and William Dieterle. I was especially pleased to read this section as very little is written about most of these directors. The photos accompanying the text here are real treasures.

Sybil's good humor and tender memories are a fine mix, especially for movie fans who love Warner Bros. films of the 1930s. A fine actress and a warm, thoughtful lady, she leaves a nice legacy with her film performances and also with three outstanding documents chronicling her life and career. She will be missed.

***

Like a lot of true movie buffs, I long for books about more obscure performers. I have read enough — thank you very much — about Marilyn Monroe, Cary Grant, Grace Kelly, James Dean, et al. Yes, they are deserving actors, but there has been an overabundance of books about these stars and now, out of sheer boredom with the truth, authors with dubious credentials are putting many a phony spin to the legends. So, when I get a book on a subject never covered adequately, it's a very happy day.

But, sometimes there's a problem. While many of these writers mean well, their efforts can be inconsistent. It's not entirely their fault. Their publishers simply need to do more editing of their books. Some of these volumes don't look edited at all which is a shame for film fans who eagerly buy a long-awaited book on a favorite actor or actress.

I was thrilled to get **Nina Mae McKinney: The Black Garbo** by Stephen Bourne (BearManor Media), because there has been nothing substantial written on this fascinating, beautiful and very talented African-American singer-actress. But the presentation here is iffy, at best.

Nina Mae McKinney (1912-67) is regarded as Hollywood's first African-American movie star due to her performance in King Vidor's *Hallelujah!* (1929). Fans of pre-Code also remember Nina Mae fondly for her supporting part in *Safe in Hell* (1931). However, the prejudice she encountered stalled any chance of elevating her status in the movie capital. She found more popularity in Europe, where she was dubbed "The Black Garbo." Nina Mae was also a pioneer of early television in England in the late '30s. She did a bunch of movies, including an important role in *Sanders of the River* (1935), starring Paul Robeson, in the UK. After returning to the United States, McKinney starred in "race films," intended for the small African-American film market: *Gang Smashers* (1938), *The Devil's Daughter* (1939), and *Straight to Heaven* (1939). She worked in cabaret and on Broadway, in other films and short subjects, but found her career fading in the '40s. McKinney made her last appearance in 1951, playing Sadie Thompson, in a minor stage production of *Rain*. Her final years were troubled; she died of a heart attack at the age of 53, possibly as a result of alcohol and drug addictions. Although McKinney received a posthumous award from the Black Filmmakers Hall of Fame for lifetime achievement in 1978, she has been generally overlooked —until now.

With filmography, bibliography and index, this book is 94 pages. However, there are a number of blank pages — a publishing no-no — so the book contains less than you might first imagine. I was not put off by the volume's short length, however, since there is so little written about Nina Mae. It's obvious that the author did his best to gather up all the info he could. He has done an admirable job, and we should be thankful that he took the time to put this together. He has a solid appreciation of her work. Bourne is also good at presenting the racially-charged environment Nina Mae found herself in during her career.

So, what's the problem? The text doesn't seem to be proof-read. Many sentences needed to be cleaned up, repetition pared down, and punctuation corrected. Also, since Bourne quotes from other books in the text, it would have been helpful if some of the titles had been put in the end notes. The photos are nice, although a few are reproduced poorly. The cover shot, though, is absolutely sensational.

I am definitely recommending this book, despite the flaws. Bourne knows and loves his subject — it's obviously a labor of love. I only wish an editor had shared his passion.

***

I am often very hard on books relating to film noir, simply because it is such a popular subject that anyone thinks they can successfully write about it. That's why **Noir City Sentinel: Annual #1: The Best of the Film Noir Foundation Newsletter, 2006-2008**, edited by noir maestro Eddie Muller (Film Noir Foundation), is so welcomed by me. The book's contributors, besides Muller, are Megan Abbott, Kathryn Ayres, Eric Beetner, Haggai Elitzur, Randall Homan, Don Malcolm, Paul Meehan, Anita Monga, Alan K. Rode, Marc Svetov, Arthur Tashiro, Will Viharo, Lindsey Westbrook, and Stone Wallace.

The book features an assortment of articles and reviews concentrating on different aspects of film noir. Eric Beetner's write-up of overrated vs. underrated noirs recommends little-known gems such as *Framed* (1947), *High Wall* (1947), *He Ran All the Way* (1951), *Where the Sidewalk Ends* (1950), and *Woman on the Run* (1950), etc., in favor of good, but over-hyped classics like *The Woman in the Window* (1944), *The Naked City* (1948), *Gilda* (1946), *The Postman Always Rings Twice* (1946) and *To Have and Have Not* (1944). Expanding your movie-watching horizons, not sticking to just the established classics, is always a positive, worthwhile venture. I was thrilled to see some recognition paid to *Woman on the Run*, one of my favorite Ann Sheridan movies, and a movie containing a complex role for Dennis O'Keefe.

Eddie Muller tackles a neglected art, comic book noirs, in his piece "Blood, Sweat, and Fear: The Ink-Stained Genius of Johnny Craig." "During an inspired five-year burst in the early 1950s, using only india ink and bristol board, Johnny Craig evoked a noir universe every bit as compelling as what Jim Thompson and Fritz Lang were simultaneously creating with prose and film." For my tastes, Muller does not do enough writing in the book. I consider him one of the best, most enjoyable writers of film history today. I love the crackling feel he transports to his reviews of contemporary noirs *Edmond* (2005), *Brick* (2005), *Running Scared* (2006), *Derailed* (2005) and *Kiss Kiss Bang Bang* (2005). His critiques of *Running Scared* and *Derailed*, especially, were right-on in explaining the difficulties I, too, had with these films. Will Viharo is another keen commentator, and I enjoyed his writing immensely. While praised and awarded for her film writing, Megan Abbott's mini-reviews did little for me, I must admit.

Alan K. Rode, author of McFarland's must-read Charles McGraw biography (q.v.), does some dandy tributes to Vincent Sherman, Joseph Pevney, Mark Hellinger, Richard Widmark, Glenn Ford, and A.I. "Buzz" Bezzerides. It's hard to beat Alan's film knowledge, clear-eyed but affectionate stance, and gift with a word or a well-turned-out phrase: "What remained was still a jolt of postwar nihilism—a filmic left hook to the gut."

Don Malcolm is another favorite here of mine. His short-but-sweet "Cup of Coffee with Jules Buck" is an engaging piece incorporating Buck's career as cinematographer/associate producer (*San Pietro*, *The Killers*, *The Naked City*, *Brute Force*, etc.) with personal recollections. Don's article on "Casting Against Type: Six Actors In Search of Transcendence" centers on Dan Duryea in *Black Angel* (1946), Tyrone Power in *Nightmare Alley* (1947), Peggy Dow in *Woman in Hiding* (1950), Steve Cochran in *Tomorrow Is Another Day* (1951), June Allyson in *The Shrike* (1955), and David Wayne in *M* (1951), and talks about how these actors broke out of their strict typecasting to turn in surprising portrayals in these movies. While I do not agree with his appraisal of Allyson's performance, which I think could've been much better, I applaud him for including Peggy Dow here. Another of those actresses who was boxed in as a "sweet nothing," Dow is one "blowtorch babe" in *Woman in Hiding*, she really took advantage of her rare opportunity as a "dolled-up other woman."

I was genuinely smitten by Marc Svetov's choice of adjectives, chiefly in his "Clifford Odets: Broadway's Blackest Bard." A good descriptive phrase can always make a difference, and there are many in here by all the writers. I liked much of the pithy language in these articles, especially phrases like "tossed-salad noir," "shards of hope and disillusionment that have been ground into his soul," "crackpot zeal," and "go-to bruiser," etc.

Annual #1 contains so much more that's worthwhile, it's jam-packed with excellent writing and intriguing subject matter. There's a marvelous quote herein from Jules Buck defining film noir: "We didn't know from noir in those days. Hellinger just wanted to make tough stories, filled with the passion of life versus death. What people call noir were simply movies that grabbed life versus death by the throat and hung on no matter what."

The Film Noir Foundation is a non-profit organization dedicated to preserving films in danger of being lost or irreparably damaged, and ensuring that there are high-quality prints available for future generations. They need donations to locate, restore, and exhibit these films before they're lost forever. A very worthwhile endeavor, you will not be disappointed by contributing, getting their newsletters and/or purchasing their annuals. This is primo noir writing, not to be missed.

***

James F. Broderick has written an unassuming, compact little book called **Now a Terrifying Motion Picture!: Twenty-Five Classic Works of Horror Adapted from Book to Film** (McFarland). This volume endeavors to examine works of horror literature and the classic films that were made from them: *Altered States* (1980), *The Amityville Horror* (1979), *The Birds* (1963), *Dead Ringers* (1988), *Dr. Jekyll and Mr. Hyde* (1931), *The Exorcist* (1973), *The Fly* (1958 & 1986), *Frankenstein* (1931), *Freaks* (1932), *From Hell* (2001), *Ghost Story* (1981), *The Hounds of the Baskervilles* (1939), *Jaws* (1975), *The Masque of the Red Death* (1964), *The Night Stalker* (1972), *The Ninth Gate* (1999), *Nosferatu* (1922), *The Phantom of the Opera* (1925), *Psycho* (1960), *Re-Animator* (1985), *The Serpent and the Rainbow* (1988), *The Shining* (1980), *Sleepy Hollow* (1999), *The Thing from Another World* (1951), and *Village of the Damned* (1960). Some of the usual suspects, to be sure, but a few unique choices, as well. For example, *From Hell* was a movie adapted from a graphic novel.

I was not aware of Broderick's previous work as a writer (for McFarland he wrote 2006's *The Literary Galaxy of Star Trek: An Analysis of References and Themes in the Television Series and Films*), but based on *Now a Terrifying Motion Picture*, I now wish I had. He is a tremendously readable essayist, with a flowing, succinct, and clever style that is very appealing. Too often I read writers giving out with the same old clichéd lines, without any hint of originality, but not Broderick. There are words and phrases he uses in this book that just hit me the right way, and I thought to myself, "Why couldn't I come up with that?" Adding proper, distinctive adjectives to words is trickier than it may sound, but when you get a winner it's a striking thing (e.g., "snow-spackled exteriors"). Sometimes what he does is so simple and effortless; for instance, this line about Darren McGavin's performance in *The Night Stalker*: "The veteran TV actor inhabits the intrepid reporter down to his Scotch-marinated bone marrow and captures the sense of jejune enthusiasm and broken-down careerist that the iconoclast Kolchak finds himself to be in his early-middle age."

The Shining chapter is filled with evocative goodies and bright lines. I must confess that I never liked the film, but I loved this spot-on observation: "The crazier Nicholson gets, the more idiotic he looks. Shelley Duvall transforms the warm sympathetic wife of the book into a simpering, semi-retarded hysteric." Another nice line: "[Stephen] King's story relies on emotionally charged events that leave his characters unsettled, feeling adrift, left ultimately trying to inhabit a psychic space that has not been cleared for landing."

Broderick, after laying out the details of an extremely uncomfortable torture scene in *The Serpent and the Rainbow*, notes that it's "more fun to watch than it is to describe." In *The Exorcist*, Regan's change is expressed as going from "mommy's little helper to Satan's little mouthpiece." On Peter Benchley's *Jaws*: "His fish goes deep, but the author stays mostly above the literary waterline, focusing on the thrill of the chase and the scenery-chewing (literally) finale." The line I loved best, however, the one to really make me laugh out loud, was this one, about *Phantom of the Opera*, after Christine has suddenly unmasked the Phantom: "He's aghast, she's agog, he's a ghoul."

In addition to the fine writing, Broderick supplies good, solid insights and fresh perspectives on the books and the movies, with a judicious use of quotes and incisive commentary. That's really saying something, especially when you are reading about a few movies here that have been analyzed to death elsewhere. I love books that compare source stories to film, and this is one of the best I have come across. It's briskly written, and there's a lot of good stuff packed into this little volume. To author James F. Broderick I say, "More books, please."

A fairly comparable book can be found with **Hardboiled Hollywood: The True Crime Stories Behind the Classic Noir Films** by Max Décharné (Pegasus Books/W.W. Norton & Co.). Published in England, this volume takes classic films and compares them to their sources, while also telling their backstories: *Little Caesar, The Big Sleep* (1946), *In a Lonely Place, Kiss Me Deadly, Hell is a City, Psycho, Point Blank, Bonnie and Clyde, Get Carter, Dillinger* (1973), and *LA Confidential*. First of all, the title is a disappointment; if you are expecting "noir," you ain't getting much. *Little Caesar*, noir? Only in Décharné's dreams. No, the word "noir" in the title seems to have been chosen mainly to sell books.

The chapters are a mixed bag, and I found myself disliking sections of certain chapters, while greatly enjoying the whole of others. While James F. Broderick's *Psycho* write-up was fresh, I thought Décharné's really lacked any genuine involvement. Sure, he got all the grisly details out about Ed Gein's murderous and cannibalistic exploits, but, other than that, nothing special.

The chapter on *In a Lonely Place* was splendid; his comparison between the book, written by Dorothy B. Hughes, and the film was masterful. I found so much of interest here; his use of quotes from the book and film here, and in the other write-ups, are handled extremely well. Hughes' book is totally different in its storyline (fascinatingly so);

Décharné gives some remarkable insights into the adaptation and how the tone remained the same even though it was drastically altered.

Hell is a City, a Hammer crime film, is a real oddity here, although a welcomed one. This rarely-seen movie begs for a revival, and his serious examination is a step in the right direction. It is a prime example of a writer expertly blending commentary and behind-the-scenes information together. *Kiss Me Deadly*, complete with cool quotes, is another standout evaluation that is very sharp and benefited from the author's attention to the minutest details.

Décharné's style is less fluid than Broderick's and his cleverness is pretty much hit-and-miss. The narrative has a slow, painstaking, loquacious tone that takes some time to get used to. If you are into crime films, you will definitely find some interest here. Even when I was bogged down in Décharné's at times sticky prose, I found something that I liked. He uses quotes well, gives biographical information about the authors, and has observations that more often than not hit the mark. It's a hard slog at times, but worth the trek, if you love these films. And who doesn't? This book will give you a new way of looking at these movies, and that's always a good thing.

While we are on this subject, if you want to read the original source stories for classic films, I suggest you check out **No, But I Saw the Movie: The Best Short Stories Ever Made Into Film**, edited by David Wheeler, with a foreword by Bruce Jay Friedman (Penguin Books). This sensational volume collects eighteen stories that were later adapted for film. You can see what the author initially intended, and I guarantee you that you'll be surprised by what you read here — by what you thought you knew about these stories: The Wisdom of Eve by Mary Orr (*All About Eve*), Bad Time at Honda by Howard Breslin (*Bad Day at Black Rock*), Blow-Up by Julio Cortázar, The Body Snatcher by Robert Louis Stevenson, Don't Look Now by Daphne du Maurier, The Fly by George Langelaan, Spurs by Tod Robbins (*Freaks*), The Idyll of Miss Sarah Brown by Damon

Runyon (*Guys and Dolls*), A Change of Plan by Bruce Jay Friedman (*The Heartbreak Kid*), The Tin Star by John M. Cunningham (*High Noon*), Night Bus by Samuel Hopkins Adams (*It Happened One Night*), The Greatest Gift by Philip Van Doren Stern (*It's a Wonderful Life*), The Day of Atonement by Samson Raphaelson (*The Jazz Singer*), Mr. Blandings Builds His Castle by Eric Hodgins (*Mr. Blandings Builds His Dream House*), The Real Bad Friend by Robert Bloch (*Psycho*), Rear Window by Cornell Woolrich, Stage to Lordsburg by Ernest Haycox (*Stagecoach*), and The Sentinel by Arthur C. Clarke (*2001: A Space Odyssey*).

***

How could anyone dislike actor Richard Dix (1893-1949)? Dix was an attractive, rugged, yet smooth presence on film going back to silents. Born Ernest Carlton Brimmer, he made his film debut in 1917, and stayed a star until his untimely death over thirty years later. Some of his most notable films include *The Vanishing American* (1925), *Red Skin* (1929), *Nothing But the Truth* (1929), *Seven Keys to Baldpate* (1929), and his Oscar-nominated *Cimarron* (1931). My favorite films of Dix, however, have been things like *Ace of Aces* (1933), *The Great Jasper* (1933), *Twelve Crowded Hours* (1939), *American Empire* (1942), *Buckskin Frontier* (1943) and The Whistler series he did for Columbia (1944-47).

His son, Robert Dix, born Robert Brimmer in 1935, was an actor for many years, nabbing an MGM contract in 1954. His best known films include *Forbidden Planet* (1956), Sam Fuller's *Forty Guns* (1957), *Young Jesse James* (1960), *The Little Shepherd of Kingdom Come* (1961), and some late '60s biker flicks, among others, including scads of episodic television work. Robert has written **Out of Hollywood: Two Generations of Actors** (Ernest Publishing), one of the most harrowing, moving and honest autobiographies I have ever read. Robert Dix, to put it mildly, led a very difficult life, and every bit of it is colorfully and achingly retold—sometimes to the reader's horror. His struggles with losing his dad at an early age, his frightening violent troubles with his stepfather and the law, problems with women, alcoholism, and religion are on full, head-throbbing display. I felt every torment, every loss, and every triumph.

Most of all, I liked Robert Dix. He admits to doing some bad things in his time, but you can't help but identify with him and want to root him on as he tries to find himself. When he slips, he's human; you understand what he's going through. He is a very smart, perceptive man, very introspective and spiritual. The section where drinking finally overwhelms him and he becomes homeless is heartbreaking; I was profoundly moved by his plight and the pain and helplessness he felt inside. When you read of his wife's miscarriage, you better have a strong stomach. He also has a knack for action—his descriptions of his fights are corkers, I must say!

He has some excellent stories about his movies, many boasting substantial production notes that are interesting to read—not the usual get-it-out-of-the-way treatment that some actors hand us in their respective autobiographies. Dix is a good storyteller; he knows what his readers are looking for, and gives it to them, plus some added goodies. I especially enjoyed hearing about the making of the movie *The 11th Commandment*, which had trouble with funding and distribution.

While Dix is a likable and descriptive writer, his text really needed a stronger proofreader. There are many typos, and factual errors regarding movies. I'm overlooking this, though, and strongly recommending this book because its overall message and content is inspiring, funny, and moving. His portrait of his famous father is an affectionate one, and I like the way Richard Dix's spirit seems to hang over the story in a compelling way. The photos are very nice, reproduced on glossy stock. Robert Dix brings the old and new Hollywood together in one unassuming volume.

***

I had high hopes for **Paul Bern: The Life and Famous Death of** the MGM Director and Husband of Jean Harlow by E.J. Fleming (McFarland). Just from the tone of the acknowledgments and preface, I sensed that here, finally, was a true and sympathetic portrait of a much-maligned man. Stories have circulated for years about Bern's mysterious death, ruled a suicide, and the motives behind it, and writers have built upon it. Little by little, the accusations have reached disgusting proportions. Missing from these writings is the real Paul Bern, the successful producer who was well regarded in his lifetime.

E.J. Fleming, although not known for restraint when it comes to using unsourced gossip, here in this book goes out of his way to give Bern (1889-1932), a major MGM producer, the respect he deserves. For this, I applaud Fleming most heartily. The problem with this book is that there are long stretches of monotony, mistakes (misspellings/factual errors), unwarranted detours, conjecture and a heavy reliance on plot summaries.

"Telling a story about people who lived and died almost a century ago is a difficult and often frustrating process," Fleming writes. "The story, as they say, is in the details, and biographers search for that one tiny detail that will answer a question, fill in a gap, or help bring a person to life." Details are fine, but here there are far too many that are far too trivial. The first example of this is in the very first chapter. We are subjected to the most mundane particulars about the Bern family's voyage from Germany to the United States. I assume the author wanted to paint a vivid picture, showing what little Paul went through to get here, but honestly, it was so dry and pointless that it began to read like filler. I don't care how many tables were on the boat, or how much food was consumed by the passengers, or what health problems were common aboard ship in those days. Right off the bat, the story was stalled like a sailing ship on a windless ocean.

Monotony builds as Bern's filmmaking is discussed. Okay, many of these films are lost, but that does not excuse an author's long recounting of movie plots, followed by tormenting reviews of same. Background on these films I would welcome, but not paragraph after weary paragraph of plot. I felt like crossing out whole sections with a bright red marker. This certainly would have been a quicker, livelier read if an editor had stepped in decisively to steer a true course.

Other detours were even more senseless. This is a book about Paul Bern. Just because William Desmond Taylor is mentioned, that does not justify launching off into a lengthy discourse on his life and unsolved murder. Nor do we have to hear *again* about the familiar travails of Fatty Arbuckle, John Gilbert and Thomas Ince.

With this lack of focus, it came as no surprise to me that Fleming, not content to discuss Paul Bern's supposed suicide and possible impotency, started talking, out of the blue, about other suicides and scandals taking place in Hollywood at the time. Fleming would be well advised to show more common sense when writing a book, carefully picking and choosing what to include and what to keep out.

Nor do I care to read lists of party guests. The book's interminable lists are meaningless. "Paul was seemingly invited to every party in Hollywood," he writes, and—darn it—Fleming is gonna list them all! Once is okay to show as an example the types of parties he was attending, but not more than that, especially when names are misspelled.

We also don't need to read an overview of the history of the movies—from day one, or the growth of Hollywood, or any of the asides about Joan Crawford and such. The only other people requiring substantial treatment here are Bern's first wife Dorothy, Jean Harlow, and Barbara La Marr. The rest is just filler. I felt that with all his diversions and distractions, Fleming was leaving out important facts. You got the feeling he kept forgetting that his book was supposed to be about Paul Bern.

In some of his previous books, Fleming seemed disrespectful of his subjects, but here Bern, and even Jean Harlow, are treated well. Fleming doesn't make any wild accusations. Harlow is often torn to shreds in other books, but here Fleming gives us a good idea why a sex symbol would marry the unassuming Bern. Fleming's lovely, sweet portrait of Harlow is refreshingly at odds with the harsh take on Harlow some other biographers dish out. Joan Crawford isn't so lucky, though. We get a long passage about her that is simply an unfair rehash of old gossip. And, really, what does the reader gain from a tasteless comment about Harry Rapf's nose? Hmmm?

Fleming's research is pretty good since he clearly has consulted a myriad of sources. I did find it odd, though, that he kept insisting that Barbara La Marr's son was definitely Bern's, then he quotes La Marr's son, Don Gallery, saying that he isn't even sure himself. Because Bern loved Gallery and gave him presents, Fleming seems to think we have positive proof of paternity.

One bright spot is Fleming's point-by-point rebuttal of Irving Shulman's notoriously bad Harlow book. It's terrific the way Fleming nails Shulman. (Applause, applause.) But then *why* does Fleming *use* Shulman's book as a source multiple times and quote from the volume liberally? (Boo, hiss.)

This is not an awful book, but with all the extraneous material, you're left with the feeling that Paul Bern's story has not been fully told. It shows respect, which is excellent in itself, but it left me wanting more. (For a better book about Bern's death, read Samuel Marx's *Deadly Illusions: Jean Harlow and the Murder of Paul Bern*.)

The photos are extraordinary. Some of the same images of Mr. Bern pop up over and over in other books. Here, there are some excellent and rare shots. By all means, get this book if you are interested in Harlow, Bern and MGM, but be prepared to be bored at times as you skim through, searching for the next fresh breeze to take you out of the doldrums and back to the good stuff.

***

Pier Angeli: A Fragile Life by Jane Allen (McFarland) could have been handled all wrong, but it turns out to be a biography of unparalleled class and research. The tragic life of Pier Angeli has been the subject of mostly rumors —her doomed relationship with James Dean and her early death, long thought a suicide — but Miss Allen, who has penned this first full-length Angeli biography, cuts through the trash normally written and comes up with answers.

I had no inkling as to what Pier was like personally, nor have I ever read anything substantial about her that wasn't based on hearsay. Jane Allen has captured Pier's personality vividly and completely; her insecurities, her complexities, that she was "flighty, highly-strung and sensitive, given to nervous laughter, seesawing emotions, and wild if brief enthusiasms for people." Those not in the know claim that Pier broke down when James Dean was killed, but her emotions were a little off way before that. The chapter about Dean is sure to cause people to reconsider what they thought they knew about the two. Their relationship has become legend; it takes quite an author to write against that, with the facts to back her up.

Allen's research is superb, helped considerably by Pier's family and friends, all of whom the author has interviewed. But what might set this apart from a normal biography is Miss Allen's comprehension of what made Pier tick. The author is by profession (says the press release) a psychologist, so Allen is able to better decipher Pier's motives and emotions, as well as the impact her mother's domination had on her life. She does this in a subtle way because Allen is a good writer and not just trying to show off her expertise.

I absolutely loved this thoughtful, sensitive, photo-filled, extremely fascinating bio. It really delivered the goods on the films (*Teresa, Somebody Up There Likes Me*) and on an emotional level. Pier led a sad, short life, which is a shame, but film fans remember her all-too-brief career fondly. This book contains both aspects and is a definite winner.

***

Radio Live! Television Live!: Those Golden Days When Horses Were Coconuts by Robert L. Mott (McFarland) is, first of all, mistitled because, regardless of its title, this book is primarily about television. He debates a few times which was better, radio or TV, with radio coming up on top. He argues that radio was, of course, better for the sound effects artist and the listener's imagination, yet his best stories are about television.

Oddly, when Mott does mention a story pertaining to radio, he often messes it up. As an example, there are the conspicuous errors in his discussion of Jack Benny. When referring to a classic line, one that many people know, you shouldn't paraphrase. Not only does it look dopey, but you are making the line less funny. He wrongly quotes Benny's classic "Your Money or Your Life" and, in a bigger exchange, totally mishandles the who, what, where and how of Benny's biggest laugh-getter — a bit involving opera names. It's pretty involved, and Mott shouldn't have tried to retell it without checking up on it. Benny fans will know, trust me.

With that said, as a television anecdote book, this can't be beat; I enjoyed his stories, told informally, at a fast pace. Of course, Mr. Mott was there, he was a writer and sound effects creator, a vet of some forty years in radio and television, so his reminiscences are invaluable for the readers interested in the early days of TV. I loved his story of working on Captain Kangaroo's show, where his sound effects area was in the basement near the restrooms and near the subway, and was, he says, "an acoustical time bomb."

He writes of adlibs, mishaps, the joys and trials of live television, cursing football players, the art of creating certain sounds (even flatulence), writing for Red Skelton, among many other fun miscellanea. He tells us how he got into the business and all the nonsense he had to go through. The set, technical and candid pix (53) are excellent.

Except for the aforementioned glaring mistakes in transcribing dialogue, I enjoyed this book immensely. Mott's first-hand knowledge of television's past is worth reading, and essential. He captures a whole era in just a little over 200 pages. His memories are fun and lively, and I strongly recommend.

***

There are many reasons to like **Rin Tin Tin: The Life and Legend** by Susan Orlean (Simon & Schuster), but unfortunately there are many more reasons *not* to like it. The book is an attempt to tell the story, define the mystique, and discuss the legacy of Rin Tin Tin, the wonder dog trained by Lee Duncan (1892–1960). It's also a discourse on fame, loneliness and obsession, and covers not only Duncan and Rinty, but other key figures such as producer Herbert B. Leonard and, regrettably, the author herself.

Rin Tin Tin first appeared on screen in a series of highly successful films for Warner Bros. in the 1920s, and had a resurgence of popularity on TV in the '50s with *The Adventures of Rin Tin Tin*. The story here is told as a journey, but too often it takes us on a detour into the author's mind and her relationship to the universe. Instead of focusing on the story behind the movies and their canine star, the author makes us privy to all her efforts as she sorts through her research. To make matters worse, the narrative is told in a mix of both the first and second person—a strange and incomplete mixture that remains lumpy on the pages. This approach could have worked, I suppose, but it was not done well here.

Most of the time, however, Orlean is a good writer. When she sticks to her basic story, the book has a nice, readable style. But her narrative strays too often from biography into a messy mass of adjectives that is sickening to read. Her attempts at poetic descriptions are sometimes laughable. She mentions grave markers that are as "smooth as pats of butter," while other markers are "a jumble of shapes and sizes, like a mouth full of very bad teeth." The cemetery guard is "a short man with a rosy face and the body of a bowler, a tight fit in his little guardhouse near the entrance." Orlean calls a road she drives on "as long and straight as a gunshot." In talking about the place where she is conducting research, she says that "some of the afternoons felt very gray, even as the building was baking in the harsh desert sun." Driving in her car, she passes "long rows of identical houses that from a distance look like angry welts"—products of the Angry Welt school of architecture, I suppose. I laughed out loud as she muses over the question of why a bird would make its nest near the storage unit she was about to enter—"Nature is so mysterious," she writes. Thank God she didn't follow that with a dissertation on the billions and billions of stars in the universe. One day is depicted as "a bright morning in May," while another is "a chilly fall day, the weight of the sky pressing down on a landscape stripped bare and bleached of color."

Her tin ear for prose sort of fits with her Rin Tin Tin ear for film history, but the book's main problem is a lack of focus. Are we reading this to learn about trainer Lee Duncan and Rin Tin Tin, or are we here for an author therapy session? I was surprised that no one at Simon & Schuster told her to suppress her own life story and concentrate on what was really important—the subject of the dang book. I suppose some might find Orlean's self insertions profound, but I am not one of those people. I found her continual interruptions a nuisance. We learn that, as a child, she wanted her grandfather's Rin Tin Tin figurine and this somehow led her on a personal journey into the subject of this book. Yes, it is natural for an author to mention the thing that first led her to the writing of the book, but here you feel as if the author's journey into the book's subject has become more important than the subject itself and there is something irritating about that.

I was particularly dismayed by personal comments she made about a few of the people who tried to help her. When she visited a man who collects TV memorabilia, she focused on making him look bad: "His apartment was dim and stuffy, and nearly every surface was hidden under a *Leave It to Beaver* lunchbox or a Smurf figurine. He had a collection of Rin Tin Tin memorabilia that I was excited to see, and I had skipped doing something more conventional, like going to the beach, in order to see his Fort Apache play set and Rin Tin Tin thermoses. He was a sweet, odd man who lived alone and could recite where and when he had gotten each of his television collectables. My first thought was that he was weird to have such a rarefied pursuit and I couldn't imagine fixating so completely on anything. And then I looked around the room and took note of the fact that the only people in it were this sweet, odd man and me." Describing Daphne, a lady who attempted to keep Rin Tin Tin's legacy alive in later years, Orlean says she's "compact and sturdy-looking and has an upturned nose and crinkly reddish brown hair ... She has a voice that only comes from a lifetime of dedication to cigarettes." When she admitted later that she and Daphne had some personal issues during the writing of this book, it made me cringe. That does not give Orlean an excuse to write private things about this woman. It's good to be honest, but when you are doing a biography and you start cutting someone who has *helped* you ... that is not wise. In another section, a local historian, with a vast knowledge of Corriganville, takes the time and effort to show her around what is left on the site of the famous Western exterior set used in the TV series. The tone of this passage borders on mockery as she contemplates why people become attached to a single interest. This is how you show gratitude to those who share their knowledge with you? As a writer, it made me feel ashamed when I thought about how these people would react reading this book. Writers like Orlean only poison the well for more thoughtful and considerate writers who come along later seeking help from these invaluable human resources.

It's also very obvious this was not written by someone with a good knowledge of films. It still boggles my mind, after all these years of reviewing, that the big publishing houses cannot fact check their books. Or that an author will not take the trouble to have the text proofed by an expert. All those years of research—and then you take a shortcut and end up with unnecessary errors.

She incorrectly states that Darryl F. Zanuck got his start as a gag writer for Chaplin and "By the time he was twenty-five, Zanuck was running" Warner Bros. Being head of production is not the same as running the studio, à la the brothers Warner.

Hollywood Cavalcade (1939), she claims, is "a corny, disjointed tale about old Hollywood, with walk-on parts by nearly everyone under contract to 20th Century-Fox at the time, including the Keystone Cops, bathing beauties, and the sly, snappy Don Ameche." It would be interesting to know if she actually saw the whole movie, or if she just fast forwarded it to see Lee Duncan's small part.

"Like many silent films, *The Return of Boston Blackie* is sometimes broad and overly schematic, but it is also fast-paced and engaging." Nice generalization there.

She refers to the Warner Bros. Vitaphone sound system as "Vitagraph," the name of the pioneer production company founded in New York City in the 1890s.

"In October 1927, Warner Bros. released the first all-talking feature, *The Jazz Singer* ..." All talking? No, this part-silent film was the first feature-length film with synchronized dialogue sequences.

After Rinty's success in the movie *Where the North Begins* (1923), she says that Lee Duncan gave Rin Tin Tin puppies to Greta Garbo and Jean Harlow. This would have been nice, but these actresses were not in Hollywood at that time.

The first day Duncan went to Warners seeking a job, "Harry Warner was directing a scene that included a wolf." Interesting, but something tells me that the director was someone other than producer Harry.

Another of those infamous "Tyrone Who?" moments occurs when she mentions the "Henry Fonda movie *Jesse James*." For the record, in *Jesse James* (TCF, 1939) Fonda played Frank James, but the title role was played by that Tyrone What's'isname fellow. (Don't feel bad, Ms. Orlean, you're not the only film book author who seems totally oblivious to the existence of Fox's top male star of that time.)

Ray Corrigan, who owned and operated Corriganville, a working movie ranch, made his share of movies where he donned a gorilla suit, but it is misleading to give your unsuspecting readers the impression he only worked in a gorilla suit. Among other things, Corrigan starred in the serial *Undersea Kingdom* (1936), played Tucson Smith in 24 Three Mesquiteer films, and 20 of the Range Busters.

"Robert Walker, a Hollywood veteran, directed the greatest number of episodes" of *The Adventures of Rin Tin Tin* TV series (1954-59). First of all, the author should have recorded his name properly—Robert G. Walker—otherwise it seems as if actor Robert Walker was the director. Funny thing about this "Hollywood veteran"—he directed no films and started directing for TV in 1953.

She refers to the TV series *Battlestar Galactica* (1978-79) as *Galactica*.

"*The Return of Rin Tin Tin* was released in a year dominated by comedies," she notes, and then highlights the major studio films *Welcome Stranger, The Bachelor and the Bobby-Soxer,* and *The Egg and I. The Return of Rin Tin Tin* "still managed to be a success," she says as if there is something remarkable about that. The success or failure of big studio comedies that year could have had no relevance to the box office receipts of an Eagle-Lion film about a boy and his dog.

Would Ed Sullivan and Jackie Cooper be among the celebrities posing for pictures with Rin Tin Tin in the 1920s? Would Roy Rogers be Jane Murfin's Hollywood Hills neighbor in the '20s? If you know nothing of Hollywood history, I guess the answer could be yes.

And, gee, what's with calling Jackie Cooper "chunky" in the movie *Tough Guy* (1936)? That was totally out of nowhere.

She misspells Micky Dolenz's first name as Mickey. However, to be even more accurate, she fails to note that when he was doing the series *Circus Boy* (1956-57), he was billed as Mickey Braddock. Charles Farrell is misspelled twice as Ferrell.

On the other hand, there is some great information here. The author had access to Duncan's personal archive and unfinished autobiography and producer Herbert B. Leonard's personal papers pertaining to the production of the TV series and his fascinating life in general. There's an intriguing portrait painted of Lee Duncan's daughter, who was interviewed for the book. Also interesting is the story about the man who posed as Lee Aaker about 20 years ago, before the real Lee Aaker began doing the film festival circuit. (Aaker, of course, played "Rusty" in the TV series.)

Unfortunately, the author muddles up the narrative with too much information on some unrelated subjects. We are treated to a long account of the development of the German shepherd breed in America; the start of dog obedience training; and the use of dogs in war. The whole thing about Hitler with his love of animals and disregard for human life went on far too long, but I'm guessing the reason is that the author had relatives who were victims of that evil man. Once again, however, you feel that Rin Tin Tin has gone out of focus while the author concentrates on her own agenda. Also, it seemed odd to me as she went on and on about the use of dogs in war, that she failed to mention a film centering on that very subject—1942's *War Dogs*. Then I remembered that *War Dogs* is a Monogram and obviously would have escaped the attention of a writer not too familiar with films.

By book's end, I found that I did not care why Susan Orlean has spent most of her life fascinated by Rin Tin Tin. Her story means nothing to me. I am not touched by her final conclusions. I wanted to read about Lee Duncan, a complicated, fascinating subject, his home life, his connection with his dogs. If only an editor had been on hand to rein in the writer and pare down the text. The tone, too, needs control, wavering as it does between the sensible to "Oh, wow, I can't believe these people I am writing about are so crazy." Slamming those who are fascinated by your book's subject rarely endears you to readers fascinated by your book's subject. I recommend this book, but with strong reservations. If you can ignore the mistakes and the author-at-the-core approach, you will learn a lot about Rin Tin Tin, his trainer Lee Duncan, and producer Herbert B. Leonard, and, of course, the mysterious universe we inhabit.

***

No other book has ever made me teary-eyed out of sheer joy. I never thought I'd ever see a whole book devoted to the fabulous Ann Savage, but here it is, **Savage Detours: The Life and Work of Ann Savage** by Lisa Morton and Kent Adamson, with a foreword by Guy Maddin (McFarland), and it's a good one.

It would be very easy for an author writing about Savage to concentrate mainly on her best-known film, *Detour* (1945), directed by Edgar G. Ulmer. Not only is it her most famous movie, it contains arguably the best performance by an actress in a film noir. What Ann Savage does as Vera is beyond anything I've ever seen in movies — her movement, her glassy-eyed mean look, and her voice. That voice, scratchy, brittle, nasty. It was a gutsy portrayal at a time when it was considered very risky for an actress to show herself so unflatteringly on camera. The effect is made even more potent when you watch Ann in other movies where she is lovely; it's a shame she never got close to that kind of role again, although *Apology for Murder* (1945), a rip-off of *Double Indemnity* (complete with a blatant steal of the Stanwyck-MacMurray staircase scene), is a very good showcase.

As a B movie fan I am used to ridicule; it's what we have to deal with all the time. When I open a book to read about a second feature, the author usually has something snide to say, talking down to the lowly B. After all, we are reminded, B movies are inferior to the bigger budget A movies. That is a viewpoint I despise. Authors Morton and Adamson do not make that mistake. Before I read this, I had an occasion to watch a Jungle Jim movie, *Pygmy Island* (1950). I checked a few sources, all contemptuous. Here, however, although the authors admit it's not the best movie, they point out its pros and cons, giving this just as much space as any of the other movies. The same goes for *Pier 23* (1951); it wasn't the best, but it had its moments. I don't need an "author" with no knowledge or love of B movies to tell me they stink. I will not be talked down to. So, that is one of the reasons why I love this book and the film-by-film look at Ann Savage's career. Each film is broken up into sections: The entries start with the title, date, studio, cast, and crew. Then we have a synopsis, commentary, and then behind-the-scenes info. When I reread the *After Midnight with Boston Blackie* (1943) entry the other day after watching it again, I felt I had gained a better perspective on the film. You've gotta love a book that does that, especially for a B movie.

The biography section is exceptional. The writing throughout is honest but also warm and appreciative. Ann Savage did not lead an easy life, her childhood was especially difficult, but, on the whole, it was quite a trip as an actress and aviatrix. She also comes across as such a character, someone you would dearly love to know — a great outlook, incredible sense of humor, feisty. (What can I possibly say about white-haired Ann, near the end of her life, brandishing a gun in one picture? Pure heaven.) This book not only covers an underrated career, but also allows us to get to know her. That is a rarity.

The photos are simply mouthwatering, eighty-five stills and poster images from such films as *Passport to Suez* (1943), *Dangerous Blondes* (1943), *Two-Man Submarine* (1944), *Midnight Manhunt* (1945), *The Dark Horse* (1946), *Renegade Girl* (1946), *My Winnipeg* (2006), etc. The latter movie, directed by Guy Maddin, is one that the authors describe as "a magnificent finale for the career of Ann Savage." The commentary for this, as well as *Detour*, is truly extraordinary work by the authors. They call the two films "prime examples of the power of the true cinema auteur." Capping this honey of a book is something truly terrific: The original *Detour* script with Ann's notes. I nearly blacked out when I got to that section. I cannot rave enough. I'm in love with the idea of a book about the tremendous Ann Savage, one of my very favorites, but tickled that it's actually a wonderful, worthwhile book. Thanks, Lisa and Kent.

***

It's hard to believe, but Tom Weaver has been conducting interviews for more than thirty years. McFarland & Company has recently published his twentieth book, **A Sci-Fi Swarm and Horror Horde: Interviews with 62 Filmmakers**. As with his nineteen previous books, this volume is a winner.

Tom is the king of the Q&A, but this book follows a totally different format. It's a collection of his "As told to" interviews, which reads like a series of articles written by the moviemakers themselves. There are also six chapters written in "editorial style" by Tom. Regarding this new approach, *sans* the Q&A, it works out marvelously and the stories related within are at turns interesting, funny, traumatic, and often poignant. Tom has always had a gift for cajoling the best (and worst) out of his subjects — and this time is no different. Every now and then, in brackets, there is a little prompt from Tom. My favorite: "Who thought Boris Karloff in a baseball cap was a good idea?"

First, the participants: Jimmy Lydon (on Robert Armstrong), Joanne Fulton (on John P. Fulton), House Peters, Jr., (on *Flash Gordon*), Frankie Thomas (on *Tim Tyler's Luck*), Jean Porter (on *One Million B.C.*), Jo Ann Sayers (on *The Man With Nine Lives*), Herbert Rudley and Tommy Ivo (on the 1946 stage production of *On Borrowed Time*), Henry Corden (on *The Secret Life of Walter Mitty* and *The Black Castle*), Fintan Meyler (on *Thriller*'s "Well of Doom"), Michael A. Hoey (on Dennis Hoey), Earl Bellamy (on *The Return of the Vampire*), Alex Gordon and Herman Cohen (on *Bela Lugosi Meets a Brooklyn Gorilla*), Karolyn Grimes (on *Albuquerque*), Mickey Knox (on the 1948 stage production of *Of Mice and Men*), Irving Brecher (on *The Life of Riley*), Barbara Knudson (on the 1950 stage production of *Born Yesterday*), Richard Kline (on Sam Katzman), Sid Melton (on *Lost Continent*), William Phipps and Arthur L. Swerdloff (on *Five*), Marilyn Nash (on *Unknown World*), Diana

Gemora (on *The War of the Worlds*), Fess Parker (on *Them!*), Rosemarie Bowe (on *The Golden Mistress*), Paul Wurtzel and John G. Stephens (on Bel-Air Productions), Pamela Duncan (on *The Undead* and *Attack of the Crab Monsters*), Marsha Hunt (on *Back from the Dead*), Herbert L. Strock (on *Blood of Dracula*), Peggy Webber (on *The Screaming Skull*), Lisa Davis (on *Queen of Outer Space*), Troy Donahue (on *Monster on the Campus*), Nan Peterson (on *The Hideous Sun Demon*), Richard Erdman (on *Face of Fire*), Roger Corman (on *House of Usher*), Alan Young (on Jack P. Pierce), David Whorf (on *Thriller*'s "Pigeons from Hell"), Alex Gordon (on *The Underwater City*), Arch Hall, Jr., (on Ray Dennis Steckler), Arnold Drake (on *50,000 B.C., Before Clothing*), Tony Randall (on *7 Faces of Dr. Lao*), Frederick E. Smith (on 1964's *Devil Doll*), Edward Bernds and Merry Anders (on *Tickle Me*), Ib Melchior (on the TV and movie versions of *Lost in Space*), Whitey Hughes, Richard Kiel, and Kenneth Chase (on *The Wild Wild West*), Burt Topper (on *Space Monster*), Peter Marshall (on Edgar G. Ulmer), Tom Reese (on *Murderers' Row*), Richard Gordon (on Protelco Productions), Nick Webster (on *Mission Mars*), Gary Conway (on *Land of the Giants*), John "Bud" Cardos and Martin Varno (on *Nightmare in Wax*), Jan Merlin (on *The Twilight People*), Robert Pine (on *Empire of the Ants*), and Ken Kolb (on the uncompleted *Sinbad Goes to Mars*). Added into this mix is a chapter, with multiple interviews, on the Calvin Beck-Norman Bates connection, a terrific write-up that attempts to trace the origins of Robert Bloch's inspiration for the Bates character in his book *Psycho*.

Unlike most interviewers I've read, Tom Weaver really has the ability to draw amazingly detailed and candid stories from his interviewees. This is especially evident in Michael Hoey's reminiscences of his father, Dennis Hoey, a character actor best known for playing Inspector Lestrade in six of Universal's Sherlock Holmes series films starring Basil Rathbone. Michael is a producer/director/writer himself, and his memories are clear, informative, and heartfelt. I loved reading about him roaming the movie backlots of his youth and getting into trouble. It's obvious he has deep affection for his father, but he's also honest about their sometimes "fractious relationship."

Tom's books have none of the superficiality that I get in some other interview books. There is no holding back, beating around the bush—everything is laid bare, regardless of how unpleasant it is; of course, that is exactly what makes the lives of these people more interesting—their honesty. Tom has a knack for gently pushing his subjects. Case in point: William Phipps, in talking about the movie *Five* (1951) here, going off on a little, very revealing, tirade about his good friend Charles Laughton that is a wonder to behold.

Another Hollywood child, Diana Gemora, talks about her dad, Charles Gemora, who did make-up, created movie monsters, and played gorillas in movies as a sideline. Her chapter is fascinating for many reasons, as it centers on a hurried all-night emergency session as Gemora, with the help of his 12-year-old daughter, races against the clock to create the Martian costume he was to wear in *The War of the Worlds* (1953). This will-they-finished-it-on-time scenario is framed around Diana telling us how her father started in the movies, etc. The incorporation of this real-life data helps sustain the suspense as materials fall apart in the workshop and Gemora needs to come up with different ideas to get the monster done on time.

There's an extremely fascinating chapter about the unmade Ray Harryhausen movie *Sinbad Goes to Mars*, featuring a short synopsis based on Ken Kolb's 1978 revised treatment. Included with the backstory are illustrations that Chris Foss was hired to render of weapons and spaceships.

There's a lot of funny material sprinkled here and there, but, without a doubt, my favorite story is the one relating to the conclusion of *Voodoo Island* (1957), shot on location in Hawaii. According to assistant director Paul Wurtzel, the film's director, Reginald LeBorg, had a bright idea concerning Elisha Cook, Jr.'s character's demise. After "Cookie" falls into the water, LeBorg wanted the fish to "attack" and eat his head.

They found a human skull, covered it with bread dough, baked it, and they painted it to look as much like Cook as possible. Come the day of filming, the "Bread Head" was attached to a dummy and thrown into a stream. Wurtzel was on hand as LeBorg tried to film this "gruesome" scene: "We put the body in the stream and it floated, and we had to throw some chum in so the fish would come around. But the bread was baked so hard, it never dissolved, and the fish couldn't eat it. Once we put the body in, we couldn't get it out, and now the slow-moving current started taking it downstream. Reggie, the camera operator and I ran along the bank after it, and the prop man Arden Cripe followed in a rowboat. Well, this was the stream that came down and formed the lagoon right outside the Coco Palms Hotel dining area, and sure enough, this weird-looking thing floated down to where the tourists were eating their lunches. They got to see me and Reggie and a guy with a camera running along the bank and, floating in the lagoon, a body with a bread head and the face of Elisha Cook [laughs]! They couldn't figure out what the hell was going on!" After all that, the scene didn't even make the final cut.

More highlights include Sid Melton's ego and his exaggerated notion about his talent and career: "Robert Lippert liked me very much. Why shouldn't he [laughs]? If I may be immodest, aside from working cheap, I think there are very few who can do what I do. I got [good] notices, writeups from critics—I throw 'em away, I don't even save 'em anymore. And I still get fan mail, quite a bit." I like Melton, but let's be realistic, shall we? His memories of working on *Lost Continent*, though, are fun when he isn't tootin' his own horn.

A talk with actor and stuntman John "Bud" Cardos shows how valuable a performer such as himself was in those days. Special effects being primitive in 1969, the way he nonchalantly mentions being set on fire without any kind of protection has to give you some newfound respect for these guys. (There's a recent photo of Cardos with his friend, fellow actor and stuntman Gary Kent, that's just marvelous.) Cardos, by the way, enjoyed working with Cameron Mitchell on *Nightmare in Wax*

(1960), but Martin Varno, the film's make-up man, has a totally different take on him, and what he has to say about the craziness on the set is one of the best pieces in the book. "He was a complete jerk," remarked Varno about Mitchell. You have to read this eye-opening chapter to find out why. I was a bit surprised by Alex Gordon's negative memories of William Lundigan in *The Underwater City* (1962), although I guess I shouldn't have been. And there's a laugh-out-loud moment, courtesy of Mickey Knox, when he relates what happened on stage when a prop gun didn't go off.

Another favorite is Lisa Davis, talking about Zsa Zsa Gabor's jealousy of her costume in *Queen of Outer Space* (1958). She also relates a terrific line attributed to Gabor. Actor Patrick Waltz, whom Davis later married, was in a scene where he scuffles with a giant spider in a cave. At one point the spider was on top of Waltz and, between takes, he was lying there on the ground with it on top of him. Zsa Zsa looked down at Waltz and remarked, "Dahlingk, if I vere you, I'd get myself a new agent!" It was nice reading about the underrated Waltz and what happened to him later, as sad as it was, and it was especially gratifying to hear from Lisa Davis about her underrated career. I've always liked Davis, particularly in *The Dalton Girls* (1957), where she stole the show as the most violent (and interesting) of the sisters. (Davis' big, fairly non-aggressive, moment is singing Les Baxter-Jim Baxter's catchy song "A Gun Is My True Love," which is absolutely hilarious.) Calling *The Dalton Girls* "a riot," she describes her tough role as "sort of a female Jack Palance." Rosemarie Bowe's memories of working on *The Golden Mistress* (1954) on location in Haiti are harrowing, to say the very least. You just start feeling sorry for her, as the mishaps pile up. The line, "I got hysterical, I started to cry" as a bucketful of crabs are thrown on her is one of the "tamer" horrors this poor lady had to go through.

Choice lines:

"The Jungle Jims were by-the-numbers again. They took six or seven days to shoot, and the direction was always the same when it came to

Johnny Weissmuller [Jungle Jim]: As he walked around the jungle, the direction was, 'Okay, roll 'em, speed, action. Come ahead, Johnny ... you see something ... you stop ... you react ... and now you go.' That was all the direction! He'd be walking along, and then all of a sudden he'd stop ... a blank stare when he'd see something ... and then he'd react with a puzzled look ... and then on he would go. Somebody once said that Johnny could go on a one-man theater tour, and call it 'An Evening of Blank Stares and Double-Takes' [laughs]." — Cinematographer Richard Kline.

"All these [acting] experiences, I remember them all pretty vividly. And I remember them fondly. The bad parts I forget ... That kind of attitude [is not the norm] with kid actors, though. Look at Rusty Hamer—he did himself in, he couldn't take the falls. Then I turn on A&E and I see Paul Petersen and a bunch of other [former kid actors] sitting in a circle, all saying how traumatic and how terrible it was that they lost their childhood. I just shake my head. That kid acting thing, it was like a trip to the wishing well, it was magnificent, it couldn't have been better. Chasing guys on horses in Westerns, swinging through the trees on a vine with a loincloth on, with Bomba at my side—my God, how much better does it get?!" — Tommy Ivo.

"Joan Collins was a peach. We played Scrabble all the time, and if anybody out there gets a chance to play Scrabble with Joan for money, don't do it. You heard it here first. I'm not bad, but this woman is a killer. And she's a good broad. I had a great time with her, everybody did." — Robert Pine.

There are 125 awesome photos, a vivid assortment of behind-the-scenes candids, production shots, portraits, and scene stills. I am still having nightmares, however, of the drag photo of William Phipps (on pg. 125) from the movie *No Questions Asked* (1951). The problem? He looks tooo good. I also like that Tom uses his photo captions to give us added information about his subjects and the movies. All too often captions are mere throwaways used for identification purposes. We actually learn something here, so make sure not to skip over them.

Tom Weaver's books just keep getting better and better, and after all these years that's quite an achievement. I strongly urge you to get this; whether you like horror and sci-fi is immaterial. First-hand stories from the people who were there—there's nothing better than that when it comes to Hollywood history.

***

According to BearManor Media's product description, the book **Scripts from the Crypt: The Hideous Sun Demon** will teach you "everything under the sun about producer-director-star Robert Clarke's 1959 monster classic." This, of course, begs the question, "How much do you need (or *want*) to learn about *The Hideous Sun Demon*?" Well, with Tom Weaver as the tour guide who takes you through the production process (and way beyond), it's fun and painless, and there are scores of amusing behind-the-scenes photographs along the way.

The book, first in Weaver's new "Scripts from the Crypt" series, is done in the style of MagicImage's "Universal Filmscript" books from the 1980s and '90s— and this is no doubt intentional, as Weaver created MagicImage's *Creature from the Black Lagoon* volume. The bulk of the *Sun Demon* book is comprised of two versions of the script, one an early work that's almost completely different from the eventual movie, the other a lot closer. For cover-to-cover readers, these would provide the bulk of the reading material. But the fun is in the rest of the book:

Weaver, a devoted fan of the late Robert Clarke (he co-wrote Clarke's 1996 autobiography, *To "B" or Not to "B"*), goes all-out in chronicling this sci-fi/horror adventure. First up is an intro by the movie's associate producer, Robin C. Kirkman, who died just weeks after penning it. (His death is mentioned only in a photo caption; you must never neglect to read Weaver's captions, which are often as newsy as the text!) This is followed by the 12-page "The Sun Demon Speaks!," in which Clarke tells the start-to-finish story of the making of the movie; this chapter has been lifted from Clarke-Weaver's *To "B" or Not to "B."* Weaver's "Notes on the Scripts" alerts readers to passages to watch for as they read the two screenplays (interesting script-to-screen variations, etc.). The two scripts come next, plus an Arthur C. Pierce outline for the *Sun Demon* follow-up film, *Sorceress*, which Clarke had hoped to produce in the 1970s.

After the scripts, more contributors make appearances: Bela Lugosi expert extraordinaire Gary Rhodes penned a lengthy article about *Sun Demon*'s 1958 Texas drive-in world premiere, complete with a transcript of an interview Clarke and *Sun Demon* co-star Nan Peterson gave at the event. Then fan-collector-entrepreneur Wade Williams weighs in with fond memories of his long friendship with Clarke. Weaver returns with a few pages on the making of *Hideous Sun Demon—The Special Edition* (a *What's Up, Tiger Lily?*-style *Sun Demon* spoof from the 1980s), plus one of the most entertaining parts of the book, titled simply "Fun Facts." In it, Weaver presents, in bite-sized paragraphs, scores of amusing factoids about the movie and the people who made it, many of whom are quoted first-hand. *Sun Demon*'s original Showmanship Manual, an afterword by Nan Peterson and a Supplemental Photo Gallery (yet more photos of Clarke at various stages of his life) round out the package.

The front cover is a poster-like piece of original art by the great Marty "Astounding B Monster" Baumann, and there's also artwork on the back cover — which is purposely printed upside-down so that, if you prefer the back cover, you can display the book with *that* illustration showing. The back cover artwork has an interesting story that goes with it: In 1958 or '59, *Sun Demon* sound man Doug Menville, just trying to be helpful, roughly sketched out some ideas for a poster which he hoped Clarke & Co. could use; they did not. But once Weaver got a-hold of the sketch, he not only ran it in the book (on page 358), he also had artist Kerry Gammill professionally fine-tune and colorize it for presentation on the back cover.

Another fun touch to look for: On the castlist on that back cover poster, following the names of the movie's actual three stars (Clarke, Peterson and Patricia Manning), are the names of Menville, Kirkman, Xandra Conkling and Ron Honthaner — crew members and/or supporting players in the movie, who provided many of the book's anecdotes. My favorite (found in the "Fun Facts" chapter) might be Honthaner's description of the day that the *Sun Demon*'s death scene (plummeting from the top of a giant gas storage tank) was shot. A rented dummy was dressed in the *Sun Demon* costume and carried to the top of the tank by Honthaner, who now waited for a signal from the camera guys at the base of the tank. "When they all waved down below to let it go, I pushed it off," Honthaner recalls. "Well, this dummy was stiff, it wasn't limber, and it took off like a glider. Then the wind caught it, and smashed it against the side of the tank! It burst open, and everything came out! A few days later, we had to go back and I had to take up an *old* dummy that was more limber, and do it all over again." While I enjoyed reading the anecdote, it was with the painful knowledge that I can never again watch the finale of the movie without picturing the plummeting Sun Demon suddenly soaring Rocky the Flying Squirrel-style (complete with rocket noise and whooshes) around the enormous tank!

In short, *Hideous Sun Demon* is everything you might expect from Overachiever Weaver, maybe (at over 360 pages) *too* much, although no one's twisting your arm to read the scripts which account for most of that page count. The BearManor grapevine buzzes with the news that the next title in the Scripts from the Crypt series will actually tackle two movies between its covers, *Bride of the Gorilla* (1951) and *Indestructible Man* (1956) — a combination that Weaver, in his always respectful and politically correct manner, is already trumpeting as a "Lon Chaney Jr. 'Make Mine a Double' Two-Pack."

***

It is very difficult as a writer to find a voice; one that best represents you and your personality, while entertaining your reader at the same time. I have found many an autobiography ruined for lack of one. That is one thing you cannot say about actor-writer-director-stuntman Gary Kent (*Satan's Sadists*) in his terrific new memoir, **Shadows & Light: Journeys with Outlaws in Revolutionary Hollywood** (www.garywarnerkent.com). Forget for a minute that the first half of the title is an overused cliche—what you get within these over 400 pages is original, tough, touching, intelligent, funny and damn straight. Gary Kent has style, a kick-ass attitude, wit and a gruff understanding of life and the business that will turn his readers around in circles, throw them out a window, and down to the pavement below. But it will also pick them up unhurt and have them strolling down the street, pleased with the experience.

Gary Kent comes across here as just one of the guys, a down-home, rough-and-ready wrangler with a heart of gold and an appealing fearlessness. He's an excellent writer, using a novel-like, highly descriptive approach to move his narrative along nicely. (About Chet Baker: "I couldn't believe the music—that horn, as clear and tender as a sigh directly from the soul." Amazing.) And I love his choice of words ("jaw-jacking"), sprinkling his text with tasty adjectives and phrases ("Suddenly, things got so quiet you could hear a rat cough") that punch up his story. It's never dull, that's for dang sure, even though Gary isn't the type of writer to rush from one story to the next; his laconic style works just fine.

As a stuntman, Gary participated in many movie brawls and stunt scenes. The sections he devotes to talking about the planning and the enacting of these fights are highlights. I marveled at Gary's ability to detail these scenes with both bone-crunching delight and heartbreaking realism, giving us a behind-the-scenes peek at how these sequences are handled and sometimes mishandled. He was also a special effects person on a few movies. He specifies how he created said effects, the problems on the set, etc. Rarely do we get this kind of attention to the inner workings of stunt and effect creating. And it's all written with an enjoyably breezy, witty style. His love of being a stuntman is a fine tribute to an often-overlooked profession. "Within the clouds of dust, the grease and grit, within the rolling tumult and danger of the stunt people, men and women, I have found tremendous courage, but also much beauty, caring, and in the end, an artful synchronicity of mind, body, and spirit that is almost holy in its application."

Some of the movies he talks about: *Ride in the Whirlwind, The Black Klansman, Targets, Psych-Out, The Fabulous Bastard from Chicago*, plus loads of TV work, including *The Man from U.N.C.L.E.* Gary jam-packs much in these pages. So many stories in here are worth noting, including a weird-fascinating encounter with Charles Manson and his followers, Warren Oates, Jack Nicholson and a terrific anecdote about Scott Brady stealing tiki torches. His stunt coordinating stories are priceless and pretty hardcore. Gary makes these episodes exciting. Less exciting, but more harrowing, is the drug hallucination he experienced and some of the low points of his life which he relates with a straightforward candor.

Gary has a tremendous sense of humor, relating funny incidents on the set. One moment made me totally laugh out loud. It was on the movie *A Man Called Dagger* after filming had ended for the day. Gary and some of the other stuntmen went out "for a good old macho drink fest to the nearest bar, a darkened little operation called the Pleasure Patch that hugged the sidewalk along Pico Boulevard. We threw open the doors, marched in like the manly men we obviously were. The place was full of woman. What a score! However, there was something wrong here, something very strange. None of the women seemed the least bit interested in our arrival. The Pleasure Patch, it turned out, was a gay bar, the local meet and greet place for the west-side daughters of Lesbos. 'Damn it, I can belly up to the bar just as well as you can!' They did, we did, and everyone had a mahvelous time, all things considered."

Yup, it's hard to dislike Gary Kent—or his book; so don't even try. I enjoyed myself immensely, and so will you. It's a whirlwind ride and worth the trip.

***

Before *Star Trek* and *Star Wars* there was *Space Patrol*, a groundbreaking live sci-fi television series that ran from 1950 to 1955, which still retains a cult following today. Now, the series is examined in the long-overdue **Space Patrol: Missions of Daring in the Name of Early Television** by Jean-Noel Bassior (McFarland). At over 400 pages, this is one of the most comprehensive studies of a television show I have ever read.

The book's most remarkable asset is the series of interviews the author conducted with surviving cast members, guest stars, family and crew. She really wants us to appreciate the show. In this, she succeeds—maybe a little too well. After a while you feel that there's too much here. An author less devoted to her subject would have curtailed some of the minutia that's rampant here. Normally, I would rather have too much than too little, but in this case, the effect is exhausting.

Bassior does extremely well introducing us to the main characters and actors on the show: Ed Kemmer (Commander Buzz Corry), Virginia Hewitt (Carol Carlisle), Ken Mayer (Major Robertson), Lyn Osborn (Cadet Happy) and Nina Bara (Tonga), as she describes the "uncanny resemblance" the actors had with their characters. She also, and I love this, gives us careers details on all the actors. This, however, brings us to the problem I had with the book, especially considering her treatment of Kemmer, the gorgeous lead of the show. The author seems way too smitten with Kemmer—not that I blame her—but, writers need to keep a safe distance from their subjects. Here, the author gets too close, resulting in some corny-sounding prose.

Her intense interest causes her to push a little too hard, to the point where the author's presence seems intrusive. In an interview with Kemmer, she bugs him to define his screen character, insisting that he tell her how he created the character. And that's when the hyperbole starts. "Perhaps Kemmer's reluctance to talk about the impact he had as

Corry (unless pressed) and the artistry he brought to the role stems from a belief that talking may kill the magic, says high school teacher Allan Cohen, who plays *Space Patrol* tapes for his students." Or could it be, Miss Bassior, that it was essentially a kiddie show, albeit a very successful and entertaining one, and that Kemmer, not wanting to be typecast, sought to move on with his career? You get the feeling that *Space Patrol* is all-consuming to the author, and she unrealistically expects others in the cast to feel the same, not realizing that, for them, it was just a job. She takes the show too seriously, but, hey, maybe this is what *Space Patrol* fans want to read. For me, however, fawning over the series and its stars is overkill. I'd like to see the subject through a more critical eye.

With that said, this is not a bad book — not by any means. This series, as popular as it was at the time, has been neglected by television historians, which is a shame. Other writers, if they mention the show at all, usually get facts wrong. Bassior remedies this problem nicely in her volume. This was an important show, and it merits a hearing (and viewing) after all these years.

Much of what's here is excellent and very interesting. At over 400 pages, the book includes information such as Kemmer's recollections of his time as a POW during WWII. The untimely death of Lyn Osborn is heartbreaking, as he was an up-and-coming talent, and here, the author pays him a wonderful tribute. She deserves our gratitude for going the extra mile to ensure that Osborn is not forgotten.

Since the show aired during those difficult years when television was live, and mistakes could not be edited out, the author gives us a brief history of that special time in TV history. Strangely though, she omits mentioning *I Love Lucy*'s important role in the development of filmed television. My favorite chapter is the one detailing all the crazy mishaps the stars had to endure on the show. Less memorable is the excessive treatment given to *Space Patrol* memorabilia. Too many fan stories also slow things down.

The photos are sensational—there are over 200 of 'em! The layout is attractive. Thankfully, the author includes an episode log.

***

Stand Up for B Movies

I would like to address a pet peeve of mine. There has been a plague of late with writers quoting dumb IMDb user reviews. Among other things, it shows that some writers have become so lazy they can't seek out legitimate newspaper and magazine reviews from reputable critics and authors. I'm not trying to insult any of you IMDb contributors out there — I know some of you are quite knowledgeable, but if you read *CI* and *FGA*, you're probably smart enough to know that there is a lot of drivel on IMDb. Not only are most of the postings uninformed, but too many show a pervasive lack of respect, understanding, and common sense when it comes to classic films. Why any writer would deem these reviews worthy of inclusion in a book on classic movies is beyond me. Also, any book using IMDb reviews will have buyers saying to themselves, "I've been tricked into paying to read reviews that I could have read online for free if I'd wanted to."

I admit that I am a movie enthusiast, and fully agree with my late friend Marvin of the Movies who once said, "There is no such thing as a bad movie. Some films are better than others, but no movie is truly bad." I know there are some who do not agree with this. I have one friend, who shall remain nameless, who doesn't see it my way at all. I don't know how many times he's said, "Well, that's two hours I'll never get back," after watching a movie he did not like. I, on the other hand, can find something to like in almost every movie I watch because I passionately love film and the actors and actresses who work in them. To me, there's always something of interest, so I never feel my time has been wasted. And, believe me, I have watched movies that have really stunk!

I was recently reading an excellent book, *Hammer Films: An Exhaustive Filmography* by Tom Johnson and Deborah Del Vecchio (McFarland). The authors do an topnotch job describing all the films, giving background, and utilizing many past interviews and ones they conducted on their own. Some of the critiques, however, are brusque and negative, and serve only to discourage the reader from watching the film and judging for themselves. My friend Jackie Jones, a real movie lover and an expert on film noir, recommended the Dane Clark-starrer *Five Days*, aka *Paid to Kill*, from 1954; she really enjoyed it, and was pleasantly surprised when she watched it. Yet, looking the film up in this Hammer book, the authors knock it down, saying it "failed to thrill" and it was "average." Some would read that and say, "Well, that's a film I'll skip," instead of giving it a chance. You know, not everyone responds to a film the same way. It's a good thing I trust Jackie's judgment, because I, too, enjoyed the film, and was glad I saw it.

Back to IMDb: It's probably the most negative of places, if you are seeking out a review. You'll also find a lot of smart alecks, who think they are being clever when they pick apart a perfectly fine movie. "B movie" is used as a dirty phrase on IMDb and too many other sites with movie reviews. We can't possibly say we like a B movie because we fear that people will think we're stupid. We want people to respect us so we go along with the opinions of the elite. As a devoted fan of the B, I am appalled by this constant maligning of the second feature. Everyone parrots the same ideas as original thinking is shunned and a shallow materialistic standard — low budget equals low quality — is embraced.

Take a gander at some comments I recently found. Spelling and punctuation are as they appeared in the "review":

"For a B-western, this is above average, if only because this plot is pretty far from the usual rustlers, lawmen, cattleman vs farmers, relative gone bad plots that litter the non-musical B-western. Problem is, the movie still isn't terribly compelling, because of the usual stock footage and wooden acting issues one find in these things."

"Not that bad, but clearly a B-movie."

"Bs are entertaining enough, but also tend to have lesser actors, writers and directors—sort of like the minor leagues for movie people. Because of this, most B-films are not the quality or entertainment level of an A-picture—though there are many, many exceptions."

"It's a definite B-Movie, but it's not a bad one."

"Like many B-movies, you can see this one was rushed into production—warts and all."

"This film isnt all that bad. Tim McCoy certainly doesnt really rank with the best of the movie cowboys (well, #1 problem would be his hat), but hes somewhat entertaining, gets into a lot of wimpy looking fights (he throws his hat a weapon. Ooh! Tough!) shoots his gun totally wrong and again treats us to his Mexican impersonation (like he did in *Lighting Carson Rides Again*)." [LW's note: I should point out here that Tim McCoy is *my* favorite western hero, and these comments particularly annoyed me.]

"As Poverty Row films go, this one isn't too bad. It has a pretty lively musical score, and some fairly good actors. The interiors are pretty cheesy-looking, as is usual for low-budget films, but there are some good LA exteriors."

"Lon Chaney, Jr. is the only professional connected with this amateurish production and seems trapped — he must have needed the money to appear in this, a picture in which he otherwise would not have been caught dead (no pun intended). And I'll bet he wished he could have turned into a werewolf."

"Monogram Pictures put the 'poverty' in Poverty Row. Its releases were hastily cobbled together from whatever talent (or lack thereof) happened to be around on any given day."

"I was pleasantly surprized with this one it is pretty good and has some suspense. It's not Shakespeare, but its not bad!"

"This is a minor entry in the Vincent Price catalogue but even so he's on good form. Just as well as the supporting cast is forgettable."

"Turn off your logical mind, then you can enjoy this for what it is."

Okay, I need to stop there and turn off my logical mind because all that just infuriates me. It's bad enough that this stuff gets written, but then to see an author quote it in his book! Dreadful. It isn't just on the Internet that B movies get a bad rap, but the worldwide web gives a pervasiveness to this claptrap, and this is very harmful to film appreciation.

Book authors need to step up to the plate and take responsibility — use discretion when it comes to writing about our beloved movies and use some original thought.

***

How many books have been written about Humphrey Bogart? After A.M. Sperber and Eric Lax's definitive *Bogart* (1997), I honestly don't see the need for yet another volume on the subject. Don't get me wrong; I love Bogart, he's one of my favorites, but just because he's a popular film book subject, that doesn't mean I welcome every Bogart book that comes along.

Let it be said that Stefan Kanfer, author of **Tough Without a Gun: The Extraordinary Life of Humphrey Bogart** (Alfred A. Knopf/ Random House), is a good writer. He is, in fact, a pleasure to read. However, with this new book his writing technique is not the issue. The problem here is wrong or questionable content. Let me count the ways.

While she certainly deserved it, Ida Lupino was not Oscar-nominated for *They Drive By Night* (1940) as Kanfer claims. In fact, in one of the major oversights in Hollywood history, Lupino was never nominated for any of her work, in front of or behind the camera.

The child was kidnapped, not murdered, in *The Man Who Knew Too*

Much (1934). It was another Peter Lorre film, *M* (1931), that was about a child killer.

Concerning Bette Davis' character in *Now, Voyager* (1942) he writes, "She plays an overweight, dowdy spinster, completely dominated by her mother. On a cruise, the ugly duckling meets the unhappily married Henreid, and under his ministrations turns into an enchanting and self-assured swan." It was Claude Rains who transformed her, and it was not until after her makeover that she met Henreid.

"Back in 1941, in *The Maltese Falcon*, he had acted opposite Mary Astor, who was still smarting from a highly publicized sex scandal involving the playwright George S. Kaufman." The incident, which happened in 1936, had to do with her diary entries being leaked to the press during a custody battle between Astor and her ex; the diary was deemed inadmissible in court. Anyway, it did no damage to Astor's career, as he later infers; it actually helped her. It's kinda doubtful she was still smarting in 1941 from the incident; nor does it have anything to do with *The Maltese Falcon* anyway.

On another scandalous note, he writes about Harlow: "In 1932, for example, Jean Harlow's second husband, Paul Bern, killed himself. The reason, said investigators, was because of an inability to satisfy a wife twenty-two years his junior. After the suicide, the movies' first blond bombshell was offered her biggest and most popular roles." Unlike the Astor case, this event did not help Harlow. I call Kanfer's so-called research and common sense into question here, due to the way he portrays Bern, his death, and how it affected Harlow.

Weirdly, he says that *Thank Your Lucky Stars* (1943) was a documentary; it was an all-star musical comedy. Also, *How to Marry a Millionaire* (1953) was a comedy, not a musical comedy. It has no singing or dancing. He has Lauren Bacall's family background wrong. My co-writer (of McFarland's *Killer Tomatoes: Fifteen Tough Film Dames*) Ray Hagen is one of Bacall's biggest fans, a real expert. According to Mr. Hagen, Bacall's mother's maiden name was Weinstein ("wine glass" in

German), but after her husband left she reverted to her maiden name but then changed that name to Bacal, which means "wine glass" in Russian. The two names were never hyphenated or used together as Kanfer does here.

Name Misspellings: Arthur Edeson (not Edelson); Wallace Reid (not Reidl); Joseph Cotten (not Cotton); Mae Clarke (not Clark); and Stuart Heisler (not Stewart), etc. Composer George Gershwin didn't die in 1939; he passed away in 1937. *The Miracle of the Bells* (1948) is hardly a good example of a religious movie that was a box office success, and shouldn't be mentioned in the same breath as the big hit *Going My Way* (1944). Just sayin'.

". . . and mimicked by Robert Sacchi in *Sam Marlowe, Private Eye*, adapted from *The Man with Bogart's Face*." Adapted? This 1980 film was originally called *The Man with Bogart's Face*, but later retitled *Sam Marlow, Private Eye*—no "e" at the end of "Marlow," by the way.

"When Humphrey began acting in films, demographics were irrelevant: everyone went to the picture show. Adolescent actors like Mickey Rooney and Deanna Durbin had their moments, but there were few teenage movies as such. Those under twenty were deemed insignificant, and in any case had no economic power." Whatever you want to think of Durbin and Rooney, they were huge box office moneymakers. To say they had their "moments" is to trivialize the truth. Mr. Kanfer seems to be trying to make a point based on the idea of the rise of teen power in 1950s pop culture. Like many other ideas about pop culture in the 1950s, this one seems to easily serve the cause of distorting the truth about the decades that preceded the '50s.

Criticizing John Huston's *We Were Strangers* (1949), Kanfer says it starred a "miscast John Garfield and Jennifer Jones as Cuban revolutionaries." If you're going to disparage a movie in print, at least watch the movie so you know what you're talking about. Garfield plays an American. The same goes for Bogie's own *The Enforcer* (1951). How can the author trash a movie and at the same time not relate the plot correctly? And don't even get me started on the mistakes he makes in "recalling" the plot of *Conflict* (1945).

While he mentions the Bogart-related song "All Right, Louie, Drop the Gun," and some others, I found it odd that he didn't even bring up 1949's "The Humphrey Bogart Rhumba," which was recorded by Betty Garrett (MGM) and Freddy Martin's orchestra, with a vocal by the Martin Men (RCA Victor), among others. In her autobiography, Garrett claimed that it was actually Bogart making a brief vocal cameo appearance at the end of her recording. If so, that makes the song's omission from this book doubly disappointing.

In *To Have and Have Not* (1944) Bogart played "Harry Morgan" and Bacall played "Marie Browning." "Steve" and "Slim" were the nicknames that only they used for each other; they were not the character names, per se.

The Killers (1946) wasn't Ava Gardner's first movie and it didn't "introduce" her; it was her 23rd film. Her first important lead, released before *The Killers*, was *Whistle Stop* (1946). *The Killers* was the first movie for, and actually introducing, Burt Lancaster. In *The Two Mrs. Carrolls* (1947), Alexis Smith didn't play the first Mrs. C. That wife was already dead at the start of the movie. Barbara Stanwyck was the second Mrs. Carroll, and Smith was the lady Bogart wanted as his third wife.

About Ingrid Bergman, the author writes, "Ingrid had scandalized Hollywood by abandoning her first husband and children to run off with Roberto Rossellini." It wasn't as simple as all that. She married Petter Lindstrom in 1937, and they had only one child, a daughter, Pia. Far from "abandoning" her "children," she fought Petter for custody of Pia.

James Cagney famously shoved the grapefruit in Mae Clarke's face in *The Public Enemy* (1931), not in *White Heat* (1949). Virginia Mayo, by the way, was the girl Cagney roughed up in the latter film.

Vincent Sherman did not direct Bogart in *Crime School* (1938), Lewis Seiler did. Sherman did, however, co-write the screenplay for that movie with Crane Wilbur. Kanfer makes it seem that the Oscar awarded to *The Seventh Veil* (1945) was for Best Picture; it was, in fact, for Best Writing (Original Story). Kanfer writes as if the movie was released in England in 1946.

Double Indemnity was released in 1944, not 1949. *Million Dollar Mermaid* was 1952, not '53. At one point he's got *The African Queen* (1951) as 1953, and *Casablanca* as 1944. Referring to Monogram, Kanfer claims it was, "...then considered the cheapest B-picture studio in town." Wrongo. Monogram films looked cheap compared to those of MGM, but they looked lavish compared to those of PRC.

"By 1947, Romanoff's had become a required tourist stop, like Schwab's drugstore or the Walk of Fame." Since the Hollywood Walk of Fame didn't exist in 1947, I'm thinking he meant the forecourt of Grauman's Chinese Theater with its cement slabs of star imprints. Later, he writes that Bogart was asked to leave the imprints of his hands and shoes "on the Hollywood Walk of Fame in front of Grauman's Chinese Theater." Methinks someone is a tad confused here. And methinks I'm more than confused by a comparison he makes in regard to Bacall's star-making appearance in *To Have and Have Not:* "Not since Greta Garbo's 1939 performance as a no-nonsense Bolshevik in *Ninotchka* had audiences seen so strong a female performer." Say what?!

He refers to "Wladziu Liberace." Actually, the pianist never used this first name professionally. However, when he started, he briefly went under the name "Walter Liberace." Kanfer calls Tim Holt an "underrated character actor." Underrated or not, Holt played numerous leads.

I can understand if he doesn't like the two films Stuart Heisler directed for Bogart, *Tokyo Joe* (1949) and *Chain Lightning* (1950), although I'm wondering if he's even seen them. That said, he writes, "[Heisler] had been in the business since the 1920s when he had edited such vaudeville films as *In Hollywood with Potash and Perlmutter*." Actually, his editing was not restricted to "vaudeville films." One look at Heisler's filmography would've told Kanfer that much. He could have easily cited the hit *Stella*

Dallas (1925), but it seems as if he's trying to belittle Heisler. Then, in regard to *Chain Lightning*, he says that Heisler "functioned as a foreman rather than a director." Oh, please, give me a break.

And please spare us the blaming of poor Mayo Methot. Bogie's third wife did have problems, sure, but to put all the responsibility for their rocky marriage on her shoulders is misleading. As a husband, Bogart was no peach. Both were full of frustrations, anger and alcohol during that time. Sperber and Lax were able to show both sides effectively in their book, but here the author is dead-set on blaming everything on the "irrational" Methot. I'm not saying she was an angel, but, come on, be fair. Kanfer also gets her final days wrong, resorting to that staple of riches-to-rags celebrity storytelling, claiming she died alone in a seedy motel and her dead body wasn't found for days. Her story was sad enough without making it even worse. Mayo died in a hospital.

Kanfer offers little in the way of groundbreaking theories or new insights into the films. He likes or dislikes the standard movies in the standard ways. Worse yet, you often get the idea he doesn't know the movies all that well, not having watched them recently or closely.

A very disconcerting touch, at least for me, is not only how he addresses Bogart throughout the book, but also Bacall. It's "Humphrey did this/Humphrey did that" and "Lauren said this/Lauren said that." I guess we are all so used to him being called "Bogart" or "Bogie" and her being referred to as "Betty" or "Bacall," that it's jarring to read these names over and over. It seems like a trivial criticism I am making here, but, for me, it gives the book an odd vibe.

Kanfer is a good writer, as many of his past books prove. Honestly, the last two chapters in this book, where he talks about how the Bogart legend grew after his death, is excellent, insightful writing. I enjoyed this much more than his actual telling of Bogart's life and career, which, as you can see, isn't exactly accurate—and I didn't even mention all of the book's problems.

Bogie's life might have been extraordinary, but this book is not. If you're interested in Humphrey Bogart, I recommend Sperber and Lax's *Bogart*.

***

When I review a book, I have a couple rules: I must read the entire volume, no skipping (unless there are cumbersome plots involved), and no relying on publicity materials to fill space. I have read too many reviews where a reviewer simply sums up a book. But I have come up against a roadblock.

I have tried four times to read **Up from the Vault: Rare Thrillers of the 1920s and 1930s** by John T. Soister (McFarland). I have struggled so long with this that now McFarland is republishing the original hardcover in a softcover.

I have read Soister's previous books on Universal, Claude Rains, and Conrad Veidt. *Of Gods and Monsters*, his unnecessary rehash of the Universal horror films, was a prime example of a writer who has a lot of opinions but doesn't know how to express them interestingly or with brevity. *Of Gods and Monsters* is infinitely better than the dullness of *Up from the Vault*, yes, but his sentences are interminable, convoluted, and dreary. You lose his message within the long stretches of prose. A big fan of parentheses, the author seems to use them only to create maximum bewilderment. (On the Internet, I have read another "writer," Donna Lethal, who overuses parentheses. She thinks her asides are funny; not only aren't they amusing, they simply interrupt whatever point she is trying to make. What results is confusion.)

Up from the Vault is well intentioned, I will admit, and, in its own way, much needed. I like Soister's attitude that not just the classics need to be covered. His book is filled with movies that are either lost or have a limited availability: *The Mystery of Dr. Fu Manchu* (1923), *The Unknown Purple* (1923), *The Sorrows of Satan* (1926), *While London Sleeps* (1926),

The Monkey Talks (1927), *The Chinese Parrot* (1927), *Stark Mad* (1929), *The Unholy Night* (1929), *High Treason* (1929), *The Spider* (1931), *Eran Trece* (1931), *The Monkey's Paw* (1933), *Trick for Trick* (1933), *Deluge* (1933), *The Vanishing Shadow* (1934), *The Witching Hour* (1934), *Double Door* (1934), *Black Moon* (1934), *Le Golem* (1936), *The Scarab Murder Case* (1937), and *Sh! The Octopus* (1937).

The main problem with this book is the manner in which these movies are described and discussed. Since most of these films are hard to find or lost, a plot summary wouldn't be out of order. Normally, I am not a fan of long plot recounting—plot vomiting, I like to call it—but if a writer can pithily retell the plot, make it fun, interesting, and weave in interesting trivia, I am more than willing to read that. A few writers have the ability to do this—and Soister is not one of them.

One person reviewed this book and said it was "incisively written." Reaaaly? However, I do agree with that person's other statements that the book is unique (because of the subject matter) and that it's an "important piece of history." But he should have warned us that it's also a dull, uninspired piece of history. Another critic gave Soister credit for a "fluid writing style," which made me do a spit take. The writing style was so heavily laden, I just could not finish the book—and I tried, my how I tried.

The photos are excellent, and especially welcome since these films are rare. I like the focus; I just can't handle Soister's drop-something-heavy-on-my-foot approach to writing. With the information he had, which was considerable, he should have written an entertaining, accessible book for movie lovers, not the heavy, tangled mess that resulted. I don't know about you, but sentences full of commas, semi-colons, and parenthetic asides are not fun. Especially when you have to read them at least three times before realizing that they say nothing.

***

There was always something about actress Virginia Bruce (1910-1982) that made her stand out. Watching her on screen was always magical. She had a luminous quality that came out in her looks, her movements, and her acting. Suffice it to say, I've always liked her very much, especially in *Let 'em Have It, Jane Eyre, The Garden Murder Case, Stronger Than Desire, Flight Angels, Hired Wife, The Invisible Woman*, and many others.

I honestly never thought of her as an acting heavyweight, but that never seemed to matter. She always brought a gentility to her roles that I found immensely appealing. And, of course, like many of her contemporaries from the 1930s and '40s, she was vastly under-appreciated and underused by the studios. Just witness her breathtaking performance in *Born to Dance* (1936) and her vocal rendition of "I've Got You Under My Skin." It's then that you'll see and feel her magic.

Just as he did with his excellent book on Kay Francis (*I Can't Wait to Be Forgotten*), Scott O'Brien has cleared away the cobwebs surrounding a long-neglected actress. **Virginia Bruce — Under My Skin**, with a foreword by James Robert Parish (BearManor Media), is, like the actress herself, charming and easy to like. This book is long overdue, and luckily O'Brien is the one who wrote it. There is an elegance to his writing, and this quality is so appropriate. I shudder to think of how another author would have handled Virginia's story.

Recently, I noticed online a comment made about this book. The reviewer complained that there seems to be too many books lately on "lesser" players, citing Bruce, Kay Francis and Carole Landis in particular, and that "one just wishes that the same detailed scrutiny and picture layouts were given many of the top tier stars as well." What an absurd statement. For too many years we've been inundated with too many books on biggies such as Hepburn, Dean, Presley, Hitchcock, Grant, Davis, and Stewart. Finally, and thankfully, the tide is turning a bit, with books on those who have never received their due. True movie fans should rally around books like *Virginia Bruce - Under My Skin*, written by someone obviously dedicated to her memory. Considering the problems faced by authors like O'Brien in digging up hard-to-find information on the lesser knowns, we really need to praise and value them for their efforts.

Scott O'Brien—I cannot say enough good things about him. Ordinarily, I do not enjoy reading long plotlines. I detest it when writers, with no special insight and little knowledge of film, start filling up the emptiness of their books by recounting each and every boring detail of plot. Scott, on the other hand, weaves details of Virginia's movements and reactions into his plots until you feel a rhapsody. He has full understanding and appreciation of what's on screen, making every minute worth remembering. His write-up on the pre-Code shocker *Kongo* is just sensational. His persuasive section on *Women of Glamour* should be enough to make readers go right out and get this neglected gem.

Scott is almost chameleon-like in this respect. It's as if his writing takes on Virginia's own personal characteristics. Perfectly in tune with his subject, the author also makes a very strong case for her acting, pointing out things I never noticed in her performances. Virginia needs a champion, and O'Brien is just the man for the job.

I also like his dialogue cuts from the films. He always picks choice bits of dialogue to describe the story and Virginia's character. This especially includes two quirky lines that just tickled me. In discussing *Society Doctor* (1935), a personal favorite of mine that co-starred Virginia with Chester Morris and Robert Taylor, Scott writes: "Virginia delivers another good line as she and intern Robert Taylor are about to light up in the staff lounge. She glibly offers, 'There's nothing like a cigarette before a tonsillectomy.' Soon after this remark Taylor is inspired to ask Bruce to marry him." Or, this line from *Shadow of Doubt* (1935), another goodie, when Virginia refuses to see a persistent Constance Collier: "I don't want to see you alone or in groups of five!" I might just use that line one day.

Naturally, I don't agree with some of Scott's assessments of her films. Ever since I was a teenager, I loved one of Virginia's later pictures, *State Department: File 649* (1949). He writes well about it, even in his dislike for it, but I've always had a soft spot for this Poverty Row exploiter. (Maybe because of her co-star William Lundigan; but that's another story.) To his credit, Scott does not just brush it aside, just because it was not a career highlight for Virginia.

I was also impressed by his attention to her television appearances, something you don't normally see in biographies. Since many of these shows are hard to come by, it's important to get this kind of information out there. This valuable info is supplemented by photos of the productions.

With all this refreshing attention to her work, however, Scott does not stint on poor Virginia Bruce's life; the balance between reel and real life is covered evenly, flowing together smoothly. *Under My Skin* is fascinating as it chronicles Bruce's successes and devastating failures, both on and off screen. Virginia's life was filled with "heartbreak, disappointment, tragedy and strange twists of fate." The section about Virginia's brief marriage to John Gilbert is particularly well done, giving us a better understanding of that union. I never knew much about the marriage, so it all was very informative, especially the weird stuff about Marlene Dietrich's involvement in it all.

Scott, through some marvelous research that includes interviews with family and Virginia's last husband, paints a vivid portrait of the real-life Virginia, amazing since she died in 1982. She becomes alive to the reader. Scott really takes us through the pain that Virginia's last husband, Ali Ipar, inflicted on her. It's a roller-coaster of emotions, not easily forgotten. Scott interviewed Ipar for the book and his attitude is likely to anger readers. He seems clueless as to how his deportations and legal problems affected Virginia. He is so into himself, it is not surprising that Virginia loses practically all her money.

The book's layout takes some getting used to, especially the way the photos are presented with shadows around them. After a while, though, it gives the book a dreamy quality, much like Virginia herself, so it does grow on you. The cover, by the way, by Darlene and Dan Swanson of Van-garde Imagery, Inc., is a honey.

Virginia's last portrait session, for author James Watters and photographer Horst in 1982's *Return Engagement,* proves to be a quite poignant interlude, typical of the respect Scott pays Virginia through the book. She was not feeling well that day, but agreed to pose. Just as the two men were leaving, Virginia managed a "faint smile," then wondered, "Do you think when I'm gone, anyone will remember that I had awfully dreamy eyes?"

Thanks to Scott O'Brien's moving, fascinating biography, loaded with gorgeous photos of one of Hollywood's "Most Beautiful Blondes," they'll remember.

***

Warren William (1894-1948) is an actor best known as the "King of Pre-Codes" for his roles as conniving heels, but who, previously, has not been deemed worthy of a full-length biography. This, thankfully, has changed, with the release of **Warren William: Magnificent Scoundrel of Pre-Code Hollywood** by John Strangeland (McFarland).

Some facts, first: He was born Warren William Krech in Aitkin, Minnesota, to a well-to-do family; he had a brother, who only lived four days, and two sisters, Pauline and Elizabeth. His early goal was to be a ship's captain or a marine engineer; he had a passion for building things, and would tinker with various inventions throughout his life.

Once acting became his main interest, he performed in plays in high school. In 1915, he enrolled at the American Academy of Dramatic Arts in New York City. After graduation, he appeared in plays with the Brooklyn Repertoire Company.

Drafted in 1917, he joined the 136th Infantry Division and his acting career was put on hold until he was discharged in 1919. In 1918, he had met Helen Barbara Nelson, a friend of his sister's, and seventeen years his senior. They would wed in 1923, and remained married until William's death.

After the war, he picked up where he left off; he toured with the play *I Love You*, and when it ended months later, he found work with an Erie, Pennsylvania, stock company. William made his Broadway bow in *Mrs. Jimmie Thompson* (1920), and acted with the Theatre Guild in the short-lived *John Hawthorne* (1921).

In New York, he made his film debut in 1922, billed as Warren Krech, in *The Town That Forgot God*. Fox offered him a film contract at this time, but he turned it down in favor of stage work. He returned to film the following year to appear in a serial called *Plunder*.

The 1920s were a busy time for the young actor, as he appeared on Broadway in *We Girls, Expressing Willie, Nocturne, The Blue Peter, Rosmersholm, Twelve Miles Out, Easter One Day More, Fanny, Paradise, Veils, The Golden Age, Sign of the Leopard*, etc., toured with other productions, and signed a contract with the Schubert Organization.

In 1924, on the advice of his sister Pauline, he shortened his professional name to Warren William, and he also grew the mustache that would become his trademark. (He would appear with a mustache in all his later films, except *Cleopatra* and *Dr. Monica*.)

In 1930-31 he appeared in the Broadway hit *The Vinegar Tree*. With this great success, Warner Bros. became aware of the dashing star who many thought resembled John Barrymore. He made his Warners debut in 1931, and at first the studio didn't know quite how to cast him. He had been a sophisticated, refined type on Broadway, but very soon William moved smoothly, and enthusiastically, into seamier territory, cornering the market on playing cads and amoral types with a deep voice oozing with a sex appeal that sounded positively sinful.

The pre-Code era was Warren William's heyday, as he seduced young innocents and cheated the suckers out of their cash; a magnificent bastard, he was seen to advantage in *The Mouthpiece, Skyscraper Souls, Employees' Entrance, The Mind Reader, Bedside*, etc. One of his best roles during this early period was as Dave the Dude in Frank Capra's *Lady For a Day*. He also played Julius Caesar in Cecil B. DeMille's *Cleopatra*.

The end of the pre-Code era in 1934 was a serious blow to William's career, as his predatory nature had to be toned down. Also not helping was his overall docile nature; never ambitious, he accepted whatever role Warners handed him, no matter how trivial, not realizing that this could harm his career. He came to be regarded as a solid anchor for strong actresses such as Kay Francis, Claudette Colbert, and Barbara Stanwyck.

Notably, he was the first actor to portray Perry Mason, imbuing the part with some welcome humor, in four movies; he also played detective Philo Vance (twice) and Ted Shane, the latter a stand-in for Sam Spade in the second filming of *The Maltese Falcon*, 1936's *Satan Met A Lady*.

Problems at Warners started when he wanted to be cast in the title role of *Captain Blood* (1935); they had announced him for it, but never seriously intended it for him. From then on, he became difficult, turning down parts and haggling over money. It did him no good and, soon, William found himself being cast more and more in B movies. He made his last movie for them in 1936.

After this, he signed with Emanuel Cohen's Major Pictures, an indie that distributed through Paramount. Many trace the real downfall of his career to his association with MGM, who put him under contract in 1937. Although his deal with the studio seemed like a good one, it ended up diminishing his star status, as they cast him in supporting parts. "I feel like the forgotten man of pictures," he remarked after breaking his deal with them.

In late 1938 he was assigned to play ex-jewel thief Michael Lanyard, aka The Lone Wolf, in a series of B mysteries at Columbia; he would make a total of nine movies as the character from 1939 to 1943. While they were second features, they afforded him a good chance to show his stuff, and they remain entertaining B's. While starring at Columbia, he freelanced at the other studios, and playing supporting parts, notably in Universal's *The Wolf Man*.

In 1943, he returned briefly to the stage, appearing in *There's Always Juliet*. But, he was slowing down; he said he needed rest after so many years of making movies, but his inactivity was also due to some lingering health problems, and his wife's own battle with cancer. William starred on a syndicated radio program called *Strange Wills* (1946), but he was tiring easily and was generally unable to work, and his doctors could not figure out the reason. Then, in December of '47, he was diagnosed with multiple myeloma, an incurable cancer of the bone marrow. The 53-year-old William's health rapidly declined; his suffering came to an end nine months later when he died at his Hollywood home with his wife by his side. A few months later, his wife Helen died at the age of 71, of congestive heart failure.

Warren William: Magnificent Scoundrel of Pre-Code Hollywood relates all this (better) and, naturally, adds much more, filling in the blanks of William's previously "mysterious" personal life. So little is known of this very private man. It's funny, one of the only things I can recall reading of a personal nature about him was in a questionable "biography" about Bette Davis in the late '80s. This information has since been quoted elsewhere whenever anyone writes about Warren William. Here, Strangeland seriously questions the authenticity of the claims made about William—and it's about time. It didn't sound right to me when I initially read it; to me, it came across as a biographer assuming that William was just like his pre-Code wolves, and taking pleasure in painting that comfortably false picture of him. Our thanks to Strangeland for calling him out on it.

The author is also very honest about William's stature in Hollywood. I've read enough books where the authors overpraise their subjects, making them seem bigger than they were. Or else, the author talks of a conspiracy that robbed them of their rightful fame. Worse yet are those so-called historians who ignore history altogether and are blind to their actors' lack of star quality. Strangeland knows exactly where William fit, what his troubles were, and how it affected the outcome of his career. He never overdoes it, but is very realistic about the progression and regression of Warren William's career.

No excessive plot summation here, either—thank God. Both life and career are handled equally throughout; it's an even mix of story, opinion, and behind-the-scenes. While I didn't quite agree with the author's long deconstruction of *Smarty* (1934), I did respect his observations.

The personal info here is the big reason to buy this. The author went to a lot of trouble to contact William's family and he has obtained some very rare personal data, as well as some tremendously unique photos showing William as a child. In particular, his research work in William's hometown and about his stint in the Army is marvelous.

Strangeland is a good, thoughtful writer, with a keen understanding of what the reader wants to read. His research is impeccable, and he has done his subject proud. I especially loved reading Strangeland's description of William's screen persona, and he got off many good turns of phrases in the process. Why can't all biographies be like this?

***

I was not pleased, to put it mildly, with **Western Highlights: The Best of the West, 1914-2001** by Henryk Hoffmann (McFarland). Who the hell is Hoffmann that he can tell me what the best movies, actors and actresses are for each given year? Not only that, but these are "A" Westerns, so B Western fans stay clear: you will be aggravated, indignant, alienated, not to mention teed-off at the omission of your favorites. Especially the author's ridiculous list of the Top 20 Western Leading Men. I can understand John Wayne as number one, but Randolph Scott #8? Burt Lancaster ahead of Scott? Sheer blasphemy. The Top 20 Ladies looks a bit strained, as if he really didn't have much to choose from — after all, this is not the Bs. The whole book is designed, it seems to me, to annoy everyone on the prairie.

Each year lists the "Outstanding Achievements" (how pretentious) — movie, novel filmed, nonfiction filmed, short story filmed, screenplay (original, adaptation), direction, cinematography (b&w, color), music, song, male and female lead, male and female support. Also included are Oscar listings, birth and deaths of Western people and a brief recap of the year. The photos (scenes, lobby cards, posters) are the book's best assets, but ...

As much as I love Ann Sheridan, how can he name her performance in *Dodge City* one of the best supports of the year? Yeah, she sang (briefly) three songs, but she barely had any dialogue. Yet, her lead in *Silver River* isn't even mentioned. Go figure. *Abilene Town* (1946), one of my favorite Westerns, is mentioned for best film and Randy Scott is as well, but not feisty Ann Dvorak, who absolutely rocks in this, or her catchy songs ("I Love it Out Here in the West," "Snap Your Fingers," and "Every Time I Give My Heart"). Dennis Morgan, who did his share of good Westerns at Warners, isn't rewarded anything — oh, except noting that he died. How charitable. Is *The Younger Brothers* (1949) considered an A? Then, where is Janis Paige? I guess she and Dvorak were a little too fiery for Mr. Hoffmann's taste.

Then, we have the author's statement that "No western masterpiece was released in 1947; nevertheless, the year's top achievements illustrate an interesting variety of styles and themes." Well, isn't that peachy that he ultimately approves? I was worried he wouldn't like anything that year, especially with that *Angel and the Badman* mucking up things. Note the sarcasm.

This is strictly an opinion book, Henryk Hoffmann's opinions, and for those film fans who blindly follow so-called highbrows. Take it or, better yet, leave it.

***

Western Movie Wit & Wisdom by Jim Kane (Bright Sky Press) is a collection of 2,000 quotes from 1100 movies, listed A to Z, with topics ranging from bravery, cannibalism, hate, kissing, lawyers, newspapers, punishment, self-respect, suffering, etc. "Iconic characters of the

American West offer advice, words of wisdom, humor, and the occasional historical fact. These quotations reflect our American culture and have application for contemporary living. Although they were uttered in a western setting, they were and are about life."

Some samples:

"It's lonely being a cannibal; tough making friends" — Colonel Hart played by Jeffrey Jones in *Ravenous* (1999)

"Don't intrude into another man's dreams unless you're prepared to pay for the intrusion." — Captain Pharaoh Coffin played by George Coulouris in *California* (1946)

"I figure a woman who shoots at me four times, I need to see her again." — Cherokee Kid/Isaiah played by Sinbad in *The Cherokee Kid* (1996)

"The first thing you learn in the law is you gotta catch 'em with the meat; the feathers don't count." — Sheriff Denning played by Frank Jenks in *Pecos River* (1951)

"Why don't you give your mouth the rest of the day off?" — Sam Longwood played by Lee Marvin in *The Great Scout and Cathouse Thursday* (1976)

"You can't tell how far a frog will jump by the way he squats." — Lucky Gosden played by Horace Murphy in *Paroled-To Die* (1938)

"There'll be no brawls here, gentlemen, unless they're over me." — Cherry Malotte played by Anne Baxter in *The Spoilers* (1955)

"It's easier to go around a rock than to jump over it. It's longer but it's easier. So in the end it is shorter." — Jules Vincent played by Stewart Granger in *The Wild North* (1952)

Although I found the selections purely hit-or-miss, I was impressed by the breadth of the selections. There's a lot here, an impressive gathering of quotes to hold interest.

The layout is terrific, I really loved the whole look and color of the book, particularly the illustrations by Isabel Lasater Hernandez.

***

Pretty bad in the editing department is **Whatever Happened to Prince Charming?: A Memoir by Jeffrey Stone, The Original Prince Charming** (Amazon.com). The title is a little misleading: Stone was the model (not the voice) for Disney Studios when they were working on their animated classic *Cinderella* (1950). The handsome Stone fit the bill as the Prince, but the character was voiced by William Phipps while Mike Douglas provided the singing.

Anyway …

Stone was born John Forrest Fontaine in Detroit, the youngest of three. His father died when he was two and Stone spent part of his childhood in a Knightstown, Indiana, orphanage, until he finally returned to live with his mother and stepfather. He joined the Navy, at the age of 16, during World War II. After a medical discharge, Stone moved back to Indiana, where he did some theater. David O. Selznick happened to see one of his performances, and suggested that Stone contact him if he was ever in Hollywood. Encouraged, he hitchhiked to California, and was soon under contract to Selznick and then 20th Century-Fox. Acting at this time as "John Fontaine," he did mostly bits and worked at Disney posing for the artists for *Cinderella*.

By the mid-1950s, to avoid confusion with actress Joan Fontaine, he changed his name to Jeffrey Stone. It was around this time that he was also getting bigger movie parts and he played D'Artagnan in the Italian-made television series *The Three Musketeers*. (The series was re-cut several times and distributed as feature films.) Despite a contract with Universal-International and a few good roles in *Edge of Hell* (1956), *The Girl in the Kremlin* (1957), *The Big Beat* (1958), *Damn Citizen* (1958), *The Thing That Couldn't Die* (1958), *Money, Women and Guns* (1958), etc., the good-looking Stone never became a star. He guested on several television series, including *Richard Diamond, Detective, Surfside 6, The Loretta Young Show, Private Secretary, The Californians, Johnny Midnight, The Millionaire, Adventures in Paradise,* and *Death Valley Days*. He claimed that he turned down the role of Zorro on television for Disney, and Guy Williams took his place. Stone did play Zorro in a Mexican film, *El jinete solitario' en El valle de los desaparecidos: La venganza del jinete solitario* (1960).

The 1960s saw an end to his acting career; Stone said his friendship with gangster Mickey Cohen was the reason. His last screen appearance was on a 1964 episode of *The Outer Limits*. He went to New York and became a writer. Stone wrote the story to the film *The Unearthly Stranger* (1964) and wrote and directed a low-budget film in Manila, *Strange Portrait* (1966), which starred Jeffrey Hunter. He began traveling the world, eventually landing in Malaysia, where, in later years, Stone went into several businesses and wrote a few novels. He was married to two beautiful actresses, Barbara Lawrence (1947-48) and Corinne Calvet (1955-60), with whom he has a son.

In a 2007 article in *Classic Images*, he told interviewer Mike Barnum, "Hollywood was the best time of my life. I was young and in an industry full of glamour and excitement, the whole ball of wax. Looking back, the big imponderable is what would have happened if I hadn't left the States. Famous film writer? Director? Character actor? Who knows. But I have no regrets. Nope, no regrets what-so-ever!"

I would hope, however, that Stone regrets not getting a fact-checker and editor for this book. Let me point something out right away —

I enjoyed this book. I think Stone can be an excellent and persuasive storyteller. This is why it ticks me off to no end that there seems to be so little effort put forth to make this presentable to the reader.

Readers who take the time to be interested in Stone's rather obscure career should have been treated with more consideration — and confusing the reader is not very considerate. The way he presents his story here, you might think most of it happened in the '50s. He was married to Corinne Calvet from 1955 to 1960, but movies that he did during the marriage are covered *after* that time period. Then he switches to his writing career in the early '60s, and then goes back to his '50s movies again. After awhile you just don't know where the hell you are in his story. Finally, I just gave up trying to understand his confused timeline, because, frankly, I was getting a headache.

Mistakes? We got tons of them. No actor should be expected to know the details of movie history. That's why it is essential to have someone helping with facts. It appears, however, that Stone ignored this problem. His film debut was an uncredited part in 1948's *You Were Meant For Me*. He confuses this by stating that his debut came in *Margie* (1946), "a twenties-era musical with Dan Dailey and Jeanne Crain." First of all, Dailey didn't star in *Margie*, nor did Stone appear in it. Of course, he means *You Were Meant For Me*, which did star Dailey and Crain. Stone, in claiming that Hal Wallis had Rita Hayworth under contract, obviously got Hal confused with Harry Cohn. He mentions a girlfriend being offered a Dean Martin-Jerry Lewis movie — in the 1960s. He seems to think Sammy Davis, Jr., was just a kid in the '60s, and Stone was doing live TV in that decade — no, no, he wasn't. Stone misspells names with almost boring regularity, but he really made me sit up and take notice when he wrote about "Eric Von Stromberg." Admittedly, Erich von Stroheim's name is often misspelled, but this tops them all. You gotta smile when a writer goes to such extravagant lengths to screw up a name.

On the other hand, Stone's stories are a blast. His personality comes out in almost every page, and you genuinely like him. Refreshingly, he doesn't try to present himself as perfect, but instead readily admits his mistakes. His experiences with shady characters are fascinating, and a bit harrowing. While there's nothing of note about Barbara Lawrence, French actress Corinne Calvet (1925-2001) is given ample space to shine. Always a character, Calvet comes across intriguingly, although Stone does not cover all that she put in her own, very frank autobiography, *Has Corinne Been a Good Girl?* (1983).

Too bad Stone didn't give himself a much-needed collaborator to help organize his interesting story. Let's face it, few people know him, and it would have been wise to cover all his films and the more-famous personages with whom he worked. A more comprehensible, accurate, and organized text would have bumped this one way up. A scrambled text badly harms a book, no matter how many interesting stories it contains.

***

C. Jack Lewis gives us a lively book on Westerns and their stars in **White Horse, Black Hat: A Quarter Century on Hollywood's Poverty Row** (Scarecrow Press), a real gem. His funny, yet sick, run-in with a nasty monkey was just too much for me. Hilarious. I don't want to spoil it for you, but, suffice it to say, you'll hate yourself for laughing at this little story.

This fascinating autobiography traces Lewis' career as a writer of low-budget Westerns and as a stunt performer. Sprinkled within are details of his meetings and friendships with people such as Ken Maynard, Lash LaRue, Frankie Darro, John Wayne, Al St. John, Ken Curtis, Raymond Hatton, Fuzzy Knight, William Boyd, Sabu, Don Barry, Bill Elliott, Ed Wood, John Russell, Audie Murphy, Tim McCoy, Hoot Gibson, Charles Starrett, Charles King, Tex Ritter, Jock Mahoney, Steve McQueen ... I could go on. The book is crowded with stories, and background, on actors, directors, writers and stuntmen that Lewis came in contact with through the years.

In addition to being an excellent anecdote source, Lewis gives us the full picture of what it was really like to make low-budget Westerns. To finance them, write them, stunt them — everything; he shares the whole creative process with the reader.

Every page is a treat, filled with amusing, sometimes moving, recollections of his acquaintances in the movie biz. The battle between Tex Ritter and a drunken Dennis Moore was amazing, truly disturbing. But he frames this sensational story with an affecting chapter about Moore and his disappointments in Hollywood. Moore was clearly a troubled man and Lewis sheds new light on this long-forgotten actor. His story about Ken Maynard is probably typical of some of the older, washed-up stars, but very poignant as written by a compassionate Lewis. As was, oddly enough, his little story on Frankie Darro. Mr. Lewis has the very nice ability to get to the heart of his remembrances, making these actors come to life for us.

I absolutely loved this breezy memoir. C. Jack Lewis has had an interesting life and we're lucky he's sharing it with us. I just felt bad for the poor monkey.

***

If you only know director William Beaudine (1892-1970) for his seemingly endless parade of B films in the forties and fifties, particularly the East Side Kids and Bowery Boys movies, you only know half the story. **William Beaudine: From Silents to Television** by Wendy L. Marshall (Scarecrow Press) is a real eye-opener. I have newfound respect for the artistry and professionalism that Beaudine brought to film because of this book.

I was under the false impression that Beaudine was strictly a very prolific "B" man. I've enjoyed his twin Torchys for Warners, *Torchy Gets Her Man* (1938) and *Torchy Blane in Chinatown (*1939), and lesser (but likable) Poverty Row things like *Desperate Cargo* (1941, Ralph Byrd),

The Living Ghost (1942, James Dunn), *The Ape Man* (1943, Bela Lugosi), *Hot Rhythm* (1944, Robert Lowery), *Black Market Babies* (1945, Maris Wrixon), *The Shadow Returns* (1946, Kane Richmond), *Philo Vance Returns* (1947, William Wright), and his Monogram Chans: *The Chinese Ring* (1947), *The Shanghai Chest, The Golden Eye* and *The Feathered Serpent* (all three 1948). Maybe these aren't classics to some, but very enjoyable, nonetheless.

What I didn't know is that, in the silent era, Beaudine was a big deal, considered an "A" director, directing Mary Pickford in *Little Annie Rooney* (1925) and *Sparrows* (1926). From other sources, we are led to believe that he was always just run-of-the-mill, a lower-bracket director who put forth an amazing amount of work. Well, this book should clear that absurd notion right away. The turning point in his career came when he went to England in the thirties to make a series of highly successful films. When he came back, quality work was hard to find at the major studios. Much later, in the fifties, Beaudine successfully turned to television and, among many other things, directed episodes of *Lassie* and did a bunch of work for Disney.

Wendy L. Marshall is William Beaudine's granddaughter and, while she's objective — a rare feat for a granddaughter — she gives us a personal portrait that none of the other books on directors can boast. She is committed to getting his story down and she does so in an appealingly professional manner. At times she does tell us her relationship with her grandfather, and these warm moments add much to the text. She does not, however, go overboard. She's a film historian, foremost.

The research is impressive, utilizing personal scrapbooks, letters and interviews with people associated with Beaudine (as well as family members): Patsy Ruth Miller, Camilla Johnson Jones, Harry Carey, Jr., Edward Dmytryk, Dorothy "Chili" Bouchier, Delmar Watson, Louise Currie, Huntz Hall, Howard W. Koch, Aubrey Schenck, Robert Easton, Billy Benedict, Roddy McDowall, Kevin Corcoran, Jon Provost, etc. Marshall's style is enjoyable. I do wish, however, she had gone against some of the written reviews more. Just because the *New York Times* disliked a movie, doesn't mean the film had no merit. This is a minor criticism in a book that had me thoroughly engrossed. I reveled in learning about Beaudine, and the author does not disappoint on this front.

"It's a daunting task to recreate seventy-eight years of a man's life and sixty years of his career, and do it honestly," writes Marshall. "Others have been duped by studio publicity department releases and gossip that acquired legend status as time passed. I've attempted to dispel the myths that attached themselves to William Beaudine." The fact that she succeeds in her intentions is happy news for B movie fans. And for those jaded by the plethora of Hitchcock books flooding the market, this should be a rare treat — to look into the work of a mostly neglected artist. No one can compare to Hitchcock, that's a given, but for the real film fan, this unique study will open up a whole new side of Hollywood. And it finally gives the director the respect he deserves, for his amazing outpouring of films that on the whole were quite good in spite of the budgets.

The filmography/TV listing is the most complete yet of Beaudine's prolific work. The photos, many very rare on-set shots, are priceless.

***

John Zacherle isn't a name that every Book Points reader will recognize because his claim to fame was as a star on local TV stations, first in Philadelphia and then in New York, starting in the late 1950s. In Philly he was the on-camera host of late-night horror movies under the name Roland, and subsequently in New York he had the same duties but called himself Zacherley. "Zach" emceed the TV debuts of many of the Universal horror classics, from *Dracula* (1931) on up, doing schtick between reels and sometimes even interjecting himself into the movies. He cut a simultaneously spooky and silly figure with his ghoulish white face, frock coat and loud, exaggerated laugh, but the activities in which he engaged on his dark, dungeon-like set were all for fun: attempting to dig to the center of the Earth, singing opera, etc. His brand of fearsome fun helped make the Universal chillers (and other monster movies) ratings hits in their late-night slots.

Rich Scrivani, who first met Zach in the mid-1960s and later reconnected with him, wrote about the TV horror host and their friendship in the now out-of-print 2006 book *Good Night, Whatever You Are: My Journey with Zacherley, the Cool Ghoul;* and now with the help of warhorse Tom Weaver he has provided the follow-up, **The Z Files: Treasures from Zacherley's Archives** (BearManor Media).

The Z Files tells the story of Zach's showbiz career in an unusual way: by reprinting scores of vintage newspaper and magazine articles published back in his heyday. It begins with reviews of a 1954 play in which Zacherle, then new to acting, appeared, and continues on through his Roland and Zacherley movie-hosting days and even *Disc-O-Teen*, an *American Bandstand*-type series from the mid-1960s; Zach, still doing his Mad Transylvanian bit, was the ringmaster amidst garage bands and dancing girls.

Besides the articles, there are a lot of other ephemera sprinkled throughout: ads for personal appearances, his contract with WABC, hate mail from horror movie fans who disliked his mood-disrupting antics and had to get it off their chests, etc. This part of the book is followed by reproductions of several of his (typed) horror-hosting scripts and (handwritten) notes and prop lists, and then there's a "Photo Ghoullery" with pics of Zach at various functions and conventions that brings him right up to the present day.

Casual fans can read some of the livelier clippings and enjoy all the photos while readers with a greater devotion to the Cool Ghoul will savor every last page; what was designed as a scrapbook can actually be read as though it were a career bio (the many articles about his professional life are arranged in chronological order). It's hard to read (or even browse) the book without a smile; the light, spoofing tone of most of the articles and the outrageous photos are an effective one-two assault on the funnybone.

Photo-wise, just for starters, there are shots of Zach in a coffin being carried by college students, running amok in his lab, dancing with high-school beauties, swinging on a swing, posing with "monsters" (fans in costume) at various conventions—and even a lot of pictures of the man contending with a large duck. A *lot* of pictures of Zach and the duck. The book is even dedicated to the duck!

In short, *The Z Files* achieves its goal by being as weird, wild and woolly—and uninhibited—as Zach himself. It's a perfect tribute.

APPENDIX

Addresses of Publishers:

Alfred A. Knopf/Random House. 1745 Broadway, New York, NY 10019 or 212-782-9000 or www.randomhouse.com

www.amazon.com

Andre Deutsch/Carlton Publishing Group. 20 Mortimer Street, London, W1T 3JW or www.goodmanbooks.com

Avon Books/HarperCollins. 10 East 53rd Street, New York, NY 10022 or 212-207-7000 or www.harpercollins.com

Back Stage Books/Watson-Guptill/The Crown Publishing Group. 1745 Broadway, New York, NY 10019 or 212-782-9000 or www.crownpublishing.com

BearManor Media. P.O. Box 1129, Duncan, OK 73534-1129 or 580-252-3547 or www.bearmanormedia.com

Bright Sky Press. 2365 Rice Blvd #202, Houston, TX 77005 or 713-533-9300 or www.brightskypress.com

Da Capo Press/W.W. Norton & Co./ Perseus Books. 210 American Drive, Jackson, TN 38301 or 800-343-4499 or www.perseusbooksgroup.com

Ernest Publishing. www.robertwdix.com

Film Noir Foundation. www.filmnoirfoundation.org

www.garywarnerkent.com

Hollywood Adventures Publishing. 5915 Corbin Avenue, Tarzana, CA 91356 or www.julieadams.biz

iUniverse. 1663 Liberty Drive, Bloomington, IN 47403 or 800-288-4677 or www.iuniverse.com

Lake Claremont Press. P.O. Box 711, Chicago, IL 60690 or 312-226-8400 or www.lakeclaremont.com

Limelight Editions/Applause/Hal Leonard. 33 Plymouth St. Suite 302, Montclair, NJ 07042 or 800-637-2852 or www.halleonardbooks.com

McFarland & Company. Box 611, Jefferson NC 28640 or 800-253-2187 or www.mcfarlandbooks.com

Penguin Books. 375 Hudson Street, New York, NY 10014-3657 or 800-847-5515 or www.penguin.com

Scarecrow Press. 15200 NBN Way, P.O. Box 191, Blue Ridge Summit, PA 17214 or 800-462-6420 or www.rowman.com

Simon & Schuster. 1230 Avenue of the Americas, New York, NY 10020 or 800-223-2336 or www.simonandschuster.com

University Press of Kentucky. c/o Hopkins Fulfillment Service, PO Box 50370, Baltimore, MD 21211-4370 or 800-537-5487 or www.kentuckypress.com

University Press of Mississippi. 3825 Ridgewood Road, Jackson, MS 39211 or 800-737-7788 or www.upress.state.ms.us

University of Wisconsin Press. c/o Chicago Distribution Center, 11030 S. Langley Ave., Chicago, IL 60628 or 800-621-2736 or www.uwpress.wisc.edu

Word Association Publishers. 205 Fifth Avenue, Tarenrum, PA 15084 or 800-827-7903 or www.wordassociation.com

www.ingramcontent.com/pod-product-compliance
Lightning Source LLC
Chambersburg PA
CBHW071712160426
43195CB00012B/1658